Gotcha Covered!

Gotcha Covered!

More Nonfiction Booktalks to Get Kids Excited about Reading

Kathleen A. Baxter
Michael Dahl

LIBRARIES UNLIMITED

UNLIMITED

A Member of the Greenwood Publishing Group

Westport, Connecticut ● London

British Library Cataloguing in Publication Data is available.

Library of Congress Control Number: 2005927741
ISBN: 1-59158-225-3

First published in 2005

Libraries Unlimited, 88 Post Road West, Westport, CT 06881
A Member of the Greenwood Publishing Group, Inc.
www.lu.com

Printed in the United States of America

∞™

The paper used in this book complies with the Permanent Paper Standard issued by the National Information Standards Organization (Z39.48–1984).

10 9 8 7 6 5 4 3 2 1

Contents

List of Figures

Introduction:
Searching for the Right Book

I am always booktalking and always looking for books that appeal to kids. It's not easy. I look at some of the current nonfiction that is being published and find it well-written and interesting, but I cannot imagine students being attracted to it. On the other hand, some of the series nonfiction out there is both attractive and appealing to look at, but dull as dishwater to read. Research shows that kids will read appealing books, enduring the dull writing, just to find out more about a topic that fascinates them, and, as book selectors, we must remember this. I have recently done a great deal of research on the topic of boys and reading, and one point on which all the experts agree is that *choice* is the most important factor in creating good readers. Let them choose what they want to read. Give them a variety of books of all types, on a variety of interesting topics, then stand back and let them read whatever captures their interest.

Girls, of course, feel the same way. Who wants to read what someone else wants you to read? As a voracious reader all of my life, I am still pretty picky when it comes to pleasure reading. There are genres I love and others I won't even dabble in. There are writers whose every new work I await with eager anticipation, and other writers I have no desire to try. My mystery-loving friends are completely annoyed with me for my adamant refusal to even pick up a Dick Francis title, but a childhood encounter with the heart-breaking *Black Beauty* led me to a permanent avoidance of books involving horses.

Gotcha Covered! is a compendium of booktalks that we hope will provide a great number of books that will capture a reader's interest. Most of the booktalks are fairly brief, as I believe attention spans are getting shorter and shorter. At conferences, I do show listeners at least one image from inside the book so they can get a feel for it, and I try to vary my booktalks within any given session—a fast and funny one, a slow and serious one, a joke, a poem, an interesting fact about science or history. Once in a while I will tell a much longer story, such as Christopher Crowe's *Getting Away with Murder: The True Story of the Emmett Till Case*. Students and their teachers are riveted by this horrifying episode in U.S. history.

I select books for a booktalk in several ways. First of all, I am blessed that many publishers send me review copies, and some of these titles leap out at me the second I open the box. The highest compliment I can pay a book is to set it on my reading chair for immediate attention. Second, I subscribe to several review magazines, reading each review and paying special attention to anything that gets a starred review. I keep an actual spreadsheet of those reviews so that I am certain not to miss anything really important. Third, I subscribe to and spend time looking carefully through *The Horn Book Guide,* which reviews books twice a year, January through June, and July through December. I find titles in the *Guide* that I may have previously overlooked.

Fourth, I delight in receiving recommendations from colleagues wherever I go. Tell me to read a book and I am hooked. Some excellent and appealing titles often fall through the cracks and do not get reviewed at all or receive poor reviews. Word of mouth becomes a helpful guide to finding these lost treasures. Also, I often scan bibliographies for other interesting titles.

A book might come to my attention in a really unusual way. Such was the case with *Bones Rock: Everything You Need to Know to Be a Paleontologist,* by Peter Larson and Kristin Donnan. I was a guest speaker at the Denver Book Fair in September 2004, when Jody Gehrig, the director of media services in the Denver school district, asked me to talk to Donnan and Larson, who had a booth at the fair. Jody told me that *Bones Rock* was published by a tiny publisher in Vermont, and the writers were inexperienced, and she asked if there were anything I could do to help. My heart sank. My previous experience with books like this did not lead me to believe that the book would be one I wanted to even examine! But Jody said it looked good, and Jody is one intelligent lady, so I walked over to the booth and started looking.

Bones Rock looked good, very good, a glossy trade paperback with hundreds of beautiful color photographs. Peter had helped dig out the famous tyrannosaurus skeleton named Sue, and Kristin's writing made a favorable first impression. I promised to read the book, and, if I liked it, to help. Their publisher had sent out only three review copies, ignoring some of the best review sources around.

I read it. I liked it a lot. I e-mailed Kristin and Peter, and they sent out review copy after review copy to anyone and everyone I suggested. I e-mailed a couple of reviewers I knew and told them I really enjoyed the book. One of those reviewers was the head of the Book Review section in *School Library Journal,* the number one magazine that school and public children's librarians look to for guidance. By November, *School Library Journal* had given the book a starred review. In December, they chose it as one of the 58 best children's books of 2004! I hope and pray *Bones Rock* is bought by many schools and libraries. It is just too good to miss. This experience taught me that you never know where you are going to find just the right book!

In *Gotcha Covered!,* my partner Michael Dahl and I offer you a selection of books we hope will be the right ones for you!

Kathleen Baxter
kabaxter@comcast.net
January 31, 2005

CHAPTER 1

Great Adventures, Disasters, Explorers, and Heroes

High adventure calls! The wild winds of fortune are beckoning us onward! Death-defying escapes, shipwrecks, shark attacks, trekking through sub-zero wind-storms on a life-and-death mission. Whose blood doesn't run faster under the spell of a hero's tale? And who doesn't yearn for marvelous surprises and dazzling discoveries?—rounding the dark side of the Moon for the first time in humanity's history, or buying a prehistoric creature in the bustling street markets of Indonesia.

We all have a bit of the hero in us, as Spider-Man's Aunt May confides to him. Hearing and reading about intrepid explorers, cunning survivors, and single-minded trailblazers tugs at that heroic nature buried inside each one of us. And one of the surest ways to hook a booktalk audience is to snare their attention with a web of true-life adventure.

DISASTERS: HANGING BY A THREAD

"Once there were two towers side by side. They were each a quarter of a mile high: one thousand three hundred and forty feet. The tallest building in New York City." This is the way Mordicai Gerstein's 2004 Caldecott-winning book starts, and I'll bet everyone knows the name of those two towers.

The Man Who Walked Between the Towers is the story of something special that happened before the towers were even completely finished being built. Phillippe Petit, a French tightrope walker, saw the rising buildings and *knew* he must walk on a rope stretched between them. It would be difficult, and it would take a lot of planning and hard work, but he knew he would attempt the risky feat, even if the police came to arrest him!

And this is the amazing story of how it happened. Gerstein's text is lyrical and poetic. His illustrations will make you dizzy and gasp for breath. Show the incredible triple-page spread of Petit walking between the towers.

Long before the twin towers began to rise, a hundred years ago in America, life was peaceful. It was a time almost impossible for us living in the 21st century to comprehend. Although a terrible war was raging in Europe, Americans enjoyed quiet and prosperity on their side of the Atlantic. Scientific knowledge was growing, and more people had leisure to enjoy its fruits. People living near the ocean enjoyed some of their free time by going swimming.

In July 1916, a young man went swimming far out in the water off a beach in New Jersey. He was a strong swimmer, and he had no reason to be afraid. The water had always been safe. No one could know that a solitary great white shark was also swimming near Charles Vansant. Even if Charles *had* known that a great white shark was swimming near him, he probably would not have worried. Everyone in America, including the experts, believed that sharks would never attack or bite human beings.

They were wrong.

Close to Shore: The Terrifying Shark Attacks of 1916 by Michael Capuzzo tells us exactly how horribly wrong they were. The shark bit Charles's leg and artery. Hard. Charles flew out of the water, screaming. Helpers swam out and were horrified to see that the shark had grabbed Charles again. His companions ended up playing a tug-of-war with Charles's body. They formed a human chain and tugged him up onto the beach. The giant shark followed, almost all of the way, its thick, muscular body thrashing on the sand. Then it opened its jaws and disappeared.

Charles bled to death in spite of the medical care his own father, a physician, tried to give him. And that was just the first attack. The shark was still hungry. It needed more food, and there were lots of unsuspecting humans in the area.

Capuzzo's book is a true horror story. Your video-literate audience might find it interesting that young Charles's deadly encounter with the great white inspired another writer who created a best seller that led to one of the world's first blockbuster movies—*Jaws!*

If you were asked to name the most deadly American disasters of them all, could you? What was the worst flood? Where was the worst earthquake? The deadliest disease? The worst hurricane and the worst blizzard? The worst fire? What shipwreck claimed the most lives?

A lot of your guesses will probably be wrong, because many of the worst disasters in our history are not that famous. Fortunately, Martin W. Sandler has made a list of them for us in his terrific *America's Great Disasters.*

One surprising fact Sandler tells us is that the worst fire in American history took place on the same night as the notorious Chicago Fire of 1871. The worst fire of all was the Wisconsin forest fire in and around Peshtigo, Wisconsin. Peshtigo is 50 miles northeast of Green Bay. About 1,500 people were killed in the fire, and many of their bodies were never found. In the town alone 800 were killed. About 50 of those people sought shelter in the town's only brick building and were literally baked alive when the temperature of the brick walls rose to over 2,000 degrees F!

The Johnstown, Pennsylvania, flood is by far the worst flood in American history. A dam, badly in need of repair, broke without warning, sending thousands of tons of water down the valley into the city of Johnstown. On its way to Johnstown, the floodwaters completely destroyed the village of East Conemaugh, shoving aside locomotives and houses in its path. People were killed by the debris in the river, not just the water. The town of Woodvale was next, and the flood destroyed every house there.

One of the best-known disasters of all time is revisited in Mireille Majoor's *Titanic, Ghosts of the Abyss.* The book is a companion to the film of the same title made by Hollywood director James Cameron, who was responsible for the mega-block-buster and 1997 Oscar winner, *Titanic.* Majoor's book is a feast for the eyes. Full of photos taken from *Titanic* archives, the book also boasts original paintings done by Ken Marschall. Marschall is called the "world's leading *Titanic* artist" and accompanied Cameron on an expedition to the sunken ship. Most of the artwork is rendered in 3-D, and each book comes with a pair of 3-D glasses. You know that everyone will want to take a look for themselves! Although the story is familiar, the photos of real people and real-life objects (mirrors, teacups, life jackets) that disappeared beneath the waves are still as haunting as ever. And getting a glimpse of the *Titanic*'s actual boiler rooms, or the steering wheel (which still survives at the bottom of the ocean!), will give your booktalk audience a chance to immerse themselves in one of the most famous of all calamities.

Did an unspeakable disaster strike down the colonists of Roanoke? This classic American mystery is recounted in Zachary Kent's *The Mysterious Disappearance of Roanoke Colony in American History.*

After Christopher Columbus made his voyage to what was called the New World in 1492, Spain launched into action. It sent adventurers to North and South America, who returned with treasure and tales of even more wealth waiting to be found. The people in England grew jealous. Sir Humphrey Gilbert suggested to the English Queen, Elizabeth I, that England establish a settlement in North America. It would be a great base for pirate ships to prey on the Spanish ships and steal their treasure. Elizabeth agreed, and granted Gilbert permission in 1578.

Humphrey's settlement never became a reality. His ships encountered storms, and Humphrey himself drowned in 1583. His younger brother, Walter Raleigh, took over the project. Raleigh was a great favorite of the queen, and in 1584 two ships funded by Raleigh reached what is now North Carolina. The captains and crews not only made friends with the natives, but they brought two of them, Wanchese and Manteo, back to England with them. The explorers also brought reports of the wonderful land they had found.

Raleigh acted immediately. A new expedition, including a scientific research team, set out in 1585. This second group had trouble dealing with the natives and trouble with supplies as well. Almost all of them returned to England, leaving only 15 men still on Roanoke Island, guarding a fort. And thus began the mysteries that have intrigued us ever since. When another group of Englanders arrived on Roanoke in 1587, they could not find the original 15 (or their houses within the fort!), and the complete disappearance of that second colony is one of the enduring questions of American history. Were they all killed? Did they go to live with the natives? Where they killed by the Spanish? Some experts proposed a deadly flood, but what kind of flood would sweep away buildings and leave the fort's surrounding walls intact? This book is a good starting point for the amazing Roanoke enigma.

A great sideline in Kent's book is the character of Thomas Hariot. Hariot was one of the scientists on the second voyage and was keenly interested in a native crop called "Uppowoc". He wrote that the natives picked and then dried the leaves of the plant, crushed them into a powder, and then smoked them in a pipe. The Spaniards called the plant "tobacco." Hariot enjoyed smoking this plant, and later after he returned to England, he became the first recorded case in history of a tobacco smoker getting cancer!

Jane Yolen and Heidi Elisabet Yolen Stemple investigate the same notorious puzzle in *Roanoke: The Lost Colony: An Unsolved Mystery from History.* They tell us that the first English child born in North America was Virginia Dare, the granddaughter of John White, one of the leaders of the Roanoke colony.

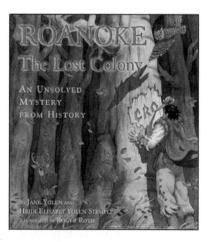

Figure 1.1. *Roanoke: The Lost Colony: An Unsolved Mystery from History* by Jane Yolen and Heidi Elisabet Yolen Stemple.

White and his companions had a rough time in the New World. The colonists also had troubles with the Native Americans, who had been badly treated by the earlier colony. The people of Roanoke needed help, and John White went back to England to get it on August 27. White told the colonists what to do in case they had trouble while he was gone. "If you leave, carve your destination on a tree. Put a cross if there has been trouble."

It took White more than *three years* to return. What he found when he came back to Roanoke is a mystery that has haunted American history ever since—an empty fort, no colonists, no supplies, no boat, and three letters, CRO, carved on a tree, with no cross above them. On a palisade post was carved the word CROATAN, which was the name of a nearby island where the natives were friendly. But no one ever found a single trace of that lost colony, on that nearby island or anywhere else. Whatever happened to Virginia Dare and her neighbors? There are several theories about what happened, and you will have a blast trying to figure it all out.

Seymour Simon describes the blasts of smoke (and lava and boiling ash) in *Danger! Volcanoes*. Booktalk audience always seems to be fascinated by volcanoes. Here is a small sampling of what you will learn when you read this book:

- Every year about 50 volcanoes erupt throughout the world.

- The Roman god of fire is named Vulcan—and the word "volcano" derives from his name.

- Some volcanoes are extinct, such as Crater Lake in Idaho. Its top is now filled with water.

- There are more than 500 active volcanoes around the world—and more than half of them surround the Pacific Ocean. They are called the Ring of Fire.

Show the picture of the second two-page spread of the volcano erupting. The fine color photographs throughout Simon's book are compelling.

Simon turns his attention to another powerful force of nature in *Hurricanes*. As Simon tells us, the worst effect of these deadly storms is not the wind, but the water they bring with them. During a hurricane in 1900, the streets of Galveston, Texas, were swamped with waves 15 feet high. The same storm killed 12,000 people and swept thousands of homes into the sea. Simon details the devastating effects of a number of storms: Opal, Camille, Fran, Hugo, and the fearsome Andrew, whose winds whipped at 120 miles per hour as it roared across Florida and Louisiana. We also learn that hurricanes go by a number of names, depending on where they take place. Australian hurricanes are called willy-willies. In the North Pacific they are called typhoons. The word *hurricane* itself comes from the ancient Maya storm god *Hunraken*. There are some eerie photos in this book. You worry about the safety of the photographers who took these fabulous shots! Besides the pictures of crushed buildings and blowing palm trees, look at the car about to sink, on the 19th page. Flip to the back and watch the wind and water crash through the glass doors of a home, with the homeowner still standing there, staring into the camera! Simon also includes a list of safety measures for those of us who may face the onslaught of a hurricane.

More incredible photographs fill the pages of Louise Spilsbury and Richard Spilsbury's *Shattering Earthquakes*. You may have heard of the notorious San Andreas Fault, which causes some of California's tremors and quakes. But on page 7 you can get an amazing aerial glimpse of the fault. On page 14 you can show your booktalk audience a landslide that buried a small town in El Salvador. Some earthquakes shove land into the ocean, where the impact can cause a new danger called a tsunami, a giant wave of crushing water.

Earthquakes are measured on the Richter scale, which is based on the degree of destruction a quake can cause. The famous quake that hit California during a World Series baseball game in 1989, and was captured on television, was 7.1 on the Richter scale. That particular quake injured more than 3,000 people, killed 60, and resulted in $10 billion in damage. Aftershocks are one of the more dangerous aspects of an earthquake. While people return to their homes, or rescue workers are searching the rubble for survivors, more shocks and tremors can suddenly occur, causing even more damage and death.

Several million earthquakes hit the planet each year! But your booktalk listeners shouldn't worry. Most quakes are too small to be felt.

One of the most notorious earthquakes on record is the focus of Shelley Tanaka's *Earthquake! A Day That Changed America: On a Peaceful Spring Morning, Disaster Strikes San Francisco.* Imagine waking up to find your house shaking. Glass is breaking; objects are falling off shelves. But it's probably only a small earthquake. If you lived in San Francisco in 1906, you got used to small earthquakes. They never caused much damage and were seldom anything to worry about. The one Tanaka writes about, however, turned out to be completely different.

The earthquake struck at 5:13 A.M. on April 18, 1906, and it was a colossal one—the *big* one—and only the beginning of the troubles of the people who were its victims. Buildings crumbled in the streets. Water mains broke, and the water drained away. Streets slid out of place, making them difficult to navigate by horses. When chimneys cracked and stoves fell over, hundreds of fires started. And there was little or no water to put them out.

This book tells the true stories of some of the people, especially young people, who were in the fire. One boy, Hugh Kwong Liang, lived with his cousin in Chinatown. Hugh's father had died. He ran away from the fire and then later found out that his cousin had taken all of the money from Hugh's father store and run away. DeWitt Baldwin was only eight when he slipped out of his house and onto the street to see what was going on. One thing he saw was the wreckage of what used to be the Valencia Hotel. "It looked as if the earth had tried to swallow the building whole. The bottom three floors sank into the ground, and the stores that used to line the sidewalk on the main floor had simply disappeared. The top story had fallen out into the street" (page 14). Many people fled to parks, where they camped out in tents and lined up for food and water. Water was practically impossible to get. People were hungry and thirsty and dirty. There were no toilets and no places to wash clothes.

Historians now estimate that as many as 250,000 people were homeless, many for weeks or months. But Americans in other parts of the country rushed to give them help, in all sorts of ways, and, somehow, San Francisco became bigger and stronger than ever before.

HIGH ADVENTURE AND HIGH SEAS

The Pacific Ocean is the setting for Rhoda Blumberg's tale of a reluctant hero, *Shipwrecked!: The True Adventures of a Japanese Boy.* When he was only nine years old, Manjiro had to earn enough money to support his family. This was not easy. The pre-teen was forced to become a fisherman, for in Japan in 1836, laws dictated that everyone perform exactly the same work as their fathers had done for centuries.

By the time he was 14, Manjiro's hard work led to a new job on a small fishing boat. In 1841, his boat set out on an ordinary fishing trip but was soon swept up in an extraordinary storm. Manjiro and his four companions were shipwrecked. They were cast away on a small island 300 miles from Japan. Finding food was difficult. Their luck changed when an American whaling ship appeared and its sailors came on the island looking, ironically, for food and fresh water. The Japanese castaways got their attention, and they were rescued.

None of the Japanese fishermen had ever seen an American. And none of them spoke English. The resourceful Manjiro, however, was speaking English within a few weeks, and did all sorts of odd jobs on the ship. The Americans offered to return the fishermen to their homes. The whalers were unaware, however, of the crueler aspects of Japanese law. Seventeenth-century Japan was nervous about foreign influence and therefore unkind to strangers. A strict edict declared that anyone who left Japan and came back would be executed. No exceptions.

Manjiro's companions chose to stay in Honolulu, but the boy sailed on two whaling boats and became a surrogate son to the captain of the ship that had originally rescued him.

Eventually Manjiro grew homesick and missed his family. He decided to take the unthinkable risk of returning to Japan, seeing the faces of his loved ones again, and then undergoing swift execution. What would your booktalk listeners do? Is family worth the risk of possible death? Show the picture of Manjiro above the title page. Look into the eyes of a real boy who had to face that question, and then tell the audience to read on.

Making a living from the ocean has always been dangerous and unpredictable, especially for whalers. The fate of the notorious *Essex,* whose exploits inspired Herman Melville's *Moby Dick,* is the focus of Nathaniel Philbrick's *The Revenge of the Whale: The True Story of the Whaleship* Essex.

In 1819 the whaleship *Essex* was one of many to leave Nantucket Island in search of whales and profits. The Quaker businessmen on the island were wildly successful in the whaling business, and they favored born and bred islanders for their crews. Anyone not native to Nantucket was an undesirable. The *Essex* had a crew of 21, including a 14-year-old cabin boy, Thomas Nickerson. Young Nickerson was one of the lucky ones. He came back.

The ship itself had been harvesting whale blubber for more than two decades and was not in the best condition. Its captain was as green as they come; this was his first command of a ship. And many of the crew were not from the island. To the folks of Nantucket, the *Essex* had bad luck written all over its timbers.

Early in the voyage, the whalers almost turned back. The trip threatened to be long and disheartening. The sooner a ship filled up with whale oil, the sooner it could sail back home. But the men of the *Essex* had trouble spotting any whales. Even in 1820, a lot of whales had been killed off. In many parts of the ocean, the great mammals were scarce. The *Essex* struck out west for a remote area of the Pacific Ocean, prompted by rumors of plentiful whales. But their luck headed south.

On November 20, 1820, an angry whale, covered with scars, rammed their ship, for no apparent reason, and sank it. The creature swam away and no one knows what became of it. This had seldom happened to a ship before. The *Essex* wasn't even chasing that particular whale.

All crew members survived. They were able to retrieve some provisions and navigation equipment during the next two days. But when the ship eventually submerged, the sailors were left alone in the middle of the ocean in three small whaling boats. They were thousands of miles from land, and, furthermore, they were not very good at figuring out in which direction lay the nearest land.

Would they starve to death or die of thirst? Would they have to eat each other? Would they ever find land? And, if they did, would they be eaten by cannibals? This book is almost impossible to put down. What a story!

Although few people ever dream of becoming a whaler, there are many who imagine leading adventurous lives in a less honorable profession—piracy. Deep down inside, don't you think that pirates were sort of neat? There are a few really famous ones, including Captain Kidd and Blackbeard. And a lot of people are fond of Long John Silver, the old one-legged swashbuckler in Robert Louis Stevenson's book *Treasure Island.* But real pirates were not the matinee idols or action-film stars we see grinning and romping on screen at the local Cineplex. Milton Meltzer's *Piracy and Plunder: A Murderous Business,* tells us the truth about pirates, and it is not fun.

A real pirate was the worst sort of criminal—vicious, cruel, with a ruthless habit of capturing and selling slaves, the quickest way for a seafaring outlaw to make a buck. Pirates enslaved friends, neighbors, even children. Sometimes a man with a particular skill was needed on a pirate ship and was captured and forced to choose between joining the crew and suffering a violent death.

Meltzer tells us that thousands of crusaders in the Middle Ages were captured by pirates and forced into slavery. Some became galley slaves, chained to benches for the remainder of their lives and forced to row the ships called galleys. They were starved, beaten, and did not live long. Modern-day pirates deal in drugs and weapons. After an excursion through Meltzer's chilling book, your booktalk audience will never again think a *real* pirate was a cool guy.

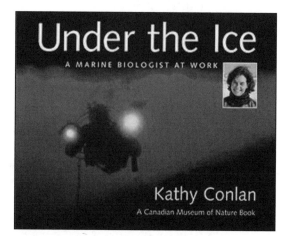

Figure 1.2. *Under the Ice: A Canadian Museum of Nature Book* by Kathy Conlan.

Kathy Conlan is cool, and has a really cool job. Risky, but definitely cool. Conlan is a marine biologist, and she dives beneath the ice of the Arctic and Antarctic. Not only is the water in those regions lethally cold, but the currents are strong, and drifting ice can capsize boats and crush divers who are too slow to get out of their way. Ordinary diving gear is useless in those extreme conditions. In Conlan's *Under the Ice: A Canadian Museum of Nature Book,* she describes how she went to Antarctica for the first time as part of a group that was studying the effects of human waste on animals on the ocean floor. Antarctica is considered a polar desert—98 percent of it is covered in ice. Conlan took hundreds of photographs of the animals that live there, and as she says, "Most of their activity occurs over eating—or attempting to avoid being eaten" (page 29). She took a wonderful shot of the ocean floor (page 28).

As people have done throughout history all over the world, the people who lived in or visited Antarctica just dumped their garbage in the ocean. Conlan says you can still see "crates, barrel hoops and jars from Scott's and Shackleton's expedition, and even the skeletons of some of their sled dogs" (page 34). The scientists in Conlan's group wanted to study what was happening to that garbage. Conlan had to dive through a tunnel cut in the solid ice and then examine the garbage piles up close and personal, which she says are smelly and messy and beyond disgusting. Shackleton was there in 1909! Can your audience imagine how gross it would be to encounter 100-year-old trash in their own neighborhoods? Conlan's photographs are great. Even the pictures of the garbage.

SURPRISE AND DISCOVERY: FROM FOSSILS TO THE MOON

What if you found something in your garbage that was 360 million years old? In Sally Walker's *Fossil Fish Found Alive: Discovering the Coelacanth,* a museum employee in South Africa saw a dead fish. A friend of hers who owned a fishing trawler often gave weird tidbits from his daily catches to the museum, but the specimen the employee saw on December 22, 1938, was beyond her wildest nightmares. She wanted to freeze the odd blue fish to preserve it, but the museum did not have the space. She did her best to take care of it, but eventually part of the carcass rotted, so the museum employee had the fish stuffed.

And a good thing, too. What her fishing friend had so blithely given her was something no scientist had ever seen before—a living coelacanth. Show the picture of the fish on page 65.

The coelacanth, which means "hollow spine" for the long prickles in its upper fin, was believed to be extinct. Paleontologists and fossil hunters thought the coelacanth had died out 70 million years ago, long before the dinosaurs, definitely before mammals or people roamed the earth. But here was a creature that had recently been swimming in the Indian Ocean.

How this all happened makes for a greatly entertaining and entirely true story. There are all sorts of twists and turns—such as that, in 1997, a scientist saw one for sale in a market in Indonesia. He did not realize that no one knew coelacanths lived anywhere near Indonesia, but the truth was that no one did know. If he had not taken pictures that day, we might still not know.

Do you think that being a paleontologist is one of the coolest jobs in the world? Do you like tons of color photographs showing exactly how dinosaur hunting is done? Do you want to get digging equipment and start immediately? Then Peter Larson and Kristin Donnan's *Bones Rock! Everything You Need to Know to Be a Paleontologist* is the book for you.

Larson, nicknamed Paleo Pete, is a world-famous paleontologist. He has dug up six *Tyrannosaurus rex*es, including the dinosaur named Sue, whose spectacular skeleton is on exhibit in Chicago's Field Museum. Larson thinks being a paleontologist is the most exciting job in the world, and he says there are a lot of dinosaur fossils out there that still need to be discovered. Probably millions! While he finds it absolutely amazing that so many fossils have survived, Larson notes that fossils never tell us the whole story; they only give us clues. But the more fossils we find, the more clues we get.

Even having thousands of dinosaur bones doesn't stop scientists from arguing about their previous owners. For example, for a hundred years scientists debated about how *Triceratops* walked. Some thought it walked like a lizard, with elbows pointing out; others believed it walked like a rhinoceros, with elbows held close to its body. Read the book and find out what scientists think today.

Lots of kids have helped find great dinosaur fossils; Larson and Donnan tell their stories and show us photographs of them along with their finds. Paleo Pete gives us a checklist if we want to hunt dinosaurs: what kind of equipment we need; that we must always have a mentor, a knowledgeable adult, with us; and that we must never ever go out dinosaur hunting alone. Special care must be taken when fossils are dug out in order to not damage them. And dino hunters always need to ask permission from landowners before they dig. Digging is not a solitary job. It takes a lot of people to unearth buried bones. Larson points out that it would take 12 1/2 years for one person to dig out and clean a whole *T. rex!* Read this book and catch some of Paleo Pete's enthusiasm. You'll want to get your gear together immediately.

If you can't get enough of discoveries about the prehistoric world, turn to Albert Marrin's *Secrets from the Rocks: Dinosaur Hunting with Roy Chapman Andrews*, which tells the story of Roy Chapman Andrews. The photo on page 3 is old-fashioned, but it shows us a lot about Roy Chapman Andrews. He is a very good-looking young man who looks as though he knows exactly where he is going and what he wants to do. And that was Roy!

Some people say Andrews was the original Indiana Jones. He did hate snakes, and he had a lot of adventures. He was born in Beloit, Wisconsin, and he was interested in animals and figuring them out. He was a good shot, and he killed many and brought them home to dissect them. He wanted to know all about them.

When he graduated from college in 1906, he went to New York City. He knew that he wanted to work for the American Museum of Natural History, but they had no positions available. Roy said he would scrub floors. He did such a great job, and had such a passion for the natural world, that he soon caught the eye of the staff. Eventually he became the museum's director, and he led several expeditions to the Gobi Desert in Mongolia/ What his expeditions found was staggering and greatly increased our knowledge of the prehistoric world. Roy himself was not so great at digging out fossils, though. He did not have the patience for it. He would hack them out with a pickaxe and completely destroy them. A pickaxe was probably a good weapon to have handy in case a snake showed up, though.

Michael Collins traveled farther than Roy Chapman Andrews ever did. In her book, *The Man Who Went to the Far Side of the Moon: The Story of* Apollo 11 *Astronaut Michael Collins*, Bea Uusma Shyffert tells us that although Collins never did set foot on the moon, he traveled to a place that no human being had ever seen before. He circled Earth's satellite, visiting the far side of the moon, while Buzz Aldrin and Neil Armstrong made the historic moon landing. Alone in the cramped moon capsule, Collins circled the Moon 14 times. He said it was blacker than any black he had ever seen. He could not see the moon itself because it was so black, but he could tell where it was, because he could not see the stars through it.

Collins is one of America's most famous astronauts, of course, and Schyffert's book is the story of the *Apollo 11* mission to the moon in 1969. It is filled with interesting information. Did you know that all of the astronauts wore diapers? Or that the moon capsule in which all three had to sit for days was about the size of an ordinary car? Or that it was hard to get food into their mouths before it flew away? This book is translated from the Swedish, and it is beautifully designed. Take a look. You'll be hooked!

Some discoveries are still under way. Gloria Skurzynski asks the big question, *Are We Alone? Scientists Search for Life in Space.* Are there extraterrestrials? Do they fly around in saucers and make crop circles? How can we find out?

Scientists work hard at trying to learn more about the universe. One of the things that excites them most is the possibility that they may find life elsewhere. Few scientists believe that we have any proof that there is life on other planets, although some people certainly believe there is. Thousands say they have been kidnapped by aliens or have seen UFOs.

In 1947, a pilot named Kenneth Arnold was flying in the northwest United States when he saw nine mysterious objects traveling very fast. "He said they moved like a saucer would if you skipped it over water"(page 4). Although he did not say the objects *looked* like saucers, several newspapers wrote up his story, and pretty soon everyone was talking about flying saucers. That is where the phrase "flying saucer" came from. The Air Force investigated and found nothing suspicious—and believed that Arnold may have seen something called lenticular clouds. Show the picture of similar clouds on page 2.

Sometimes we see pictures of flying saucers today, but as the author points out, almost all of these pictures are very blurry. Any detailed, sharp photos of spaceships have always been proved to be altered, changed on a computer—or maybe even a photo of a Frisbee flying through the air. And most of the crop circles have been proved to be hoaxes, made by pranksters.

So scientists have no proof that there are E.T.s. And how are they looking? First of all, they look through giant telescopes, and they have equipment that can pick up sounds and radio frequencies from far, far away. Second, they study life here on Earth. How did it develop? What did it need to develop? "Scientists are pretty certain they know where a planet has to be to support life. It's called the 'Goldilocks' zone—an orbit that's 'not too cold, not too hot, but just right,' which mean's it's not too close to its star's blazing heat but not too far away, either. That's just where our Earth happens to be: in a Goldilocks zone, more formally called a habitable zone" (page 37).

Third, most scientists believe that water is necessary for life, and several other chemicals as well. But they are continually looking for unusual life forms right here on our own planet—and finding them all the time.

A good companion to Skurzynski's book is *Escape from Earth* by Peter Ackroyd. Ackroyd charts humankind's "eternal dream" of leaving Earth and voyaging into outer space. He plots his course from the early pilots who struggled to break the sound barrier, to today's moon landings, and on to spacecraft flying beyond our solar system. Yuri Gagarin, a Russian astronaut who was the first man in space, almost didn't make the return trip. During reentry, his module couldn't separate from the rest of the ship and began to heat up to several thousands of degrees. Finally, his seat ejected while Gagarin was only 23,000 feet above the ground! He landed peacefully in the Russian countryside. Farmers who saw him landing thought he was a creature from another planet.

Ackroyd's book is full of the dynamic, vivid photos that DK Publishing is so famous for. There is even a terrific black-and-white photo of the two dogs, Belka and Strelka, who flew around Earth aboard *Sputnik 5*. One of Strelka's puppies was given to President John F. Kennedy as a gift from the former Soviet Union.

When Jill Cornell Tarter was a young girl, she hated wearing dresses, liked to go camping, and fell in love with the adventures of Flash Gordon and Buck Rogers. The adult Tarter is the current director of Project Phoenix at the SETI Institute in California. What SETI stands for can be found in the subtitle of Ellen Jackson's *Looking for Life in the Universe: The Search for Extraterrestrial Intelligence.* Jackson gives us a rare glimpse of a female scientist at work on one of the hottest issues in current science: Is someone else out there in the universe? Tarter works with a team of scientists who listen for that telltale blip from the cosmos, or search for something weird on their computer printouts. Her work takes her from the mountains of California to the world's largest radio telescope in Arecibo, Puerto Rico. The telescope covers an area as large as 26 football fields! And it is in such demand by scientists from around the world that Tarter's group gets to use it only 40 days out of the year.

So far, there is no hard proof that other intelligent creatures are out there. But Tarter thinks the search is worthwhile. "People are so concerned about whether others are black or white, male or female," she says. "We're really all the same. I think if we found life on other planets, we'd see ourselves as just human. And that would be a very good thing" (pages 10–11). Jackson's book is a very good thing, with bright, vivid photos on almost every page, a clear picture of how a scientist really works, and some neat pictures of outer space. Although uncluttered, the book is very detailed; there are even photos of the tiny Puerto Rican tree frogs, called *coqui,* that sometimes share cabins with the busy scientists.

EXTREME TRAVELERS

Christina Allen relates an earthly journey in *Hippos in the Night.* Allen was a young woman fresh out of graduate school when she had the adventure of a lifetime. She begged and pleaded and did everything she could to get invited on an expedition called AfricaQuest, whose mission was "to travel the length of East Africa's Great Rift Valley to meet with scientists and local people and gather clues to the disappearing wildlife" (page 5). The young scientists would ride on mountain bikes!

Allen was very excited, of course, but a lot of her beliefs about Africa were to be greatly challenged. She was horrified at how much of the wildlife is disappearing and endangered, but she believes that, as with everything else, change here is inevitable. Along the way, Allen meets hippopotamuses, a hyena and a lion, and many, many other beautiful animals, and enjoys getting to meet the people of Tanzania and Kenya. If you like adventures and wildlife, this is the book for you.

The highest mountain in the world was not always called Everest. According to Audrey Salkeld's *Climbing Everest: The Tales of Triumph and Tragedy on the World's Highest Mountain,* the Tibetans and the Sherpas who lived nearest the awesome peak called it "Chomolunga." No one knew that it was the tallest mountain in the world until 1852, when the British Survey of India, which was supervised by Sir George Everest, found that it was indeed taller than any other.

Since it was the world's highest mountain, people wanted to know if it was possible to climb it. Would there be enough oxygen to breathe? "Three French scientists flew a balloon to the same height as Everest in 1875. Rising rapidly, they all passed out—two never to wake again. Would the same thing happen if you ascended that high on foot, even though you would be rising more slowly? No one knew the answer to that" (page 10).

We now know that it can be climbed, and more than a thousand people have done it. But more than 170 people have died on it, as well. It is a dangerous place.

Many of the people who live near the mountain now make a living working on it, guiding the climbers, carrying their gear, and selling them supplies. But they had never climbed the mountain before others came. The most famous of these people was Tenzing Norgay, who, with Sir Edmund Hillary, was the first to reach the summit, in 1953. He even saved Hillary's life!

Different expeditions have tried different routes up the mountain. One of the most famous expeditions was in 1924. George Mallory, making his third attempt to climb the mountain, died on it. No one knows whether he made it to the top. His body was found, frozen solid, 75 years later, but his camera is still missing. His companion's body has never been found.

The Chinese sent a group to conquer Everest at all costs in 1960. They did, but they had a terrible time of it. Only one man has climbed up the mountain alone, Reinhold Messner, from Italy. He wanted to do it without help and without oxygen. Salkeld also tells of one man who skied down the entire mountain in less than five hours!

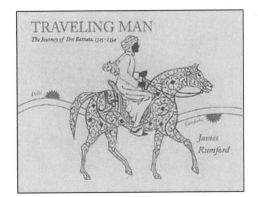

Figure 1.3. *Traveling Man: The Journey of Ibn Battuta, 1325–1354* by James Rumford.

James Rumford's *Traveling Man: The Journey of Ibn Battuta, 1325–1354* starts out like a fairy tale: "In the days when the earth was flat and Jerusalem was the center of the world, there was a boy named Ibn Battuta." Growing up in Morocco's port Tangier, the youngster Battuta became fascinated by ships, maps, and faraway places. When he was 21, he decided to make a pilgrimage to Mecca—and he kept going and did not return home for more than 25 years. He saw the Volga River in Russia, toured the crowded cities of India, and even wrote about far-flung Beijing (although he probably didn't set foot there). This is a beautiful picture book describing the expeditions of one of the world's greatest travelers.

You can show your booktalk audience photographs taken by another world traveler in Ted Lewin's *Tooth and Claw: Animal Adventures in the Wild.* What an interesting life he has led. Lewin likes to have adventures, to take pictures of them or draw them, and then write books about them. And we readers are all the luckier for it.

Open almost any page and find a photo to show your audience. Then ask them what they think it would it be like to

- see a Bengal tiger lunging at you while you were riding an elephant,

- watch a group of chimpanzees eating the small monkeys they have just killed,

- surprise a rattlesnake,

- hear the terrible cry of the howler monkey, or

- run into a huge bull shark while you are swimming.

These are just a few incidents that Lewin experienced. How would you handle them?

Wild beasts are not the most dangerous characters one can meet while traveling. Humans are far worse, according to John Farman's *The Short and Bloody History of Highwaymen.* In the 1700s, there were scores of highwaymen riding the high and low roads of England. These men were criminals, but they enjoyed a romantic reputation in spite of the fact that most of them were pretty horrible.

Many highwaymen were gentlemen who were born into good families. But if they lost all their money or didn't inherit as much as they thought they would, there was always a third option. They could acquire a strong horse and a good set of pistols and rob travelers on the highway. Roads rambled through lonely spots and there were few travelers, whether traveling singly or by coach, so highwaymen didn't worry much about being seen or having someone else stumble in during a robbery.

Fun cartoons fill the pages along with interesting facts about these low-lifes, many of whom ended their days by being hanged. Sometimes their bodies were just left to rot where everyone could see them. This was a warning to other people who were considering a "romantic" life of crime.

Farman tells us:

- Highwaymen liked to attack on roads going uphill, because their victims would be traveling more slowly.

- There were no police or highway patrol!

- There were no banks, so people usually carried their cash (all of it) with them.

- Sometimes highwaymen disguised themselves as women—but there was at least one real highwaywoman, as well.

Figure 1.4. *The Great Serum Race: Blazing the Iditarod Trail* **by Debbie S. Miller.**

If you want to find out about travelers who sought to save lives instead of take them, turn to Debbie S. Miller's incredible *The Great Serum Race: Blazing the Iditarod Trail.* In 1925, the city of Nome, Alaska, was struck by a fatal outbreak of diphtheria. Children were dying. The city council closed the schools and other public places, but one thing alone would fight the disease: antitoxin serum. The nearest serum, however, was a thousand miles away, in Anchorage. Worse yet, Nome was ice bound, and it was too cold for airplanes to fly. There was only one way to get the serum to Nome—dog sleds.

Bring on the four-footed heroes!

Alaskans organized a relay race of multiple dogsled teams to bring the serum to Nome from the nearest railroad terminus 675 miles away. Most of the teams could only travel 30 miles before cold and exhaustion defeated them. Four dogs died due to the severe weather; several more became permanently lame. But two dogs defied all odds to achieve greatness, the lead dogs Togo and Balto. Togo led his team over 260 miles. The frigid January air registered 50 degrees below zero. The trail lay over thin ice and through treacherous snowdrifts. Balto and Togo's owner, Leonhard Seppala, carried the precious serum himself, wrapped up to keep it as warm as possible.

This story is also detailed in Robert Blake's beautifully illustrated *Togo.* Balto is the dog who led the team that brought the serum into Nome, but Togo was his owner's favorite, the one Seppala considered the true leader. And both books agree that most of the glory unfairly went to Balto, who went on to star in a movie. There is even a statue of him in Central Park. Tell your listeners that the incredible race to Nome is now commemorated every year by the world-famous Iditarod race.

If your booktalk listeners can't get enough of dogs and humans sharing adventures together, then show them Carmen Bredeson's *After the Last Dog Died: The True-Life, Hair-Raising Adventure of Douglas Mawson and His 1911–1914 Antarctic Expedition.*

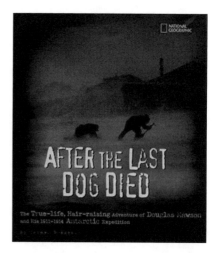

Figure 1.5. *After the Last Dog Died: The True-Life, Hair-Raising Adventure of Douglas Mawson and His 1911–1914 Antarctic Expedition* **by Carmen Bredeson.**

Even when he was only two years old, Douglas Mawson must have loved to have an adventure. When his family moved from England to Australia, he climbed right up the ship's rigging, scaring everyone around him!

From an early age Mawson was curious about science and geology, and he was especially interested in learning more about Antarctica. He went on Sir Ernest Shackleton's first expedition to the icy continent in 1907. Although that first trip found him seasick or battling 100-mile-an-hour winds, Mawson was hooked, and he decided to plan his own scientific trip. He raised money and a crew and set off a few years later in December 1911. The group settled in and divided into four parties, eager to explore and draw maps. Mawson headed east with two men and ran into big trouble.

Falling into crevasses, or cracks in the ice, was always a problem in the Antarctic. It happened to even the most observant travelers. Most of the time the crevasses were not that deep, or you could catch yourself before you fell. But on December 14, 1912, Mawson was second in line when he noticed a crevasse. He turned around to warn the man behind him, then continued on. A few moments later, Mawson turned again—and saw an 11-foot-wide crack in the ice. His friend, Belgrave Ninnis, had vanished from sight. Mawson could not see him, his dogs, or the sledge filled with their supplies, food, and their tent that Ninnis had been carrying.

Mawson and the man who had walked ahead of him called out to Ninnis for three hours. They could not hear Ninnis, but they could hear one of the dogs, trapped in its harness. They tied all their remaining ropes together but still could not reach the sledge, which dangled 150 feet below the surface of the ice. After three hours, the men gave up. Their friend was irretrievable, dead or dying. And they had almost no food at all, none for their own dogs, and were over 320 miles—and five weeks—from the base camp where they could get more.

They survived, but a month later, Mawson himself fell into another crevasse. And while he tried to climb to safety, a blizzard set in. His unfailing spirit and amazing fight for survival provide an unforgettable glimpse of a true hero's heart.

BIBLIOGRAPHY

Ackroyd, Peter. *Escape from Earth.* DK, 2003. ISBN 0756601711. 144 p. Grades 5–up.

Allen, Christina. *Hippos in the Night.* Illustrations by Rob Shepperson. HarperCollins, 2003. ISBN 068817826x. 136 p. Grades 5–7.

Blake, Robert. *Togo.* Philomel Books, 2002. ISBN 0399233814. 32 p. Grades K–3.

Blumberg, Ruth. *Shipwrecked!: The True Adventures of a Japanese Boy.* HarperCollins, 2001. ISBN 0688174841. 80 p. Grades 4–8.

Bredeson, Carmen. *After the Last Dog Died: The True-Life, Hair-Raising Adventure of Douglas Mawson and His 1911–1914 Antarctic Expedition.* National Geographic, 2003. ISBN 0792261402. 64 p. Grades 4–8.

Capuzzo, Michael. *Close to Shore: The Terrifying Shark Attacks of 1916.* Crown, 2003. ISBN 0375922318. 140 p. Grades 5–8.

Conlan, Kathy. *Under the Ice: A Canadian Museum of Nature Book.* Kids Can Press, 2002. ISBN 1553370015. 56 p. Grades 4–7.

Farman, John. *The Short and Bloody History of Highwaymen.* Lerner, 2000. ISBN 0822508400. 96 p. Grades 4–8.

Gerstein, Mordicai. *The Man Who Walked Between the Towers.* Roaring Brook Press, 2003. ISBN 0761328688. Unpaged. Grades K–4.

Jackson, Ellen. *Looking for Life in the Universe: The Search for Extraterrestrial Intelligence.* Photographs by Nic Bishop. Houghton Mifflin, 2002. ISBN 2001051312. 57 p. Grades 5–9.

Kent, Zachary. *The Mysterious Disappearance of Roanoke Colony in American History* (In American History). Enslow Publishers, 2004. ISBN 0766021475. 128 p. Grades 4–up.

Larson, Peter, and Kristin Donnan. *Bones Rock! Everything You Need to Know to Be a Paleontologist.* Invisible Cities Press, 2004. ISBN 193122935x. 204 p. Grades 4–up.

Lewin, Ted. *Tooth and Claw: Animal Adventures in the Wild.* HarperCollins, 2003. ISBN 0688141056. 112 p. All ages.

Majoor, Mireille. *Titanic, Ghosts of the Abyss.* Paintings by Ken Marschall. Hyperion Books for Children, 2003. ISBN 0786818999. 48 p. Grades 4–9.

Marrin, Albert. *Secrets from the Rocks: Dinosaur Hunting with Roy Chapman Andrews.* Dutton Children's Books, 2002. ISBN 0525467432. 80 p. Grades 4–up.

Meltzer, Milton. *Piracy and Plunder: A Murderous Business.* Illustrated by Bruce Waldman. Dutton Children's Books, 2001. ISBN 0525458573. 96 p. Grades 4–up.

Miller, Debbie S. *The Great Serum Race: Blazing the Iditarod Trail.* Illustrations by Jon Van Zyle. Walker & Company, 2002. ISBN 0802788114. 32 p. Grades 1–5.

Philbrick Nathaniel. *The Revenge of the Whale: The True Story of the Whaleship Essex.* G. P. Putnam's Sons, 2002. ISBN 039923795x. 164 p. Grades 4–up.

Rumford, James. *Traveling Man: The Journey of Ibn Battuta, 1325–1354.* Houghton Mifflin, 2001. ISBN 0618083669. Unpaged. Grades 3–5.

Salkeld, Audrey. *Climbing Everest: Tales of Triumph and Tragedy on the World's Highest Mountain.* National Geographic, 2003. ISBN 0792251059. 128 p. Grades 4–8.

Sandler, Martin W. *America's Greatest Disasters.* HarperCollins, 2003. ISBN 0060291079. 96 p. Grades 4–8.

Schyffert, Bea Uusma. *The Man Who Went to the Far Side of the Moon: The Story of Apollo 11 Astronaut Michael Collins.* Chronicle Books, 2003. ISBN 081184007778. 80 p. Grades 5–9.

Simon, Seymour. *Danger! Volcanoes.* SeaStar Books, 2002. ISBN 1587171821. Unpaged. Grades K–3.

———. *Hurricanes.* HarperCollins, 2003. ISBN 0688162916. Unpaged. Grades K–3.

Skurzynski, Gloria. *Are We Alone? Scientists Search for Life in Space.* National Geographic, 2004. ISBN 079226567x. 92 p. Grades 4–8.

Spilsbury, Louise, and Richard Spilsbury. *Shattering Earthquakes.* Heinemann Library, 2004. ISBN 1403447845. 32 p. Grades 4–7.

Tanaka, Shelley. *Earthquake! A Day That Changed America: On a Peaceful Spring Morning, Disaster Strikes San Francisco.* Paintings by David Craig. Historical consultation by Gladys Hansen. Hyperion Books for Children, A Hyperion/Madison Press Book, 2004. ISBN 0786818824. 48 p. Grades 4–8.

Walker, Sally. *Fossil Fish Found Alive: Discovering the Coelacanth.* Carolrhoda Books, 2002. ISBN 1575055368. 72 p. Grades 4–8.

Yolen, Jane, and Heidi Elisabet Yolen Stemple. *Roanoke: The Lost Colony: An Unsolved Mystery from History.* Illustrated by Roger Roth. Simon & Schuster Books for Young Readers, 2003. ISBN 0689823215. Unpaged. Grades 3–5.

CHAPTER —————————2

The Natural World: Astounding Animals and Fascinating Science

AMAZING LAND ANIMALS

Children love animals! All kinds of creatures, feathered, finny, horned, and clawed, fascinate kids of all ages. And it seems a booktalk can't go wrong when it features titles with cute, cuddly, and lovable dogs.

As Christopher Farran points out in the introduction to his *Dogs on the Job!: True Stories of Phenomenal Dogs,* "our dogs always seem eager to help us" (page x). And so they do. He goes on to tell us 18 remarkable tales about dogs that do work for people, and often do it in outstanding fashion.

Jet, for instance is a border collie. At Southwest Florida International Airport, he has an important job to do. The airport is located next to several parks, swamps, and nature areas, and all sorts of birds live nearby. Many of the birds are big, and if they get on the runways and a plane runs into them, not only do the birds die, but airplanes can be badly damaged. In the morning and evening, when it is cooler and birds tend to gather on airport grounds, it is Jet's job to clear them off the runway, thereby saving their lives and also preventing damage to the planes. He gets paid well for his efforts!

Some dogs are trained to search for explosives and drugs in airports. When they find something, they go against all doggy instincts and sit down quietly, so that the authorities can take over. And so they can get a treat for work well done!

Dogs assist blind people, people with hearing loss, and other people with disabilities. Others are dog detectives, tracking people and pets that are lost or have disappeared.

Dogs do all sorts of work for their human friends, and they are loyal companions who sometimes risk their own lives so that their owners can live. Farran ends his book by telling the story of the Greek hero Ulysses, who came home after 20 years of war and wandering only to find that no one, not even his family, recognized him. Only one being knew who he was—his dog, Argos.

"Homer's story of Argos' loyalty to Ulysses has endured for over three thousand years. Why would the old storyteller put in that little detail about the dog in his long, dramatic poem about Ulysses? History tells us that Homer was blind. And maybe—just maybe—he had a loyal dog himself" (page 110).

Dogs have helped people for thousands of years. More recently, when the World Trade Center towers were attacked on September 11, 2001, people were buried in the rubble of the buildings. Some were dead and some were alive. Almost all of them were hard to find. Searchers could not do it alone. They needed help. And the best help came from dogs.

In Donna M. Jackson's *Hero Dogs: Courageous Canines in Action,* your audience will learn that there were two guide dogs in the World Trade towers who led their owners to safety, and who kept calm even though everything and everyone around them was falling apart. Later, search and rescue dogs came in, brought from all over the United States. They sniffed through the rubble, searching for body odor, which they could smell as far as 30 feet down. They helped find the survivors—and the bodies. It was difficult, depressing work for them, and sometimes people would hide so that they could be found and the dogs could feel that they were doing their job. This book tells the story of these hero dogs, including the ones who helped at the Pentagon.

Search and rescue dogs take a long time to train. Jackson tells us the characteristics that they need (page 17):

- a friendly disposition toward people and other animals;

- a high level of focus on tasks—the dog shouldn't be distracted easily by sounds, etc.;

- a willingness to take risks and act against their instincts—for example, remaining on a moving surface instead of jumping off; and

- a strong play drive—the dog must be motivated to keep working to get a reward, which can be anything from a tug-of-war game to a favorite toy or treat.

Another special kind of dog that helps humans is the therapy dog—a dog that who people hold him or her so that they can be comforted. A therapy dog named Tikva was a wonderful help to searchers and survivors at the World Trade Center. Lots of photographs of the different kinds of hero dogs help us to realize what a great contribution they have made and continue to make.

Patricia Lauber, in *The True-or-False Book of Dogs,* tells us that every single dog is originally descended from a wolf. That seems hard to believe. They all look so different. But here we learn how they changed over the years and why they look so different—and why they make good pets and why they behave the way they do.

The book even has a chart of how a dog's body expresses its feelings. Fun illustrations light up an equally delightful text.

Stephanie Frattini gives equal time to felines in her *Face-to-Face with the Cat*. If you like cats and kittens, you are going to love looking at the photos in this book—and learning so many things about these animals that so many of us love!

For instance:

- Did you know that the reason a cat can twist and turn so well is because it has 600 separate muscles that enable it to do just that?

- After cats mate, the female shoos the male away because he will not help her with her kittens.

- Kittens like to play with other animals—especially each other.

Ragdolls are a new breed of cat that was developed in California in the 1960s. Joanne Mattern introduces readers to these newcomers in *The Ragdoll Cat.* Ragdolls have long hair and possess two coats of it, with the shorter one underneath. This means that their hair does not mat or get tangled as much as other longhaired cats. Ragdoll cats grow very slowly. It may take as long as four years for them to become fully grown. Also, their colors get darker as they get older, so they may not attain their permanent colors until they are four years old, either.

Figure 2.1. *The Ragdoll Cat* by Joanne Mattern.

They are quiet cats that like to watch what is going on around them, and they have pleasant personalities. Some ragdolls have a trait that a lot of people enjoy: They go limp when they are held. Show your readers a fun picture of a limp ragdoll on page 9. If you like cats, read about this unusual and beautiful breed.

Jane Goodall was 10 years old when she fell in love with the Tarzan stories of Edgar Rice Burroughs. But even before she could read she loved chimpanzees and had a stuffed one called Jubilee. He now has no hair because when Goodall was a child, she carried him everywhere.

Goodall knew from an early age that she wanted to live with animals in Africa and write books about them. When she was 26 years old, her dream came true: She received a grant to study chimpanzees. In her charming *The Chimpanzees I Love: Saving Our World and Theirs,* Goodall relates how she learned that chimpanzees live in communities, and, just like people, in each small community "all the individuals know one another, but there are some who do their best to avoid each other, some who meet only occasionally, and some who spend a lot of time together and are real friends" (page 21). Mother chimpanzees take excellent care of their babies, and so do older brothers and sisters.

We know that chimps are very close genetically to human beings. Humans can even use chimpanzee blood when blood donations are necessary. And although they cannot speak, some chimps have learned sign language. Jane was astounded to learn that they use tools, much as humans do. Prior to Goodall's discovery, scientists thought that only human beings used tools.

Chimps are in great danger of becoming extinct. We think that 100 years ago there were about two million chimps in Africa. Now there are probably no more than 150,000. That's less than 7 percent of their original numbers! And some of today's chimps live in terrible conditions in laboratories and zoos and circuses.

Another animal that most of your booktalk listeners know about only from visits to the zoo is the subject of Martin Jenkins's *Grandma Elephants in Charge*. Elephant families, like elephants themselves, are big. The males tend to go out alone, leaving the young ones and the females to stay in the groups. And the young do not become fully grown until they are at least 10 years old.

The most important elephants in these groups are the grandmothers, because they have been around a long time and know things about the terrain, where to find food, and how to deal with predators. "If she stops they all stop. If she moves, they all move. And if there's any sign of danger, you can be sure she'll be the first to investigate and the first to decide what the family should do" (page 18). Appealing pictures illustrate this big book.

Learn the story of the first baby elephant born in captivity in Clare Hodgson Meeker's *Hansa: The True Story of an Asian Elephant Baby*. The zookeepers at the Woodland Park Zoo in Seattle were very excited. For the first time ever in the zoo, a baby elephant was about to be born. They hoped that the baby would be born alive and that the baby's mother would accept the baby and not trample it to death—something that had happened at other zoos! Woodland Park Zoo was lucky. The new baby elephant was a girl and it weighed 235 pounds. Within a few minutes, and with a little help from the zoo workers, the baby was walking. And her mother accepted her. That baby grew like crazy. Every day she drank seven gallons of milk and gained another three pounds. Her mother got hardly any sleep because her baby wanted to nurse so often.

The zoo had a contest to name the baby, and a seven-year-old girl named Madison Gordon won. The name Hansa means "Supreme Happiness" in Thailand, the country where the baby's mother was born. Show the picture on page 16 of little Hansa walking underneath her mother.

Meeker's book tells us lots of interesting facts about elephants. Did you know that the reason their skin is so baggy is because having more skin surface helps elephants stay cool? (They don't sweat like we do.) And an elephant's trunk has more than 100,000 muscles in it, which makes it strong enough to lift several thousand pounds. The elephant uses its trunk to sniff almost all of the time. Also, elephants love to swim. Ask your booktalk listeners if they have ever used a snorkel at the beach or in a swimming pool. Then explain that elephants use their trunks as snorkels, and they sometimes swim as far as 20 miles at a stretch in the wild.

Ann Whitehead Nagda and Cindy Bickel introduce your booktalk audience to another amazing zoo inmate in *Tiger Math: Learning to Graph from a Baby Tiger.* At the Denver Zoo, a Siberian tiger named Bukra gave birth to a baby whom the zoo staff named T.J. T.J. only weighed three pounds, and, although he had a good mother, he did not gain weight very rapidly. Soon everyone found out what was the matter. Bukra died, apparently of cancer, when T.J. was only 10 weeks old. Being sick, she had not been able to give him the nutrition he needed.

Now the zoo staff really had to be creative and work hard, because T.J. needed to eat, and eat a lot. But T.J. had no appetite. The story of how they saved him and how he grew is great fun—show the pictures of T.J. opening the refrigerator by himself on page 25. An extra attraction of the book is that you can learn how to make graphs! This is an excellent choice for an integrated classroom lesson on math and animal science.

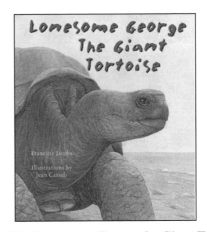

Figure 2.2. *Lonesome George the Giant Tortoise* **by Francine Jacobs.**

George the Giant Tortoise is lonely for a good reason. He is, as far as scientists know, the last of the Pinta Island giant tortoises. He has never been able to mate and is clearly not interested in female sea tortoises from anywhere else but home. This amazing land animal is featured in Francine Jacobs's *Lonesome George the Giant Tortoise.*

George weighs almost 200 pounds. He is a land turtle, and he is called a saddleback turtle because his shell's high opening (resembling a saddle) lets him stretch his neck to nibble on tall bushes. George gets almost all of the moisture he needs from the food he eats. There is no fresh water on Pinta Island except for some puddles after it rains.

The tortoises on Pinta Island have had it bad for a long time. People killed them for food. Later visitors brought goats to the island, and they ate everything in sight, leaving no food for the tortoises. By the time wardens from the Galapagos National Park found George, he was the only tortoise left. He was relocated to the Charles Darwin Research Station in 1972, and he has lived there ever since. George has had quite a life. Scientists are still hopeful that somewhere they will find a female tortoise to keep George company.

Figure 2.3. *Polar Bears* by Gail Gibbons.

Did you know that when a polar bear is born, it weighs only one pound and cannot see or hear? Gail Gibbons gives us some great facts about Earth's northernmost mammal in *Polar Bears*. Polar bears live at the top of the world: the Arctic, where it is so cold that not many animals can live there at all. The polar bear is the biggest and strongest of those that do. A male polar bear may be able to stand as high as 10 feet tall and weigh between 750 and 1,100 pounds! Its paws may be as wide as 12 inches and as long as 18 inches! But when it is born, it weighs only one pound and cannot see or hear.

Polar bears have a great sense of smell. Scientists believe they may be able to smell seals, their favorite food, as far as three miles away. Show the picture of the bear waiting for a seal to come up to the hole in the ice. And did you know that polar bears can eat up to 150 pounds at one meal?

Gibbons also turns her sights on a famous mammal that lives only in the imagination: unicorns. In *Behold . . . the Unicorns,* she relates that around the world, people have told stories of unicorns. Writers and storytellers of the ancient world loved them. "People in many cultures believed the strength of an animal was centered in the horns it used for protection. When the animal had only one horn, the horn was seen as twice as powerful—and magical" (n.p.).

This colorful book is full of stories about and beautiful pictures of unicorns. Did you know that, in the Middle Ages, merchants sold unicorn horns? Many people bought these, because they thought they held the magical powers of unicorns. "The unicorn still represents the qualities most people value. They are seen as being gentle, brave, strong, kind, and noble creatures" (n.p.). Show almost any pictures of the unicorns. Kids love them!

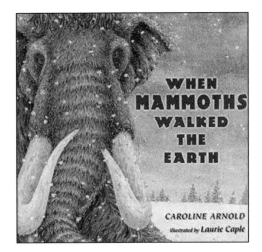

Figure 2.4. *When Mammoths Walked the Earth* **by Caroline Arnold.**

Kids also love hearing about dinosaurs and other prehistoric creatures. A terrific book about one of the earliest mammals is Caroline Arnold's *When Mammoths Walked the Earth.* The Ice Age began about 1.8 million years ago and lasted a long, long time—until about 10,000 years ago. Scientists say that about 18,000 to 20,000 years ago, nearly one-third of the earth's surface was covered with ice. But sometimes it got warmer—and then it got colder again. The huge mammoths, which first lived in Africa, were able to come to North America across the land bridge that connected what are now known as Alaska and Siberia. Different types of mammoths evolved in different places. The biggest ones of all were in Siberia.

Scientists know a great deal about mammoths, even though they have been extinct for thousands of years, because they have found so many mammoth remains—bones, and even, sometimes, entire mammoths, still frozen solid! They know they were a lot like the elephants of today. "They were plant eaters and had four large teeth in their jaws. As the teeth became worn by chewing, they moved forward in the mouth, fell out, and were replaced by a new set. Each succeeding tooth was larger than the one before it. A mammoth could have up to six sets of teeth during its lifetime, with the last set growing in at about age forty-three. After this sixth set finally wore out, the mammoth would die of starvation" (page 12).

Scientists have found excellent mammoth remains here in the United States, in places like the La Brea Tar Pits in California and Hot Springs, South Dakota.

Some great frozen mammoths have been found in Siberia. Windsor Chorlton's *Woolly Mammoth: Life, Death and Rediscovery* tells the story of one such creature that seems to be almost intact, so intact that it is possible that mammoth clones can be made from its body.

The mammoth of Chorlton's book is called the Jarkov, after the family who found it and immediately broke off its huge tusks to sell. The tusks weighed over 100 pounds apiece and were highly valuable. Scientists eventually heard about the Siberian find and started investigating. They were amazed at what they found. This exciting book also tells how experts are currently taking the woolly mummy out of its prison of ice and what they hope to learn from it. It is an amazing story. Show the double-page spread of the woolly mammoth on pages 12–13 and tell your audience that it weighed about as much as 130 adult people!

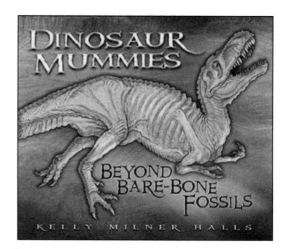

Figure 2.5. *Dinosaur Mummies: Beyond Bare-Bones Fossils* **by Kelly Milner Halls.**

Did you know that dinosaurs leave "mummies" behind, just as early Egyptians did? Of course, as Kelly Milner Halls tells us in *Dinosaur Mummies: Beyond Bare-Bones Fossils,* dinosaur mummies are different than human mummies. In place of careful embalming and linen wrappings, the dinosaur remains are mineralized. Luckily, the slow, natural process of dino decay helped preserve the body parts for modern-day scientists to study.

One of the rarest fossils comes from a young duckbill dinosaur nicknamed Leonardo. Leonardo is over 23 feet long and 77 million years old. Paleontologists can even tell what the long-dead duckbill ate on his last day on Earth!

Figure 2.6. *When Bugs Were Big, Plants Were Strange, and Tetrapods Stalked the Earth: A Cartoon Prehistory of Life Before Dinosaurs* **by Hannah Bonner.**

Do your booktalk listeners know what creatures came *before* the dinosaurs? Peruse the peculiar Permian age in Hannah Bonner's wonderfully weird *When Bugs Were Big, Plants Were Strange, and Tetrapods Stalked the Earth: A Cartoon Prehistory of Life Before Dinosaurs.* Behold the alarming *Arthorpleura,* an ancient centipede six feet long. *Hibbertopterus*, a cousin of the scorpion, was bigger than a Labrador retriever. A smart illustration by Bonner shows the relative sizes of these monsters as they lie on the beach next to a modern-day sunbather.

Before the Permian era, most animals laid their eggs in water. But then among the bizarre swamps and wetlands something startling occurred: Amphibians laid their eggs on land for the first time. Lots of new things were happening. Bonner tells us that a strange dog-like creature called *Procynosuchus* could breathe and chew at the same time. This was a new development in the animal kingdom.

And to find out more about denizens of the prehistoric world, turn to Shelley Tanaka's *New Dinos: The Latest Finds! The Coolest Dinosaur Discoveries!* Probably almost everyone today realizes that we are constantly learning new information about dinosaurs, but most of us almost certainly did not realize how *quickly* our knowledge is growing and changing. Scientists now believe that only *1* percent of the dinosaur species that lived has been found. "About every seven weeks someone discovers the bones of a dinosaur no one has ever seen before" (page 2).

Figure 2.7. *New Dinos: The Latest Finds! The Coolest Dinosaur Discoveries!* **by Shelley Tanaka.**

Some of the amazing facts the author tells us are that:

- The Sahara desert in Africa is full of fossilized dinosaurs. Because it is so remote and hot, much of it is still unexplored by dinosaur hunters—and much remains to be found.

- *Tyrannosaurus rex* had a bite that was so powerful it exerted 3,000 pounds per square inch. This could crush a pickup truck! It had the most powerful bite force of any known animal, although modern crocodiles are pretty powerful, too: 20,00 pounds per square inch.

- So far, the contest for the biggest carnivorous dinosaur of them all is between *Gigantosaurus* and *Tyrannosaurus rex*. *Gigantosaurus* had teeth like daggers, and at least one paleontologist has said that *Gigantosaurus* would kill its prey by biting it. The bite was so big and so horrible, that the prey would bleed to death while *Gigantosaurus* just watched.

- We know that all of the continents on Earth were one large continent millions of years ago—but finding similar dinosaur fossils at different places around the globe helps us learn how the continents were originally formed.

- Fossils have been found of dinosaurs with feathers. Scientists are constantly changing their opinions of how the dinosaurs really looked.

- Birds are descendants of the dinosaurs, and this book tells how it happened!

- We can learn a lot more about dinosaurs from studying fossils of their internal organs, but these are almost impossible to find. Recent discoveries have located a few, and our knowledge is growing by leaps and bounds.

In addition to this great information (and a lot more), there are colorful, informative, great illustrations that demonstrate some of the new knowledge that we have. And you can be sure that certain listeners in your booktalk audience will begin memorizing these fun facts as fast as you can tell them.

BUGS AND CREEPY CREATURES

Figure 2.8. *The Bug Scientists* by Donna M. Jackson.

Anyone want to eat a bug cookie? Along with an unbelievable recipe for Chocolate Chirpy Chip Cookies, Donna M. Jackson's terrific *The Bug Scientists* shows us what some of the people who love bugs do. These scientists are nuts about bugs! Professor Tom Turpin teaches about insects at Purdue University and conducts a cricket-spitting contest at his annual Bug Bowl. Valerie Cervenka studies insects to fight crime and determine when and how people died. She works in Minnesota as a forensic entomologist. One of the things she can do is tell how long ago a body died by studying the insects and insect eggs on the cadaver. Steven Kutcher directs insects in movies such as *Jurassic Park* and *James and the Giant Peach.* And Ted Schultz studies ants that farm—and do it brilliantly. Jackson's book also tells how school kids help study the unusual and beautiful monarch butterflies, which mysteriously migrate thousands of miles every spring and fall. Show the picture of the tagged one on page 19. No one is sure yet how these creatures know exactly where and when to migrate. This book could get your listeners excited enough to help in the discovery.

And listen to this terrific quote on page 4 from Ted Schultz, an entomologist at the National Museum of Natural History, Smithsonian Institution: "If an alien creature arrived on the planet Earth and asked what the dominant life form was here, we would have to say insects. To us, the insects seem like alien creatures, but in fact we're the aliens."

Jackson's book will give your listeners an entirely new perspective on the busy world of bugs.

Snakes! Thousands and thousands of them, all in one place! Balls of snakes! Piles of snakes! Unless you live about 50 miles north of Winnipeg, Canada, you have probably never seen anything like what you'll read about in *The Snake Scientist* by Sy Montgomery. Scientists know of no other place like the Narcisse Wildlife Management Area when it comes to observing garter snakes:

> For about six weeks each April and May, thousands of these harmless snakes awaken from eight months' sleep beneath the earth. They pour out of the pits like water—a river of writhing reptiles. At any of the three big dens here, you can see more snakes at a glance than you could find anywhere else in the world: so many snakes that they are piled two feet deep in places . . . so many snakes that you could pick up ten, twenty, even thirty of them in a handful. (page 4)

Have you ever heard of hibernation? Well, what these snakes do is called *brumination*. When they wake up in the spring they are ready for action. The males wake up first, and then they all wait together and watch for the female snakes to wake up. Scientists are not sure what happens next. The snakes form a mating ball (show the picture on page 36), and all the males try to mate the female in the center of the ball. Scientists are not even sure how the males can *tell* which snake is the female. But they now believe it is by smell, an important sense for creatures who cannot hear.

The snake scientist in this book is Bob Mason, who has loved snakes and turtles all of his life. As a kid he collected them and brought them home. Sometimes they even turned up in the laundry! It drove his mom crazy.

Crowds of schoolchildren visit the wildlife area every year and can handle the snakes and see and feel how harmless they are. You'll wish you could join them—and you can learn what they do, just by reading this fascinating book with its great photographs.

Figure 2.9. *The Tarantula Scientist* **by Sy Montgomery.**

Sam Marshall is a bug scientist who specializes in one particular bug: tarantulas! Sy Montgomery, who wrote *The Tarantula Scientist,* and Nic Bishop, who took the incredible photographs, accompanied Sam on a tarantula-gathering expedition to French Guiana in South America. In tropical spider country the three men learned a lot about tarantulas. Here are some of the facts:

- No one has ever died as a result of a tarantula bite. Tarantulas seldom bite. They only attack things they want to eat, and they do not want to eat people. They would really rather hide than fight! And, actually, they are very good at hiding.

- They protect themselves with their hair, which is sharp and barbed and very irritating to anyone the spider lands on.

- Tarantulas can live for up to 30 years. Most spiders live only a season or two.

- Tarantulas have been around for a long time, more than 150 *million* years.

- They are neat and clean and have very tidy burrows.

- Like other spiders, they weave webs. Their silk is incredibly strong.

- The Goliath birdeater tarantula can have a leg spread of almost 12 inches!

When Sam returns to Ohio with a few hundred tarantulas, he gets his students to help him study them. They love it! Sam tells his students: "You have to wait a number of hours to have some secrets revealed. You never know when you'll see something so cool that the other ninety-nine hours of watching are worth it" (page 66).

Sometimes scary movies tell us that insects are going to take over the world. Cathy Camper tells us that they already have: "For every pound of people on earth, there are three hundred pounds of insects" (n.p.). Wow! That is an *awful* lot of insects. Camper explains in *Bugs Before Time: Prehistoric Insects and Their Relatives* that our neighbor insects were here before the dinosaurs and have successfully outlasted those gigantic creatures. Insects have always adapted and evolved, so that they could survive. Cockroaches, she says, have been here for over 325 million years. One pair of cockroaches can have as many as 100,000 babies in one year. No wonder there are so many of them!

Figure 2.10. *Bugs Before Time: Prehistoric Insects and Their Relatives* **by Cathy Camper.**

How do we know that insects were here long ago and that they changed? Fossils tell us, and there is other evidence as well. But this book is full of fun information—did you know that prehistoric dragonflies had wingspans as wide as 30 inches? Or that millipedes had as many as 400 legs?

For information on one of the most fascinating and ubiquitous of bugs, turn to Melvin Berger's *Spinning Spiders*. We see spider webs all around us when we go outside. "New spiderwebs are beautiful patterns of thin threads. Old webs may be covered with dust and dirt. We call them cobwebs" (page 5). In simple language, this beautifully illustrated book describes the different types of spider webs and how they work. Children will be delighted by the information on page 17: Becausespiders do not have teeth, they drink the flies they catch. They wrap them in thread, and then inject poison into their bodies to turn them into mush! Kids will love it!

While many kids think that most spiders are poisonous, or at the very least dangerous, Seymour Simon calms our fears in *Spiders,* and reminds us that very few spiders are deadly. In fact, spiders do a lot more good than harm. The best thing they do is eat other bugs that cause damage to crops, and therefore they help protect human food. Spiders come in all shapes, sizes, and colors. Some spiders look like grapes. Others look like bird droppings. Birds, who hunt spiders, will see the "droppings" and steer clear of these particular bugs. The orb-weaver spins a beautiful web. You can see it in full color. You can also show your audience a terrifying close-up of a wolf spider in all its bristly, grisly glory. Spiders may indeed be scary to some younger kids, but your listeners will thrill to the amazing abilities of these bugs. Some jumping spiders, for example, can jump a distance that is 40 times the length of their own bodies. That translates to a third-grader being able to jump the length of two basketball courts. Cool!

Figure 2.11. *The Life and Times of the Ant* by Charles Micucci.

Ants may be little, but compared to a lot of insects, they are big. Like Camper, Charles Micucci in *The Life and Times of the Ant* reminds us that ants have been around for over 100 million years, and they are very strong. "Ounce for ounce, an ant is one of the strongest animals on earth. An ant can lift a seed five times its weight, while an elephant can lift a log only one fifth of its weight" (page 3).

Most insects live solitary lives; not so ants. Ants are very social and never live alone. They need each other to survive, to be fed, to build homes, and to exist. Show the amazing picture of the inside of an anthill.

For more information about the ant world, open April Pulley Sayre's *Army Ant Parade.* When the army ants go marching, it is quite a sight—and a human being would be very lucky to see it. They come out at dawn and go looking for food. They eat just about anything that gets in their way: other insects, spiders, scorpions, lizards, frogs, snakes, small birds, and mice. The animals and insects in the area run away to avoid being eaten, but birds frequently follow them, hoping that the presence of the army ants will make the insects come out of hiding so they can be easily caught.

Would they bite you? Or try to eat you if you were watching? Show the picture of the frog being eaten by the ants. Then read this book to find out what happens next.

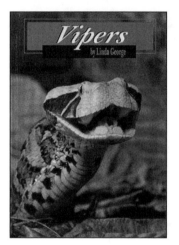

Figure 2.12. *Vipers* by Linda George.

If you know someone who needs to write a report about snakes, Linda George's *Vipers* is a good place to find some great facts about some of the most amazing ones.

Vipers are snakes with long, hollow fangs. "Venom flows through the fangs and into the snake's prey" (n.p.). These snakes also have fangs that are hinged. "The fangs lie flat against the roof of a snake's mouth when its mouth is closed. The fangs swing forward and lock into place when the snake is ready to bite" (page 8). Can you imagine having teeth that lie flat against your mouth and only come out to lock in place when you are ready to bite something?

Viper venom is poisonous and kills its prey fairly quickly. But vipers do not usually slither around looking for food. They wait for it to come to then. They lie quietly, and when something comes close to them, they strike. After they bite something, they often let it run away—and then they follow its scent to find its body and eat it. For a vivid example, show the photo of the viper eating a rodent on page 31.

One particularly deadly snake is called Russell's viper, named after Dr. Patrick Russell, who discovered it in Asia more than 200 years ago. This snake, along with cobras, causes more snakebite deaths than all of the other snakes in the world combined!

Like to have your own creepy creature as a pet? A great handbook is Tristan Boyer Binns's *Hermit Crabs: Keeping Unusual Pets.* Binns is good at giving clear, visual fun facts ("Hermit crabs can be smaller than a penny or bigger than a softball."

[page 7]), and lots of good info for potential owners ("Some hermit crabs move their toys around at night—so you may want to glue anything heavy to the back wall of your crabitat." [page 19]). Great word, crabitat! There are helpful tips on how to choose a crab, how to clean a shell—boil it for five minutes, *before* the crab crawls inside—and even how to bury your pet when it dies. And remember, they may be called hermits, but these crabs need company. You can't just have one! So, be warned.

ANIMALS OF WATER AND AIR

Pink dolphins! Who has ever heard of such a thing? Sy Montgomery introduces your booktalk audience to these amazing creatures in *Encantado: Pink Dolphin of the Amazon*. Pink dolphins exist in the wild, in only two places in the world: the Amazon River and the Orinoco River, both in South America. There is also one dolphin in captivity, in the Pittsburgh Zoo, and that is the one that is displayed in most of the photographs. The zoo dolphin is the only member of its species that anyone has ever been able to see clearly.

Figure 2.13. *Encantado: Pink Dolphin of the Amazon* **by Sy Montgomery.**

Wild pink dolphins live in dark water, permanently stained by natural rain forest chemicals. As they swim by, you might be able to get a glimpse of them, but one thing that confuses everyone is that they seem to change colors. Sometimes they appear pink, and sometimes they seem to be gray. No one gets a good look, as the water they live in is so dark.

These mammals don't look like regular dolphins, and they can do some things regular dolphins cannot do, such as twisting themselves around (show the picture on page 17). They navigate the same way bats do, by echolocation. They emit sounds that bounce off objects and give them an almost three-dimensional picture of the watery world around them.

This book is not only about the pink dolphins, but also about the Amazon itself, which holds half of the world's river water—14 times the flow of America's Mississippi River. The Amazon nurtures more than 2,500 different kinds of fish within its depths. The photographs by Dianne Taylor-Snow are spectacular. Her images will give you the urge to see the wild pink dolphin's home in person after you read this amazing book.

Sailors used to believe the ocean was a "silent world" (page 5), but we know now that it's not silent at all, and a lot of the undersea noise is made by dolphins. In her marvelous *Dolphin Talk: Whistles, Clicks, and Clapping Jaws,* Wendy Pfeiffer lists the ways in which dolphins communicate: "These dolphin sounds are made like the sounds you make when you stretch the neck of a balloon between your fingers and then let the air escape slowly" (page 10).

Dolphins don't rely on just squeaks and clicks to "talk" with each other; they also use their entire bodies, similar to the way humans use body language. For instance, if your mother is mad, does she usually have to tell you so? Or do you know the minute you see her?

Dolphins find each other using echolocation. Dolphins hear extremely well, and their sound beams can help them locate the tiniest objects.

Jeffrey L. Rotman presents some lovely photographs of sea turtles in Mary M. Cerullo's *Sea Turtles: Ocean Nomads.* Sea turtles possess their own un-stereotypical beauty and are graceful animals in the water—but clumsy and awkward on the land. Turtles come on land, however, whenever they lay eggs; they always lay their eggs on the same beach that they themselves were born on. No one knows how the reptiles find that beach, but they often navigate great distances to reach it.

There are seven, possibly eight, different species of sea turtles. Scientists are not exactly sure. But they are certain of one thing: The greatest enemies of this endangered animal are people. People build homes and resorts on the same beaches where turtles lay their eggs. People throw garbage in the ocean and the turtles eat it or get hurt by it, entangled in plastic, cut by sharp metal. Fishermen frequently catch sea turtles by accident and then kill them in nets.

Sea turtle babies have a hard time of it. Right after breaking out of their eggs and climbing up onto the sandy beach, the babies all join together and head toward the water. Birds flying overhead are aware of this and swoop down and eat them. Very few babies make it to the ocean alive—and those that do may encounter larger and more dangerous predators underwater. Scientists figure that roughly one out of every thousand babies lives long enough to become an adult.

Oceanography is a relatively young science. Sneed B. Collard III explains in *The Deep-Sea Floor* that "as recently as the mid-nineteenth century, many people believed that the ocean was bottomless or that no life existed in the deep" (page 9). They were wrong.

Figure 2.14. *The Deep-Sea Floor* by Sneed B. Collard III.

A great deal of life swarms and scurries at the bottom of the ocean. Scientists believed for a long time that food could only be created by energy from the sun and that life, therefore, was totally dependent on sunlight. Oceanographers now know this is wrong.

Animals that live on the bottom of the ocean sometimes eat each other—but their main sources of food are three things: whalefall (like roadkill, only bigger!), fecal pellets, and marine snow. Sometimes a large animal, such as a whale, dies on the surface of the ocean and sinks to the bottom. This animal becomes a banquet for the animals at the bottom. Or animals may eat food that has been pooped out by other animals—that is fecal pellets. Kids love this tidbit of information. Some deep-sea creatures may eat marine snow, which is made up of "mucus, small pieces of dead plants and animals, and bacteria" (page 17). By the time Collard's book was written, scientists had discovered more than 1,000 species of fish at the bottom of the ocean.

Richard Sobol tells us about a sea creature that likes to be touched in *Adelina's Whales.* Ten-year-old Adelina Mayoral has lived all of her life in a very special place—La Laguna in Baja California, Mexico. La Laguna is the only place in the world where gray whales, which can weigh many tons, seek out human beings and let them touch them. Sobol's photographs show the beauty of the gray whales and the poverty of the residents in this unusual and lovely place.

In *Surprising Sharks* by Nicola Davies, simple, brightly colored illustrations will attract kids to this excellent introduction to sharks. Several sharks are pictured in the text and many others are shown on the endpapers—all labeled. Two two-page spreads show the anatomy of the shark. Davies points out that sharks do kill people, about six every year, but that every year people kill 100 million sharks. Your booktalk audience might be surprised to learn that humans can also be predators.

All About Sharks by Jim Arnosky is full of illustrations, charts, tips, and diagrams of these underwater hunters. The skin of a shark, for example, is "covered with tiny tooth-like scales that make it feel like sandpaper" (n.p.). And did you know that sharks have no eyelids? A hammerhead has eyes positioned on the far ends of its weird, T-shaped head. Angel sharks hide themselves by burying themselves in the sand. And how many kinds of sharks are there in the world? At latest count, 250 species prowl the seas. This book is an excellent introduction to the fearsome fish. Arnosky also includes a page covered with pictures of different kinds of shark teeth. One of the teeth is a life-sized illustration of a prehistoric shark's teeth.

Deborah Diffily leads us down into the ancient hunting grounds of those prehistoric monsters in *Jurassic Shark.* Karen Carr's clean, detailed, and sometimes-eerie paintings show how the ancestors of modern-day sharks spent their days. Mostly eating. Or being eaten. The Jurassic shark, known as *Hybodus,* stretched seven feet in length but would attack creatures more than twice its size. Seven rows of razor-sharp teeth filled its mouth. One of *Hybodus*'s enemies was the incredible *Liopleurodon,* 80 feet long with jaws 10 feet wide. Although this book is thoroughly researched and stuffed with amazing information, it reads more like a storybook than a nonfiction title. Thankfully there is a pronunciation guide on the last page, to help wrap your tongue around these mighty monster monikers.

Christopher Sloan guides us through the world of another super-predator in *Supercroc and the Origin of Crocodiles.* Millions of years ago, supercrocs were eating dinosaurs for dinner. Supercroc was twice as long and many times heavier than any crocodile alive today. This book tells its story and the story of the crocodiles we have on Earth now.

Figure 2.15. *Supercroc and the Origin of Crocodiles* **by Christopher Sloan.**

The supercroc found in the Sahara desert had a skull that was more than five feet long and a body length of 36 feet. Digging it out took a lot of work and a lot of time, but the fossil taught us a lot about the crocodiles of long ago. Apparently this animal was quite common in North Africa, and often fought dinosaurs.

As the author says, "Crocs are often called 'living fossils' because of their long history on earth. . . . Crocs have always had long armored bodies, powerful tails, and very toothy snouts. Like their reptile cousins, turtles and lizards, crocs have a body plan that has worked well for a very long time" (page 16). In fact, he explains, crocodiles are closely related to birds!

> Crocs are distinguished from other reptiles by their hearing. . . . Perhaps this explains why crocs . . . have social behavior that is organized around sound. For example mother alligators bury their eggs deep in a nest of dirt and vegetation. When baby alligators are ready to hatch from their eggs, they make grunting noises. On hearing them, the mother, who has been guarding the nest for 65 days, tears the nest open and carries the hatchlings in her mouth to the water. She will continue to protect her young for weeks, listening carefully to their calls. In some cases, they will stay together for years. (page 19)

This book is jam-packed with information about the different kinds of crocodiles and their history and about how we can tell them apart. Show the picture of the crocodile fighting the dinosaur on pages 12–13 and the one on pages 42–43 of the crocodile playing with the dog-sized horses before it eats them.

Compared with the ruthless, predatory crocs, codfish are sitting ducks. Codfish swim around with their mouths wide open ready to eat absolutely anything that comes near them. Consequently, that makes them very easy to catch. And, once upon a time, there were a lot of them. Mark Kurlansky's *The Cod's Tale* may not sound interesting, but wait until you open it up and start reading!

Fish almost never swim alone. That is why a fisherman who has caught one fish will quickly throw his hook or net back in the water and try to catch more. Fish swim, hunt, eat—and spend their lives in groups. A group of fish is called a school. This is not because it is a place of learning. It is an old word from Holland that means a crowd. Fish live in crowds.

The largest school of fish ever known lived in the Atlantic Ocean off Canada and the northeastern part of the United States. So many fish lived in this school that they would bump into one another when swimming.

These fish were the Atlantic cod, and they were to become not only the most commonly eaten fish in the Western world, but also one of the most valuable items of trade. Like gold or oil, the valuable cod played a central role in the history of North America and Europe. (page 6)

And now there are hardly any of them left.

How this all happened and what it all meant makes for a great true story, full of surprising information. Did you know that one of the things that took the longest to settle in the treaty that ended the American Revolution was a discussion of fishing rights? And that cod fishing was heavily involved with slavery? The book also includes some fun and funny recipes for cod. Show the picture of the cod eating anything on pages 8–9.

Figure 2.16. *Growing up Wild: Penguins* **by Sandra Markle.**

Everybody loves to look at penguins, and Sandra Markle's *Growing up Wild: Penguins* is a great book to look through for some fine photographs. It has photos of Adelie penguins, who live in Antarctica and who breed in the Antarctic springtime, which is September and October.

The male penguins are the first to begin building the nests, and the nests are made of pebbles. Some of them are stolen from other nests! When the females arrive, they each lay two eggs, a few days apart. And both penguin parents take turns warming and guarding the nest.

The worst enemy of the Adelies is the skua, a gull-like bird that keeps a bloodthirsty eye out for penguin eggs and penguin chicks. Show the picture on page 11. The clever skuas even work in pairs—one distracts the parents while the other snatches the chick or the egg.

If your booktalk audience can't get enough penguin pics, then grab Betty Tatham's *Penguin Chick* (Let's-Read-and-Find-Out Science). You will love looking at the pictures in this book! Did you know that some penguin mothers lay only one egg a year? And that she takes wonderful care of that egg along with the father? The father spends a lot of time sitting with the egg and sometimes on it, keeping it warm. The parents share equal egg-time responsibility due to the fierceness of the climate and the scarcity of food. They have to take turns so that one of them can find food while the other gives necessary warmth to the unborn chick.

When the baby penguin is born, the parents still have to take very good care of the new, helpless, hungry baby chick. Show the picture of the parent tenderly brushing the baby's coat on page 23.

Figure 2.17. *It's a Hummingbird's Life* **by Irene Kelly.**

Few of your listeners will have seen a penguin, but they may have watched a hummingbird go whizzing by. Or spied it while it zipped quietly around a special hummingbird feeder. In *It's a Hummingbird's Life* Irene Kelly explains that these tiny birds work hard almost constantly. They build little nests, lay two eggs, and need to feed their babies every three minutes. Hummingbirds eat eight times their body weight in nectar from flowers every day. That would be like human beings drinking 500 cups of juice in a day. They have amazing flying abilities and can go straight up in the air. Their wings revolve like helicopter blades. And they migrate hundreds of miles every fall. Hummingbirds are amazing, and this book tells us all about them.

Figure 2.18. *Chicks & Chickens* **by Gail Gibbons.**

If you like to eat chickens or like to watch chickens, or want to know more about chickens, Gail Gibbons's *Chicks & Chickens* is the book for you. It has all sorts of interesting information about them:

- We know that people raised chickens in China as long as 4,000 years ago!

- They have weak wings so they cannot fly very far.

- There are about 113 breeds of chickens.

- There are more than 10 billion chickens in the world!

- Chickens can live to be as old as 12 years.

- Once a chicken laid an egg that was 12 inches long!

Any of the colorful double-page spreads is good to show your listeners.

Figure 2.19. *Beaks!* **by Sneed B. Collard III.**

One thing all birds have in common, from penguins to hummingbirds to chickens, is a beak. As Sneed B. Collard III sums up in *Beaks!:* "Birds have no teeth. No hands. No antlers, horns, or spines. But birds have beaks. And beaks are enough" (first page of text).

Have you ever really looked at a bird, or even a picture of a bird? Have you ever thought of how many different kinds of beaks birds have? Mr. Collard tells us all of the things that they can do and all of the different ways that they work to make it easier for the bird to get food. Think of a hummingbird beak. How do hummingbirds use their beaks? How about an eagle beak? Or a duck beak? You can review the fun facts in this book with the "Test your 'beak-ability'" quiz at the end.

ANIMAL DISCOVERY AND BEHAVIOR

The Lewis and Clark expedition had many important tasks to accomplish. One was to discover animals that, while familiar to Native Americans, were still unknown to the people who had migrated from Europe. The expedition did better than expected: They found the Western rattlesnake, mule deer, pronghorn, and mountain goat, among many others.

Today a lot of people still believe that all of the earth's animals have been discovered, but this is not true. Laurence Pringle tells us in *Strange Animals, New to Science* that new animals are being discovered all of the time. Like Lewis and Clark, Pringle points out some creatures that are unfamiliar to most Western eyes.

Take a look at the picture of the Javan rhinoceros of Vietnam on page 17. Scientists thought that this animal had become extinct about 100 years ago, but they were wrong. It certainly is endangered, however. Only 15 are known to exist. The Cuban frog on page 18 is so small it easily fits on a dime! The forest owlet of India is only eight inches tall and also was believed to be extinct. You will be delighted by the pictures of these unusual animals.

Figure 2.20. *What Do You Do with a Tail Like This?* **by Steve Jenkins and Robin Page.**

Steve Jenkins and Robin Page have come up with a great concept, and a terrific booktalk activity, in *What Do You Do with a Tail Like This?* Each two pages show five different animal parts: noses, eyes, tails, feet, and mouths. The book asks us to guess which animals the body parts belong to and what they do with them.

There is some great information here. Do you know that the horned lizard shoots blood from its eyes when attacked? Or that the humpback whale can hear other humpback whales hundreds of miles away? Or that the field cricket's ears are on its front legs?

Keith DuQuette, in *They Call Me Woolly: What Animal Names Can Tell Us,* reminds us that names of animals may tell us a lot about them. Have you ever thought you might want to get close to a vampire bat? Or a Komodo dragon? Or a Tasmanian devil? How about a rattlesnake? Its name describes the noise it makes when it is about to strike.

Names might tell you where an animal, such as the rat snake, lives, in what kind of a place or on which continent, for instance; or how an animal moves; or what kind of food it eats—. There are some great pictures, and a couple of pages of good facts in the back. Show the picture of the white shark, the blue marlin, and the yellow goatfish, which all have names that describe their color, on pages 14–15.

Hop Frog by Rick Chrustlowski gives us a good overview of a frog's life. When two leopard frogs mate, they produce a mass of 3,000 eggs. This book describes, in colorful, appealing pictures, exactly what happens to those eggs. First a black dot appears in each, and eventually a tiny tadpole breaks out. Then its lungs develop, it grows and changes, and it must avoid being eaten by predators. Simple and a fine introduction to life cycles.

Figure 2.21. *Spy Hops & Belly Flops: Curious Behavior of Woodland Animals* by Lynda Graham-Barber.

Have you ever seen a fox hop on its hind legs? Or an otter slide on its stomach? Or a chipmunk stuff nine nuts in its mouth? You will have fun looking at the pictures in Lynda Graham-Barber's delightful *Spy Hops & Belly Flops: Curious Behavior of Woodland Animals*. Little listeners will also have a lot of fun copying the curious creatures. See how many behaviors they can copy!

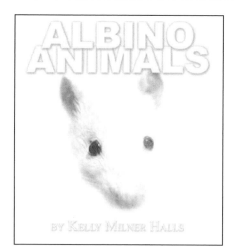

Figure 2.22. *Albino Animals* **by Kelly Milner Halls.**

Frogs are one of the many animals included in Kelly Milner Halls's eye-popping *Albino Animals.* Albinos are animals with no pigment. Pigment absorbs color from all of the colors in light, which is called the spectrum. An animal with no pigment cannot absorb color from light, so it appears white. When there is no pigment in the eyes, we can see the blood vessels, which make the eyes look pink or red. This is all related to genetics. Almost all of the species on Earth have some albino members, including human beings.

This book is chock-full of wonderful photographs. The aforementioned albino frog appears on page 15. And there are an albino hedgehog, pug, hummingbird, and locust (!) along with dozens of other beautiful specimens.

Many albinos lead difficult lives. First of all, they tend to sunburn very quickly, and this can even cause death. Second, because they have no protective coloring or camouflage, they are frequently killed at an early age by predators. Albinos, unfortunately for them, can be spotted from a great distance. Often, the albinos that live longest are those raised on breeding farms.

Halls includes some wonderful anecdotes. For instance, in 1970, an owner of a tourist aquarium was cruising in the waters near Vancouver, British Columbia, when he saw an albino orca. Five members of the orca's pod were captured for the aquarium that day, and it was later discovered that all of the members of the albino's pod had some physical defects. Scientists believe that possibly the whole group was made up of outcasts, orcas who had grouped together because they were unacceptable to their own pods.

Many albinos have vision problems or are blind because sunlight damages their unprotected eyes. Albino buffaloes are considered sacred to many Native American tribes. A photo of one can be seen on page 38.

In another of her easy-to-read books about pets, Joan Holub shares lots of information about another group of hopping animals in *Why Do Rabbits Hop? And Other Questions About Rabbits, Guinea Pigs, Hamsters, and Gerbils.* Only one animal out of the four, the rabbit, is not a rodent, but all of them have one thing in common: Their front teeth keep growing throughout their lives!

Other great information:

- There are about 50 breeds of rabbits.

- The biggest rabbit is the Flemish giant, which weighs up to 22 pounds.

- The most popular hamsters are the golden hamsters, and they were found in Syria around 1930.

- The most popular kind of gerbil is the Mongolian gerbil.

A great animal book for young readers is Mary Ann Fraser's *How Animal Babies Stay Safe.* A lot of animal babies are very much like human babies. They need someone to take care of them. Their parents take good care of them just like a human baby is taken care of by its parents. But, in fact, human babies need their parents around longer than any other kind of animal.

There are some great pictures of the different ways animals take care of their little ones—and you will get some new information about the different ways they need help.

Show the picture of the alligator with its babies in its mouth (no other animal would dare attack them there) on page 17.

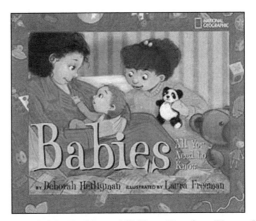

Figure 2.23. *Babies: All You Need to Know* **by Deborah Heligman.**

For young booktalk audiences, one of the most fascinating of all animal babies is the human! Open up Deborah Heligman's *Babies: All You Need to Know* for a light and fact-filled introduction to the world of infants. Anyone who has ever had a new baby come to live with them has a lot of questions! Those babies don't do much at first. It seems like they just eat and cry and go in their diapers.

But, as this book tells us, every one of us was once a baby, even our grandpas and grandmas! We have all grown up quite a bit, and most babies weigh three times as much on their first birthday as they did on the day they were born. "If you grew at that rate every year, you'd weigh more than a thousand pounds by the time you were five" (page 6).

This book will tell your booktalk listeners some of the things they will want to know about their new baby—or their baby cousin or their baby friend. Heligman gives ideas for playing with the baby and for understanding what the baby means when it tries to communicate. This is a fun and helpful book for kids who like babies.

Kids are as interested in babies and toddlers as are their parents. After all, they have to live with them too! Robie K. Harris and Michael Emberley tell us what to do to make a baby happy in *Hello Benny!: What It's Like to Be a Baby.*

What do babies see? What do they know?

This great book gives all sorts of information. For instance, "If you smile, talk, whisper or sing to a baby who is many weeks old, most often the baby will smile back at you. For a few months after that, babies smile at everyone they meet and sometimes even at a photo. People who smile, make noises, and move their mouth, eyes, and eyebrows are what babies like to smile at most" (n.p.).

You can learn that when babies kick their legs or wave their arms, it may be because they are excited. And that sometimes thumbs, fingers, toes, and feet are babies' favorite toys. And babies all around the world make the same noises, no matter what language their parents speak. There are lots of great pictures, too. Show the one of the baby sucking on its foot.

The world's biggest creatures start out as tiny babies. But it's sometimes hard for kids to wrap their brains around the idea of just how large (or tiny) animals can be. Steve Jenkins solves this problem, and creates a delightful book, in *Actual Size.* It's a terrific concept book and a marvelous resource for any animal lover. You'll find the answers to a lot of interesting questions in this book:

- What tarantula is big enough to eat birds?

- Which animal's tongue is two feet long?

- What is the world's largest bird?

- What animal has eyes that are about one foot across *each?*

- What is the biggest cat ?

- What kind of an earthworm grows up to one yard long?

- What is the world's smallest fish? Clue: It takes *7,000* of these fish to weigh one ounce!

Not only are these answers amazing, but Jenkins lavishly illustrates his pages with actual size (!) pictures of at least *part* of every animal described in this book. You will have a lot of fun with this one.

Show the picture of the Siberian tiger, the biggest of the big cats. How would you like to see that face up close?

A good addition to any booktalk on animals would be a title on one of the people who helped change the way we view Earth's other inhabitants. A good start is Amy Ehrlich's *Rachel: The Story of Rachel Carson.*

Rachel Carson was five years old when she found a fossil of a sea creature in Pennsylvania, far from any ocean. Her mother told her that the land they lived on had once been covered by the ocean. Rachel was amazed. As she grew older and older, Rachel's interest in writing and in nature increased. She knew she wanted to be a writer, and her first story was published when she was 13. But in college she switched her major to biology. Once she graduated, she got a job at the Woods Hole Marine Biology Laboratory on Cape Cod, and there she became more and more interested in the ocean and the life living within it, both plant and animal. Because of her passionate concern, and because she was a terrific writer, Rachel Carson changed the world! This book tells how she did it.

FASCINATING SCIENCE

Food is always a topic that perks up the ears of a booktalk audience. And when science is served up as a side dish, as skillfully as Elaine Landau presents it in *Popcorn!,* it makes for a satisfying combo. If you are feeling even a little bit hungry, and you do not have any popcorn on hand, don't read this book until you are not hungry at all. *You will want popcorn!*

Figure 2.24. *Popcorn!* **by Elaine Landau.**

You probably have already figured out that Americans love popcorn. In fact, every year, each adult and each child eats, on the average, 68 quarts! That is a lot of popcorn.

Only one kind of corn is, in fact, popcorn. Not every kind pops. Popcorn seals water inside it, which expands when heated and then bursts. People have been eating it for thousands and thousands of years. In New Mexico, scientists found popcorn that is more than 5,600 years old! In the last century popcorn was usually made for sale in carts on the street—until World War II. There was a big shortage of sugar, and people wanted snacks. Popcorn was cheap and tasty and served that need—and people started to really like it.

When TV became popular in the 1950s, popcorn sales dropped until popcorn producers started telling people how to make it at home, in pans and in electric poppers. Then, in the 1980s, microwave popcorn became WILDLY popular.

More popcorn is eaten in the United States than anywhere else on earth. Hungry now?

Food gives us energy. And energy is something your booktalk audiences are loaded with! But do they know where it comes from? Kimberly Brubaker Bradley says in *Energy Makes Things Happen* that unless you are not feeling well, you probably always have lots of it. Most of our energy, in fact, comes from food. Heat and light and all sorts of movement come from energy.

As the book tells us, "Energy is transferred from one thing to another. When a boy throws a baseball, he transfers energy from his arm to the ball. Then the ball can move through the air. (The more energy he gives the ball, the faster it goes!" (page 8). This book tells us where energy comes from and how we get it. Have fun finding out how it works! Show the picture of the kids getting their energy from drinking milk and eating cookies on pages 16–17.

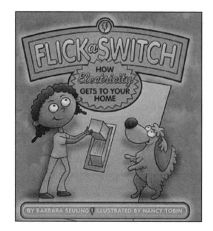

Figure 2.25. *Flick a Switch: How Electricity Gets to Your Home* **by Barbara Seuling.**

Barbara Seuling talks about a popular form of energy in *Flick a Switch: How Electricity Gets to Your Home.* Have you ever wondered how electricity really works? It seems like magic. You walk into a dark room and turn on a switch and suddenly the room is filled with light. It seems so easy. But it really isn't.

It took a long time for people to discover that things they saw, such as lightning, were made of something, which could be very useful to them—electricity. Benjamin Franklin was the first to prove that electricity and lightning were the same thing, and that was more than 250 years ago. Show the picture of Ben Franklin with his kite. Inventors who came after him worked on it, and in 1800, a man named Alessandro Volta invented the battery, which is an electric cell. The word "voltage" comes from his name.

By 1882, Thomas Edison had invented the light bulb and opened the first power plant, in New York City. This book tells us what happens inside that power plant and how the electricity gets from there into our houses.

Americans and Canadians are so familiar with electricity that they take it for granted, but about one-third of the people in the world have no electricity at all. That means no computers, no electric lights, no refrigerators, no TV, and no electrical medical equipment. Ask your booktalk audience if they could live in a world without electricity? How would they go through a normal day without power in their schools and homes? Then ask them if the power has ever gone out in their homes. What did they do, and how did they cope? Seuling also includes some fun experiments to do with electricity.

Kids usually know how tall they are, or how much they weigh. David M. Schwartz in *Millions to Measure* explains that people didn't always know those simple facts. People needed a way to measure long, long ago. When they ran races, how far did they run? How big should they make things?

Different countries had different ways of measuring. Sometimes people measured by the length of their feet—but not all feet were the same size. Then at least one king said that one foot was the size of *his* foot. His foot was the one everyone else needed to measure by. Eventually measurements became standardized, so that everyone was measuring the same thing. But the system was complicated and hard to remember.

Along came the metric system, in the late 1700s. This system is now used almost everywhere—except in the United States of America. This has led to complications. One was the spaceship that was lost in space in 1999—the *Mars Climate Observer.* The builders of the ship used inches and yards to measure. The operators used the metric system. You cannot use both kinds and get things right. Steven Kellogg's strong visuals go a long way in helping explain some of this tricky stuff. You can also show kids the pullout spread of the metric system.

Need a few more tricks to spice up a booktalk? Turn to J. Patrick Lewis's *Scientrickery: Riddles in Science.* If you like riddles and jokes and science, you will have a lot of fun with this book. It's a guessing game, and the pictures give you clues to the answer. See how many you know without guessing!

Read the poem "T-bones" aloud to your audience.

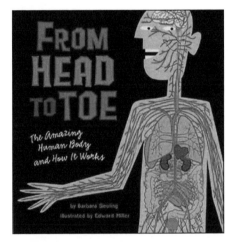

Figure 2.26. *From Head to Toe: The Amazing Human Body and How It Works* **by Barbara Seuling.**

You will really be amazed at what you learn about your body when you read Barbara Seuling's fun *From Head to Toe: The Amazing Human Body and How It Works.* As the author tells us, every single part of our body has a purpose—except for one part: the appendix. Nobody is sure why we have that. But bones do a lot of work, joints help us move, our thumbs help us do all sorts of things that animals cannot do, muscles enable us to move (show the double-spread of the muscles on pages 14–15), and the brain is the main headquarters. There are great color pictures here and terrific information. Do you know which four tastes—and *only* four—are recognized by the human tongue? (Sour, salty, sweet, and bitter.) Do you know that our hair grows out of tiny openings called follicles? If your follicles are oval-shaped, you will have curly hair. If you have round follicles, your hair will be straight. Ask your booktalk kids what shape follicles they have. Scientists and doctors have learned a great deal about the human body, and we can now replace or renew many of its parts. Read all about it!

Seymour Simon has teamed up with Nicole Fauteux to produce a series of marvelous hands-on science books on a number of topics. Even if you think you don't like to try science experiments, you will have fun with the ones in these books. The authors of the books make these experiments into games that are really fun to play! *Let's Try It Out in the Air* introduces kids to that great invisible element that we can't live without: air. How can we find out about air? We can't see it—or can we? Maybe sometimes we can see it move things—like when it is windy. But what does air do? What can it hold up? *How* can it hold things up? Try it and find out! All of the two-page spreads are terrific. The one with the balloons is especially fun.

Let's Try It Out in the Water asks kids if they have ever played on a beach near an ocean or a lake or even near a swimming pool. Why do some things sink and other things float? Why can you throw a tiny pebble in the ocean and it sinks, but a great big ship carrying hundreds of people stays afloat? What helps things float? What doesn't? What makes them sink? Figure it all out by following the easy and fun experiments.

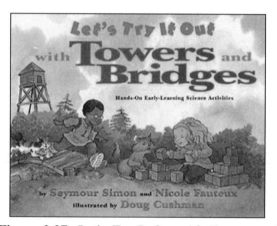

Figure 2.27. *Let's Try It Out with Towers and Bridges* **by Seymour Simon and Nicole Fauteux.**

And finally, *Let's Try It Out with Towers and Bridges: Hands-On Early-Learning Science Activities* is a wonderful concept book. The authors start out by imagining that you are a pioneer family who need to build a shelter on the trail. The shelter is temporary and therefore pretty rickety. But suppose you want a house—or a bridge—that will stay put and last a long time? What can you do to make it strong and durable? A grand idea truly well executed. Kids will have a lot of fun while they learn with this one.

Vicki Cobb has her own series of science books, illustrated by Julia Gorton. These titles focus on simple, recognizable phenomena, and make science a part of the reader's daily life. In *I Face the Wind,* she asks if kids know what the wind really is. Can they explain it? Why is it sometimes really hard to walk when the wind is strong? Why is it sometimes hard to even stand up straight? What can wind do? And what is it made of? This book has some quick experiments that show kids how wind works. Everything needed for the experiments is easy to find. You probably have it in your library or classroom right now.

If your kids are interested in finding out about how water works and what it can do, then turn to Cobb's *I Get Wet.* Teachers in primary grades will find it helpful for doing simple experiments, and it asks questions that children can figure out the answers to—and then see demonstrated.

Find out:

- What shape is water?

- Does water stick to itself?

- Why does it flow?

- Does water stick to you?

The pictures are vivid and the directions are easy to follow.

Cobb presents a clever introduction to the science of light and mirrors in *I See Myself.* When you want to see what you look like, what do you do? Where do you go? Do you ask a friend to tell you if your hair is messed up? Probably not. Most of us would go straight to a mirror. But what if a room were completely dark? Could we look in a mirror then?

We could, but it absolutely would not work.

A mirror is the very best place to look at yourself (although this book tells us some other places we could look at ourselves—see if you can guess them), but it also needs light.

As always, Cobb includes strong, simple experiments, along with easy-to-grasp information about mirrors and light in this book. Look at the second double-page spread that shows places you can see yourself.

Lola Schaefer and Lindsay Barrett George have created a beautiful book about flowers with *Pick, Pull, Snap!: Where Once a Flower Bloomed.* Single-page illustrations and foldout spreads tell us the story of how various flowering fruits and vegetables grow. Peas, corn, raspberries, peanuts, peaches, and pumpkins are included. Die-cuts and people's pleasure at seeing the new produce add to the fun.

Gail Gibbons has another own book on growing things, *The Berry Book.* Think any of your kids like berries? Strawberries, raspberries, blueberries, cranberries, blackberries? In this delightful book, Gail Gibbons tells us about the different kinds of berries, including a few that are poisonous. She tells us how they grow and how they are used. Not every berry that we grow, however, ends up in our stomachs. Bayberries, for example, are often used in making candles. Gibbons even tells us how to grow our own strawberries and how to bake a blueberry pie.

On the last page we learn that grapes, bananas, cucumbers, and tomatoes, among other foods, are also classified as berries. That means chimpanzees are berry lovers, too.

Gibbons turns her hand to other growing things with *Tell Me, Tree: All About Trees for Kids.* Did you know that:

- Many trees have as many roots below the ground as they have branches above.

- Most of the oxygen we breathe comes from trees.

- There are really only two groups of trees—broadleaf trees and evergreen trees.

- The largest living things in the world are trees.

- Trees cover about one-third of the earth's land surface.

Gibbons's book has some neat pictures of trees, including a great illustration of "Inside a Tree."

Nature isn't always pretty. For example, look at the picture of a bald eagle eating the rotten fish and feeding it to its chicks in Lee Ann Landstom's *Nature's Yucky! Gross Stuff That Helps Nature Work*. Many things that people consider to be gross and disgusting are normal and natural and wonderful when they happen in nature. Animals do many amazing things, such as

- eat rotten, smelly meat and fish;

- don't poop for months;

- throw up every day;

- poop on their very own legs; and

- put their stomachs outside their bodies in order to eat!

These are just a few of the things that some animals do. Kids always seem to enjoy topics that appeal to their slightly squeamish side. And this title is a good book for doing just that.

Figure 2.28. *Life on Earth: The Story of Evolution* **by Steve Jenkins.**

Steve Jenkins takes another controversial science topic and treats it with his typical flair and masterful artistry. *Life on Earth: The Story of Evolution* is an amazing introduction to a difficult concept. Have your kids ever heard of the theory of evolution? Would you be able to explain it? This beautiful book is easy to read and easy to follow, and, in it, Steve Jenkins shows us what evolution is and how it affected life on Earth. Jenkins fills his clean, white backgrounds with intricate and breathtaking portraits of creatures from long ago as well as current fauna. And each illustration is done in Jenkins's painstaking, signature style of cut and torn paper collages. These amazing pictures look as if they were painted and polished. Show your audience the *T. rex* on page 15, and the flightless bird on the next spread. You can almost feel the texture of their skins. An elaborate continuous spread on pages 4 through 7 is an updated version of the "Peaceable Kingdom"—from peanut worm to black rhino to bowhead whale—with a key to each creature's name and habitat at the back of the book.

For billions of years, Jenkins explains, there was no life on Earth. The planet was very hot. There was no water. The air was full of poisonous gases. But at some point the earth cooled down, water collected, and oceans formed—eventually leading to the growth of tiny bacteria. All of life on Earth today—the birds, the mammals, the fish, and the humans—is descended from those original, tiny bacteria—and you can clearly see how this happened by reading this book. For those booktalks that want to add a deeper, richer layer of scientific thinking, this is a spectacular source.

The rain forests on our present Earth are the fertile backdrop for April Pulley Sayre's *Tropical Rain Forest.* Did you know that:

- There are many species of animals in tropical rain forests. Birdwatchers can see as many as 300 species of birds in one day. In most places, you cannot see that many in a year. In Peru, a scientist found 43 species of ants on one tree.

- Rivers flood the Amazon rain forest for up to five months every year.

- Many rain forest trees have epiphytes on them. These are plants that grow on other plants. Orchids are one kind of epiphytes, and once a scientist counted 300 orchids growing on one tree!

- Many insects pollinate plants. The rafflesia flowers attract pollinators by smelling like rotten meat! Flies love that smell!

This book is easy to read and contains some beautiful pictures. Look at the glass-winged butterfly on page 33 and be dazzled!

Rain forests are full of creatures that use camouflage to hide, survive, or make themselves effective hunters. But John Woodward points out in *Clever Camouflage* that animals that use this special trait can be found in habitats all around the globe. There are two main types of camouflage: cryptic coloration and mimicry. The first method allows an animal to blend in with its surrounding, like the well-known chameleon. But an even more amazing example is the leaf-tailed gecko of Madagascar. Show your booktalk group a picture of this creature on page 9. Can they see it? The lizard's skin looks exactly like the flaky, gray bark of the tree branch it perches on. Turn the page, and show your kids the row of icky thorn bugs. You'll see how the exotic little critters got their name. Decorator crabs attach plants and shells to special hooked hairs protruding from their skin. Eventually they look just like a section of ocean floor. And the stone plant of Africa (it's alive!) resembles the smooth desert pebbles that surround it.

The mimic octopus of Indonesia, on the other hand, uses its camouflage to look like other creatures. It can swim like a jellyfish, crawl like a crab, or wiggle like a poisonous sea snake. Clear, bold text and dramatic photos make this book a "Where's Waldo" of the animal kingdom. A surefire hit!

Figure 2.29. *Dirt* **by Steve Tomecek.**

Steve Tomecek gets down and dirty about his favorite topic in *Dirt*. Tomecek is frequently called "The Dirtmeister." And for good reason. He loves the stuff! "Some people just think that dirt is something to be cleaned up—like the stuff you wash out of your clothes. But dirt is really one of the most important things on earth" (page 6).

Tomecek wants us to love dirt as much as he does. His arguments are pretty persuasive. Most people don't think about dirt much at all. But dirt helps feed us. Most of the food that we eat is grown in dirt, and, without dirt, we would be in bad shape.

This fun book tells us about the different kinds of dirt, how dirt is created, and what things live and grow in dirt. Did you know, for instance, that "by tunneling through the soil, earthworms give plant roots places to grow? These tunnels also make spaces for water and air to get into the soil. Some scientists think that, over the course, of a year a single earthworm can eat several tons of soil" (page 17).

There's more to dirt than mud pies and pickup truck commercials.

BIBLIOGRAPHY

Arnold, Caroline. *When Mammoths Walked the Earth.* Illustrated by Laurie Caple. Clarion Books, 2002. ISBN 0618096337. 40 p. Grades 3–5.

Arnosky, Jim. *All About Sharks.* Scholastic, 2003. ISBN 0590481665. Unpaged. Grades 4–7.

Berger, Melvin. *Spinning Spiders.* Illustrated by S. D. Schindler. HarperCollins, 2003. ISBN 0060286962. 33 p. Grades 1–3.

Binns, Tristan Boyer. *Hermit Crabs* (Keeping Unusual Pets). Heinemann Library, 2004. ISBN 1403408254. 48 p. Grades 4–7.

Bonner, Hannah. *When Bugs Were Big, Plants Were Strange, and Tetrapods Stalked the Earth: A Cartoon Prehistory of Life Before the Dinosaurs.* National Geographic, 2004. ISBN 079226326X. 48 p. Grades 4–8.

Bradley, Kimberly Brubaker. *Energy Makes Things Happen.* Illustrated by Paul Meisel. HarperCollins, 2003. ISBN 0060289082. 33 p. Grades K–3.

Camper, Cathy. *Bugs Before Time: Prehistoric Insects and Their Relatives.* Illustrated by Steve Kirk. Simon & Schuster Books for Young Readers, 2002. ISBN 0689820925. Unpaged. Grades 3–6.

Cerullo, Mary M. *Sea Turtles: Ocean Nomads.* Photographs by Jeffrey L. Rotman. Dutton Children's Books, 2003. ISBN 0525466495. 40 p. Grades 3–6.

Chorlton, Windsor. *Woolly Mammoth: Life, Death and Rediscovery.* Scholastic Reference, 2001. ISBN 0439241340. 40 p. Grades 3–6.

Chrustlowski, Rick. *Hop Frog.* Henry Holt, 2003. ISBN 0805066888. Unpaged. Grades K–3.

Cobb, Vicki. *I Face the Wind.* Illustrated by Julia Gorton. HarperCollins, 2003. ISBN 0688178405. Unpaged. Grades K–2.

———. *I Get Wet.* Illustrated by Julia Gorton. HarperCollins, 2002. ISBN 0688178383. Unpaged. Grades K–2.

———. *I See Myself.* Illustrated by Julia Gorton. HarperCollins, 2002. ISBN 0688178375. Unpaged. Grades K–2.

Collard, Sneed B., III *Beaks!* Illustrated by Robin Brickman. Charlesbridge, 2002. ISBN 1570913870. Unpaged. Grades K–3.

———. *The Deep-Sea Floor.* Illustrated by Gregory Wenzel. Charlesbridge, 2003. ISBN 1570914028. 29 p. Grades 2–4.

Davies, Nicola. *Surprising Sharks.* Illustrated by James Croft. Candlewick Press, 2003. ISBN 763621854. 29 p. Grades K–3.

Diffily, Deborah. *Jurassic Shark.* Paintings by Karen Carr. HarperCollins, 2004. ISBN 0060082496. Unpaged. Grades K–3.

DuQuette, Keith. *They Call Me Woolly: What Animal Names Can Tell Us.* G. P. Putnam's Sons, 2002. ISBN 0399234454. 32 p. Grades K–3.

Ehrlich, Amy. *Rachel: The Story of Rachel Carson.* Illustrated by Wendell Minor. Silver Whistle/Harcourt, 2003. ISBN 0152162275. Unpaged. Grades K–3.

Farran, Christopher. *Dogs on the Job! True Stories of Phenomenal Dogs.* Illustrated by Pat Bailey. Avon Books, an imprint of HarperCollins, 2003. ISBN 0064411208. 116 p. Grades 3–8.

Fraser, Mary Ann. *How Animal Babies Stay Safe.* HarperCollins, 2002. ISBN 0060288035. 33 p. Grades K–3.

George, Linda. *Vipers* (Snakes). Capstone High-Interest Books, 2002. ISBN 0736809104. 48 p. Grades 4–up.

Gibbons, Gail. *Behold . . . The Unicorns.* HarperCollins, 2002. ISBN 0688179584. 32 p. Grades K–3.

———. *The Berry Book.* Holiday House, 2002. ISBN 0823416976. Unpaged. Grades K–4.

———. *Chicks & Chickens.* Holiday House, 2003. ISBN 082341700x. Unpaged. Grades K–3.

———. *Polar Bears.* Holiday House, 2001. ISBN 0823415937. Unpaged. Grades K–4.

———. *Tell Me, Tree: All About Trees for Kids.* Little, Brown, 2002. ISBN 0316309036. 32 p. Grades 1–3.

Goodall, Jane. *The Chimpanzees I Love: Saving Our World and Theirs.* A Byron Preiss Book, Scholastic Press, 2001. ISBN 043921310x. 80 p. Grades 4–8.

Graham-Barber, Lynda. *Spy Hops & Belly Flops: Curious Behavior of Woodland Animals.* Illustrated by Brian Lies. Houghton Mifflin, 2004. ISBN 061822291x. Unpaged. Grades K–2.

Halls, Kelly Milner. *Albino Animals.* Darby Creek, 2004. ISBN 1581960190. 72 p. Grades 4–8.

———. *Dinosaur Mummies: Beyond Bare-Bone Fossils.* Darby Creek, 2003. ISBN 158196000X. 48 p. Grades 4–8.

Harris, Robie K. *Hello Benny!: What It's Like to Be a Baby.* Illustrated by Michael Emberley. Margaret K. McElderry Books, 2002. ISBN 0689832575. Unpaged. Grades K–3.

Heiligman, Deborah. *Babies: All You Need to Know.* Illustrated by Laura Freeman. National Geographic, 2002. ISBN 0792282051. 32 p. Grades K–3.

Holub, Joan. *Why Do Rabbits Hop? And Other Questions About Rabbits, Guinea Pigs, Hamsters, and Gerbils.* Illustrations by Anna Di Vito. Dial Books for Young Readers, 2003. ISBN 0803727712. 48 p. Grades 1–3.

Jackson, Donna M. *The Bug Scientists.* Houghton Mifflin, 2002. ISBN 0618108688. 48 p. Grades 3–6.

———. *Hero Dogs: Courageous Canines in Action.* Megan Tingley, 2003. ISBN 0316826812. 48 p. Grades K–4.

Jacobs, Francine. *Lonesome George the Giant Tortoise.* Illustrations by Jean Cassels. Walker & Company, 2003. ISBN 0802788645. Unpaged. Grades 1–3.

Jenkins, Martin. *Grandma Elephants in Charge.* Illustrated by Ivan Bates. Candlewick Press, 2003. ISBN 0763620742. 29 p. Grades K–2.

Jenkins, Steve. *Actual Size.* Houghton Mifflin, 2004. ISBN 0618375945. Unpaged. Grades K–3.

———. *Life on Earth: The Story of Evolution.* Houghton Mifflin, 2002. ISBN 0618164766. 40 p. Grades 2–5.

Jenkins, Steve, and Robin Page. *What Do You Do with a Tail Like This?* Houghton Mifflin, 2003. ISBN 0618256288. Unpaged. Grades K–3.

Kelly, Irene. *It's a Hummingbird's Life.* Holiday House, 2003. ISBN 0823416585. Unpaged. Grades K–2.

Kurlansky, Mark. *The Cod's Tale.* Illustrated by S. D. Schindler. G. P. Putnam's Sons, 2001. ISBN 0399234764. 44 p. Grades 3–6.

Landau, Elaine. *Popcorn!* Illustrated by Brian Lies. Charlesbridge, 2003. ISBN 1570914427. 32 p. Grades 2–5.

Landstrom, Lee Ann. *Nature's Yucky! Gross Stuff That Helps Nature Work.* Illustrated by Constance R. Bergum. Mountain Press Publishing Company, 2003. ISBN 0878424741. Unpaged. Grades K–4.

Lauber, Patricia. *True-or-False Book of Dogs.* Illustrated by Rosalyn Schanzer. HarperCollins, 2003. ISBN 0060297670. 32 p. Grades K–3.

Lewis, J. Patrick. *Scientrickery: Riddles in Science.* Illustrated by Frank Remkiewicz. Silver Whistle/Harcourt, 2004. ISBN 0152166815. 32 p. Grades 1–4.

Markle, Sandra. *Growing up Wild: Penguins.* Atheneum Books for Young Readers, 2002. ISBN 0689818874. 32 p. Grades 2–4.

Mattern, Joanne. *The Ragdoll Cat.* Capstone, 2001. ISBN 0736808973. 48 p. Grades 4–8.

Meeker, Clare Hodgson. *Hansa: The True Story of an Asian Elephant Baby.* With Photographs from the Woodland Park Zoo. Illustrations by Linda Feltner. Sasquatch Books, 2002. ISBN 1570613443. 48 p. Grades 3–7.

Micucci, Charles. *The Life and Times of the Ant.* Houghton Mifflin, 2003. ISBN 0618005595. 32 p. Grades K–3.

Montgomery, Sy. *Encantado: Pink Dolphin of the Amazon.* With photographs by Dianne Taylor-Snow. Houghton Mifflin, 2002. ISBN 0618131035. 73 p. Grades 4–8.

———. *The Snake Scientist.* Photographs by Nic Bishop. Houghton Mifflin, 1999. ISBN 0395871697. 48 p. Grades 4–6.

———. *The Tarantula Scientist.* Photographs by Nic Bishop. Houghton Mifflin, 2004. ISBN 0618147993. 80 p. Grades 4–9.

Nagda, Ann Whitehead, and Cindy Bickel. *Tiger Math: Learning to Graph from a Baby Tiger.* Henry Holt, 2000. ISBN 0805062483. 30 p. Grades 2–5.

Pfeffer, Wendy. *Dolphin Talk: Whistles, Clicks, and Clapping Jaws.* Illustrated by Helen K. Davie. HarperCollins, 2003. ISBN 0064452107. 33 p. Grades 1–3.

Pringle, Laurence. *Strange Animals, New to Science.* Marshall Cavendish, 2002. ISBN 0761450831. 64 p. Grades 4–8.

Sayre, April Pulley. *Army Ant Parade.* Illustrated by Rick Chrustowski. Henry Holt, 2002. ISBN 0805063536. Unpaged. Grades K–3.

———. *Tropical Rain Forest.* Scholastic Reference, 2002. ISBN 0439355230. 48 p. Grades 1–3.

Schaefer, Lola. *Pick, Pull, Snap!: Where Once a Flower Bloomed.* Illustrated by Lindsay Barrett George. Greenwillow Books, an imprint of HarperCollins, 2003. ISBN 0688178340. Unpaged. Grades K–3.

Schwartz, David M. *Millions to Measure.* Pictures by Steven Kellogg. HarperCollins, 2003. ISBN 0688129161. Unpaged. Grades 1–3.

Seuling, Barbara. *Flick a Switch: How Electricity Gets to Your Home Featuring Jojo and Her Dog Willy.* Holiday House, 2003. ISBN 0823417298. Unpaged. Grades 1–3.

————. *From Head to Toe: The Amazing Human Body and How It Works.* Illustrated by Edward Miller. Holiday House, 2002. ISBN 0823416992. 32 p. Grades 2–5.

Simon, Seymour. *Spiders.* HarperCollins, 2003. ISBN 0060283912. Unpaged. Grades 4–7.

Simon, Seymour, and Nicole Fauteux. *Let's Try It Out in the Air.* Illustrated by Doug Cushman. Simon & Schuster Books for Young Readers, 2001. ISBN 0689829183. Unpaged. Grades K–3.

————. *Let's Try It Out in the Water.* Illustrated by Doug Cushman. Simon & Schuster Books for Young Readers, 2001. ISBN 0689829191. Unpaged. Grades K–3.

————. *Let's Try It Out with Towers and Bridges.* Illustrated by Doug Cushman. Simon & Schuster Books for Young Readers, 2003. ISBN 068982923x. Unpaged. Grades K–3.

Sloan, Christopher. *Supercroc and the Origin of Crocodiles.* Introduction by Dr. Paul Sereno. National Geographic, 2002. ISBN 0792266919. 56 p. Grades 2–6.

Sobol, Richard. *Adelina's Whales.* Text and photographs by Richard Sobol. Dutton Children's Books, 2003. ISBN 0525471103. Unpaged. Grades 2–5.

Tanaka, Shelley. *New Dinos: The Latest Finds! The Coolest Dinosaur Discoveries!* Illustrated by Alan Bernard. Paleontological consultation by Dr. Philip J. Currie. An Atheneum Book for Young Readers/Madison Press Book, 2003. ISBN 0689851839. 48 p. Grades 4–8.

Tatham, Betty. *Penguin Chick.* Illustrated by Helen K. Davie. HarperCollins, 2002. ISBN 061356829x. 33 p. Grades K–3.

Tomecek, Steve ("The Dirtmeister)". *Dirt.* Illustrated by Nancy Woodman. National Geographic, 2002. ISBN 0792282043. 32 p. Grades K–3.

Woodward, John. *Clever Camouflage.* Heinemann Library, 2004. ISBN 1403447039. 32 p. Grades 4–7.

CHAPTER  3

A World at War, a World of Wonder

THE HOLOCAUST AND WORLD WAR

D-Day does not mean one special day in history. It is a term that started in World War I, and it refers to the day, any day, when a planned attack will take place. But almost everyone now believes that D-Day means only one special day—June 6, 1944, the day when the Allied forces landed on the beaches at Normandy to invade Europe and attempt to win World War II.

Figure 3.1. *Remember D-Day: The Plan, the Invasion, Survivor Stories* by **Ronald J. Drez.**

In *Remember D-Day: The Plan, the Invasion, Survivor Stories*, Ronald J. Drez points out that D-Day did not come a moment too soon. For almost four years, most of the people in Western Europe had lost their freedom, and many, in particular the Jews, had lost their most basic rights, including the right to live. But Hitler and his allies had strong and powerful armed forces, and the time had to be right for an invasion.

The Supreme Commander of the Allied Forces was General Dwight D. Eisenhower, and the decision when and where to invade was his. The invasion was incredibly complicated. Secrecy was vital. Spies were everywhere. The Germans knew an invasion was coming and they needed to be prepared. But how could they be prepared if they did not know when and where it was coming? Their best guess was that the invasion would come at Calais, France, only 25 miles from Dover, England. That was the closest spot to launch an attack on European soil.

But Eisenhower knew the Germans would think that, so he wanted to make sure the invasion landed someplace less likely. He chose the beaches at Normandy, the *farthest* point away across the English Channel, and then he built fake armies, using balloon-like equipment, to convince the Germans that he was headed for Calais—or maybe even Norway! The Germans sent in spies, who turned out to be useless. As unlikely as it seems, every single one of the spies was captured by the Allies.

The spies for the Allies, however, were doing great work. One, whose code name was Garbo, was able to keep 20 different identities separate and never lose track of who he was being at the moment. He did an amazing job of fooling the Nazis.

Drez includes a lot of stories beyond just what happened on the beaches, which, in many cases, was absolutely horrifying. And the photographs are great. Turn to page 39 and see the anti-aircraft fire coming up toward the planes of American paratroopers approaching their drop zones. What kind of courage did it take to face that kind of fire?

The story of D-Day is one of the greatest stories of all time.

In *D-Day: They Fought to Free Europe from Hitler's Tyranny: A Day That Changed America*, Shelley Tanaka states that every military leader on both sides of the war knew that an Allied invasion was inevitable. Even Hitler knew.

For the soldiers who fought on D-Day, it was probably the most horrifying experience of their lives. Thousands of troops arrived under deadly fire, and thousands died that day. Read the story of paratrooper Don Jakeway. He had enlisted in the airborne forces two years earlier, when he was fresh out of high school. He went through extensive training (only 120 men out of every 2,500 made it into the paratroopers) and bulked up his body an additional 40 pounds—from 138 to 180 pounds. He could do 25 deep knee bends with a grown man slung over his shoulder, and he had to jump out of a plane with a 150-pound pack on his back. Jakeway made his jump the night before the big ground invasion of Normandy. The night was foggy and he had no idea where he had landed, only that he got caught in a tree and had to cut himself out of his parachute. Jakeway had to hide from the Germans and hunt for his unit. Many of his fellow paratroopers were already dead.

Bob Giguere invaded the beach. He was a demolitions man. Ducking enemy bullets, he was ordered to crawl through a tunnel and explode an enemy gun emplacement. This task was insanely dangerous, but Giguere did it and survived. Later during the battle, however, he heard a nearby explosion and lost consciousness. Giguere ultimately survived, but the shrapnel that pierced his body still sets off metal detectors in airports.

This is an incredible book.

Soldiers were not the only people who watched the horrors of D-Day. Reporters and photographers followed the fighting. And in World War II, women became an increasingly important part in reporting the day-to-day battles. Penny Colman's *Where the Action Was: Women War Correspondents in World War II* tells us that just like their male counterparts, women reporters wanted to be where the action was—but it was not always easy. Female reporters and photographers who tried to cover World War II often had a hard time of it. A lot of people thought that women had no business traveling to dangerous places, or doing dangerous things. War, writing about war, and taking pictures of war, were for men only.

Women correspondents finally came into their own during World War II. They managed to get some scoops and take some incredible photographs. Margaret Bourke-White, one of the most famous photographers of all time, managed to become the first woman to accompany an air force on a bombing mission. Ruth Cowan went to a reception at the French embassy in Algiers. There she ran into the famous American, General George Patton. " 'So,' he asked her, 'you want to be in a war. What is the first law of war?' Without hesitation, she replied, 'You kill him before he kills you' " (page 39). General Patton decided she could stay in Algiers and cover the war right on the spot!

By the middle of 1944, as D-Day approached, more women were able to cover the war because so many men were in the army. Women did daring and courageous things to get a story. They were also among the first to see the concentration camps and were horrified at what they saw.

One woman, Dickey Chapelle, survived WWII only to die 20 years later in another war, in Vietnam, when she stepped on a land mine. Colman's amazing book is loaded with moving and exciting stories.

On D-Day a group of 100 girls walked out of an orphanage and into the night. The Allies were invading France, and the girls' home was no longer safe. In *The Orphans of Normandy: A True Story of World War II Told Through Drawings by Children* by Nancy Amis we learn of the girls' true-life adventures, including their taking shelter in an old iron mine and being fired upon by German soldiers. Photographs of the home and the girls conclude this moving book.

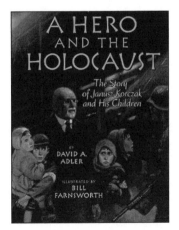

Figure 3.2. *A Hero and the Holocaust: The Story of Janusz Korczak and His Children* by David A. Adler.

David A. Adler tells the story of a popular Polish physician in a children's hospital who also wrote children's stories in *A Hero and the Holocaust: The Story of Janusz Korczak and His Children.* Janusz Korczak was a celebrity in Poland. He was a physician who worked in a children's hospital and wrote stories for them—as well as books for adults. He became the director of a Jewish orphan's home, and even let the children draw on his bald head. The children loved him.

He hosted a very popular radio program of stories and advice. This was in the days before there was television and everyone was excited about the radio.

But Janusz had a secret. Like his beloved orphans, he too was Jewish, and not a lot of people knew that. To be Jewish in Poland in the late 1930s was a death sentence. When the Nazis invaded Poland in 1939, it was the beginning of the end for Janusz and his children.

Read this fine book to learn what happened to Jewish people at that time. It is a good introduction to the Holocaust for early readers.

Show the picture of Janusz's bald head being drawn on.

The most famous young person who lived during World War II is Anne Frank. Her story still resonates with young booktalk audiences around the world. And your listeners will enjoy being introduced to Anne's pen pal, Juanita Wagner, through Susan Rubin Goldman's *Searching for Anne Frank: Letters from Amsterdam to Iowa.*

In 1939, Juanita Wagner was 10 years old and lived in the tiny town of Danville, Iowa. Her teacher, who loved to travel, had started a pen-pal project with a group of teachers from a Montessori school in Amsterdam. Juanita, whose nickname was "Nita," chose a girl named Anne Frank. She wrote her a letter and Anne wrote back.

There were only two letters from Anne, for soon war broke out. But the one letter from Anne that still survives is priceless.

Almost everyone knows what happened to Anne. Her family, who were Jewish, watched their world grow smaller and smaller and their rights as human beings disappear, until finally, in July 1942, they went into hiding on the top floor of a factory owned by Mr. Frank. There they remained for over two years, helped by non-Jewish friends, until the Nazis discovered them, stormed the house, and hauled them away.

Nita and her sister Betty watched their own lives change as America went to war following the attack on Pearl Harbor in December 1941.

Susan Goldman Rubin shows us what happened in both countries and both families as the war took over the girls' lives. And she shows us how amazing it was for Nita to realize her pen pal was the internationally famous Anne Frank.

For those children who have never heard of the Franks' harrowing story, a terrific introduction is *Anne Frank in the World 1929–1945,* compiled by the Anne Frank House in Amsterdam. Show your audience the pictures of little Anne. They will find it hard to believe that this pretty, ordinary baby had to live and die the way she did. She looks just like everyone does, not disgusting, not dirty, and not evil—as the Nazis said all Jews were.

If you have read *The Diary of a Young Girl* by Anne Frank, you probably love her. Her story is horrible and moving and wonderful. She and her family were forced to live hidden in an attic when the Nazis invaded their homeland of the Netherlands, vowing, ultimately, to get rid of all the Jews.

This book tells the story of Anne's life during that time. Born in Frankfurt, Germany, in 1929, she moved as a young child to Amsterdam with her mother, father, and older sister Margot. Her father loved to take photographs, so we have many of her to stare at here—and many to see of the world outside her own little family. There is an overview of what the Nazis were doing in Anne's town as well as the rest of the world. It is terrifying to read. If you are at all interested in World War II, or Anne, or the Holocaust, this book is a great one.

Show the double-page spread on pages 48–49 of mothers and children who look Aryan, which Nazis considered the only acceptable kind, and of mothers and children who do not. This single spread would be a great springboard for a discussion on what your kids think about different types of people.

Yehuda Nir, another child of the Holocaust, shares his life story in *The Lost Childhood: A World War II Memoir.* Yehuda Nir was 11 years old in 1941, and he was definitely in the wrong place at the wrong time. He was Jewish and he lived in Poland, and the Nazis were after him and every other Jew they could find. They found his father in the summer of 1941 and executed him on the day they arrested him. Yehuda and his mother and sister did not learn about his father's death until the war was over, four years later.

Yehuda's family went into hiding. Many Jews did that, some successfully, almost all miserably. What was unusual about the way the Nir family hid was that they hid in the open. They pretended to be Catholics and went out into the Nazi-controlled world and lived openly. They took whatever work they could and managed to get through the war alive and together, something extraordinary in that time. The worst exposure came when Yehuda made a mistake in a conversation with a friend, asking what date Christmas was coming that year. Any Christian would know that Christmas always comes on December 25, and his friend realized immediately that Yehuda was not a Christian. Read this book to find out how Yehuda was saved from this near-fatal slip.

Lili Jacob was another lucky survivor of the war. In 1945, Lili Jacob was a prisoner in the Dora/Nordhausen concentration camp in Germany. She was in the camp hospital on May 2 when American soldiers arrived and freed the prisoners. As she was leaving the camp, Lili saw a photograph album. When she opened it, she found photographs of people from her hometown—and also photographs of her own family. She kept the album, and brought it to America when she came here as an immigrant.

What Lili had was a great treasure and a horrifying statement. The album became the basis for Clive Lawton's stunning *Auschwitz* by Candlewick Press. Most of the photographs in this fine book revealing the world's most infamous concentration camp came from her album, which now resides in a museum in Israel. The photos show us the faces and bodies of people who were about to die and people who were already dead. They show bodies being stacked up high to be burned. They show slave laborers. They show us the story of Auschwitz.

Like all of the concentration camps, Auschwitz was chosen at least partially because it had a train station. The Nazis came up with a plan, "The Final Solution," to kill all of the Jews in Europe. They set up incredibly efficient murder camps. Estimates of the number of people killed at Auschwitz range from one to four million. Most people were killed almost immediately when they arrived at the camp. Look at the large picture on pages 22–23 of the Hungarian Jews who have no idea that they are about to be gassed. Others, mostly men and strong young women, became slave laborers.

The guards were German criminals who were released from prison to take charge of the camps. The camp itself was originally an army barracks, near a small Polish town. How Auschwitz was planned, how it grew, how it operated, and how it was freed is the subject of this haunting book.

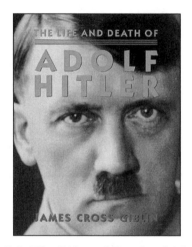

Figure 3.3. *The Life and Death of Adolf Hitler* by James Cross Giblin.

Confronted with the horrors of a place like Auschwitz, some people feel certain that Adolf Hitler was the most evil person who ever lived. He was responsible for the deaths of millions of people before and during World War II. His story, recounted in James Cross Giblin's *The Life and Death of Adolf Hitler,* is both fascinating and horrible.

Hitler started out life in a fairly ordinary way, born into a middle-class family in Austria. He wanted to be an artist, and moved to Vienna, living in poverty and making few friends. His life changed with World War I. He became a soldier and became more and more interested in the fate of his country, especially after the war ended and Germany had been defeated.

The German people felt weak and hopeless, and Adolf discovered that he had both a gift for speaking and a talent for raising those hopes. His passionate speeches began to attract a following to his National Socialist, or Nazi, political party.

Then disaster struck. A plot went bad and Adolf and some of his followers ended up in jail. Hitler took the opportunity to write his life story, *Mein Kampf* ("My Struggle"), which became a huge success after his release from prison.

He began, slowly and irresistibly, his return and rise to the top. You may know parts of this story—the stories of the "Phony War" and the London Blitz, the Final Solution, the invasion of the Soviet Union, the Battle of the Bulge, the plot to assassinate Hitler, and the final suicide in the bunker. The author ties this all together for us in a way that is an absorbing read and an excellent overview.

While hearing about Hitler's life, some of your booktalk listeners might be surprised to learn that there were two world wars. A great companion book, and one that will introduce them to one of the greatest disasters of World War I, is Diana Preston's *Remember the* Lusitania*!*

Figure 3.4. *Remember the* **Lusitania***!* **by Diana Preston.**

On the morning of May 1, 1915, there was an ad in a New York morning newspaper. It was underneath a notice that the *Lusitania*, a ship of the Cunard Line, was sailing for Liverpool that day from New York. It said, simply,

> NOTICE! Travelers intending to embark on the Atlantic voyage are reminded that a state of war exists between Germany and her allies and Great Britain and her allies; that the zone of war includes the waters adjacent to the British Isles; that, in accordance with formal notice given by the Imperial German Government, vessels flying the flag of Great Britain, or of any of her allies, are liable to destruction in those waters and that travelers sailing in the war zone on ships of Great Britain or her allies do so at their own risk. (opposite page l)

It was signed "The Imperial German Embassy."

The *Lusitania* was, in fact, a British ship. The United States was not yet in the war, however, and many American citizens were on the ship. Most people seemed to think there would not be a problem. Surely the Germans would not kill American citizens! Most passengers refused to cancel their trip, although the sinking of the *Titanic* a few years earlier must have been in their minds.

The truth was that the big ships could sail a lot faster than the German submarines. It seemed extremely unlikely that a German submarine could be in the right place at the right time to sink such a powerful ship. But as the *Lusitania* neared Ireland, it did not realize that a German U-boat shared the same waters. The U-boat launched a torpedo at the perfect moment—and the *Lusitania* was under water in 18 minutes. There was no time to launch most of the lifeboats. In fact, according to the rules of war, the U-boat should have warned the ship that it was to be sunk and let the passengers get on lifeboats before launching that torpedo.

What happened next was a true horror story. The people still alive were in agony. Some had been sucked into the smokestacks of the ship as it sank and then shot out like human cannonballs when the ship exploded. They were covered with soot and oil and some of them had their clothes ripped off.

Many people believed that the United States entered World War I on the side of Great Britain due in great part to this terrible disaster.

THE ANCIENT AND MODERN WORLDS

Imagine that you are a poor Chinese farmer, working on land that has not enough water. With two of your neighbors, you decide to try digging a well. You have to dig deep, and when you do, your shovel strikes something hard. What is it? You see a head. Not the head of a real person, but a pottery head. You have never seen anything like it in your life. You decide you had better tell a government official.

As Jane O'Connor recounts in *The Emperor's Silent Army: Terracotta Warriors of Ancient China*, in March 1974 a Chinese farmer made one of the most incredible discoveries of all time. For there was not just a single head buried in the ground; it was attached to a life-sized body of a solder, also formed of pottery. Eventually, scientists dug up over 7,000 of these soldiers, and no two of them are exactly alike. They are an army, each soldier with his own individual face, and they have been underground for over 2,000 years. Their weapons, kept in a separate location, were also discovered. The ancient spears and swords were still amazingly sharp after cleaning—so sharp, in fact, that they can split a hair!

The man who buried the soldiers in the ground was the first emperor of China. He felt, as did the ancient Egyptians, that he needed his belongings (including an army) to take with him to the next world when he died. There are no written records of the emperor building this massive army, but we now know more about it, such as his making sure that none of the workers who assisted in his burial would ever tell the secret. He had them all bricked up in the tomb, to die, after they placed his body there.

To see this army is an incredible sight, but it used to be even more amazing. The figures were originally painted. Over the last 220 years, the paint has disappeared, but show your audience the picture on page 31 of the current, ongoing reconstruction.

Fiona MacDonald brings a welcome touch of humor in her reconstruction of early Mexico in *You Wouldn't Want to Be an Aztec Sacrifice! Gruesome Things You'd Rather Not Know*. The Aztec people arrived in Mexico about 1200, and by 1325, they pretty much had taken charge of the place. They conquered most of the neighboring lands, and one thing they liked to do was to capture people and offer them up as sacrifices to the gods.

The hero of this story is captured in a "flowery war," fought mainly to acquire captives. He is marched through the hot, dry land, to a huge city where he is kept in a cage with other captives. If he is fat or ugly, scarred or ill, he will have to work as a slave, but if he has "good skin, good hair, good teeth, and a strong body," he is just right for a sacrifice. David Antram's cartoon illustrations add just the right touch of goofiness to a fascinating topic.

Before the Aztecs created their civilization, Central America was already home to the Maya. According to Elizabeth Mann's *Tikal: A Wonders of the World Book,* the Mayan city of Tikal, which is in modern Guatemala, was settled about 2,800 years ago, and it grew quickly. It sat in the heart of the Yucatan peninsula, and it covered about 25 square miles. Tikal was a rich city, the traders who traveled its lands were taxed heavily, and it was ruled wisely and well. But sometime around 1,400 years ago, Tikal was conquered by other cities, and it spent about 100 years recovering from the horrors of that conquest. Then a new, young ruler arose named Hasaw, who made the city of Tikal even more beautiful than before.

"Hasaw was a majestic figure, taller than his people by a head, and beautiful by Maya standards. Thanks to the boards that had pressed his head when he was an infant, his forehead was regally flattened. The small ball that had been hung inches in front of his tiny face had done its work too. His eyes had focused on it and now were crossed fetchingly above his long, magnificently hooked nose" (page 18). Obviously Mayan standards of beauty were not the same as standards of today.

The story of how the Maya lived and how their beautiful city was abandoned and taken over by the jungle is a mysterious and fascinating tale. There are many gorgeous illustrations. Show the pull-out one on pages 35–38.

Another ancient civilization of the Western Hemisphere comes to life in Ted Lewin's *Lost City: The Discovery of Machu Picchu*. In 1911, a Yale professor named Hiram Bingham desperately wanted to find a special place: the lost city of the Inca, which was named Vilcapampa. He had heard it was beautiful and located in the Andes Mountains, and he led an expedition to find it.

He did not find it, but he found something better. He discovered the lost Inca city of Machu Picchu, which is one of the most beautiful cities of all time, even though it now lies in ruins. It is also one of the highest cities in the world, lying at an altitude of roughly 8,000 feet above sea level!

Ted Lewin painted wonderful pictures of this incredible place, and tells the story of how Bingham found it—with the help of a little boy. Show the last two-page spread of the city, or any of the wonderful illustrations.

One of the reasons that everyone likes to look at mummies is that we know that they were real people once—alive, walking, talking people, but people who have been dead a long time and are mysterious to us. Joyce Filer's *The Mystery of the Egyptian Mummy* is the true story of one mummy. He was a man name Hornedjitef, and his mummy is now in the British Museum in London. He lived over 2,000 years ago in a city named Thebes, which is now called Luxor. He was a priest of the god Amun and he worked in the temple at Karnak.

"If Hornedjitef lived, worked, and was buried in ancient Thebes, how did he come to be lying in a glass case in the British museum?" (page 5). That's the first mystery! Wouldn't he have been surprised if he knew he was coming to a place that didn't even exist when he was alive? This book tells us that the museum bought the mummy in a sale in 1835 and paid about $500 for it. It had been collected by Henry Salt, the British consul-general in Egypt, who did a lot of excavating and collecting while he was there.

But why did the Egyptians mummify people anyway? What gave them the idea? How did they figure out how to do it? Did they just mummify people, or did they mummify animals too? What did the people who look so spooky and weird as mummies really look like in real life? (Show the picture on page 24.) How can we find out about the lives of the people who were mummified? Were they married? Did they have kids? All of these questions and more are answered in this interesting book. People who like mummies will want to learn more!

Gail Gibbons has created a terrific intro to the art of mummy-making for younger readers in her colorful *Mummies, Pyramids, and Pharaohs: A Book about Ancient Egypt.* The reasons for the complicated, 70-day process of mummification are set in a clear context by Gibbons's explanation of the everyday life of the early Egyptians. She touches on hieroglyphs, houses, lucky charms, the diverse society, clothing, and the ornate interiors of burial tombs. Why does Egyptian art always show people from the side? The artists thought that view gave the best perspective of the human body. Did you know that Cleopatra was a *Greek* Pharaoh? Or that historians believe the three famous pyramids of Giza were once topped with gold capstones? Think of how they would have gleamed in the desert sun! Gibbons's book is a strong, solid resource; an easy-to-follow pageant that guides the first-time traveler through ancient Egypt.

Did you know the Sphinx stretches one average city block long from front to back? It is almost six stories tall. Its mouth is seven and one-half feet wide. This mysterious statue has the body of a lion and the face of a man, a pharaoh, a ruler of ancient Egypt. And James Cross Giblin tells us in his *Secrets of the Sphinx* that the lion-man has been staring across the desert for about 4,500 years. When Jesus Christ was born, the Sphinx was already 2,500 years old!

Today, the stony stare does not gaze at the limitless desert horizon. Now, it stares about 200 yards, at souvenir outlets and fast food shops, and the rapidly growing suburbs of Cairo, Egypt. And that is a problem.

The huge population of Cairo, about 40 million people, has created pollution, and its effects are slowly but effectively destroying the Sphinx. Every day, pieces of stone the size of potato chips flake off the ancient monument, blowing away in the wind or falling to the ground. No one knows how much longer the statue can survive.

The Sphinx's story starts about 3100 BC, when the then-current pharaoh united the two halves of Egypt, north and south, into one country. The workers who built the Sphinx and the pyramids were probably not slaves, but rather skilled laborers, whose work was hard but highly valued. They painted the original Sphinx (show the two-page picture of the construction). The statue was built on the site of a natural rock formation that somewhat resembled a crouching lion.

The Sphinx was covered by sand for almost 1,200 years, from about 1400 BC to 200 BC , and Giblin tells a lovely legend about how it was found again.Followers of the American prophet Edgar Cayce, believe that the secrets of the lost continent of Atlantis are buried somewhere beneath the Sphinx. The giant statue never fails to fascinate, and this book tells us why.

Figure 3.5. *Hatshepsut: His Majesty, Herself* **by Catherine M. Andronik.**

Catherine M. Andronik sheds light on a dark and fascinating corner of ancient Egypt in *Hatshepsut: His Majesty, Herself.* Has your booktalk audience read or heard anything about life in ancient Egypt? One thing they probably know is that it was ruled by pharaohs, which was the Egyptian name for kings. This book tells the story of one of those kings, one who was very unusual. She was a woman!

Hatshepsut was the daughter of the Pharaoh Tuthmosis (tooth-MOE-sis) and his queen. She had a sister, but no brothers. She did, however, have half-brothers, sons of the women in her father's harem.

Hatshepsut was not trained to be pharaoh, because that was something only a man could become at that time. She was trained, instead, to serve as the wife of one of her half-brothers. People in Egypt's royal families intermarried with their brothers and sisters. Hatshepsut did the same, but her husband died a few years later. She had no children of her own, so her dead husband's son by one of the women in the harem was designated to become pharaoh. Unfortunately, the dead pharaoh's son was too young. He needed someone to be in charge. Hatshepsut took the job. And Hatshepsut took full power. She ended up becoming the first and only female pharaoh in Egypt's long and complicated history.

This is quite a story. Hatshepsut wore a false beard and had paintings and sculpture made of herself as a man. Show the picture on page 21 of Hatshepsut with her false beard. Thousands of years later, these artifacts would baffle historians. Who was she/he? Why had his/her name been crossed out of many inscriptions? And why has her mummy still not been found?

Confucius is famous not for his appearance, but for his way of thinking. But the picture on the cover of Russell Freedman's insightful *Confucius: The Golden Rule* may surprise you. Freedman tells us, "He has been described as a homely giant with warts on his nose, two long front teeth that protruded over his lower lip, and a wispy beard. What people remembered most, however, wasn't his odd appearance but his undeniable charm" (page 6).

Confucius got the name we now call him in the 1500s, when Jesuit missionaries visited China and Latinized his Chinese name. That was about 2,000 years after he was born. He loved learning, this we know for sure, and he cared deeply about other human beings. He thought about many things, and thought about them deeply. Some of his ideas, which seemed new and strange at the time, are now our common beliefs. "Confucius told his students that it was their duty to criticize any ruler who abused his power—even at the risk of their lives" (page 15). About 2,300 years later, the Continental Congress, which met in Philadelphia, completely agreed with his teachings when they voted on the Declaration of Independence.

Confucius did not found a religion, but, rather, a way of thinking. He was not just a piece of paper in a fortune cookie, but a thoughtful, caring human being who made a difference in many countries and in many, many lives.

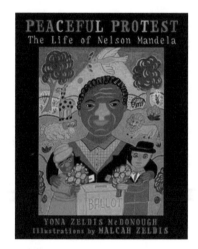

Figure 3.6. *Peaceful Protest: The Life of Nelson Mandela* by Yona Zeldis McDonough.

The life of a modern-day giant is retold in *Peaceful Protest: The Life of Nelson Mandela* by Yona Zeldis McDonough. Nelson Mandela grew up in a divided country. The white people, the rulers of the land, had one set of rules for their lives, but the black South Africans lived under a horrible, unfair set of rules that tried to regulate their lives.

Mandela was born in 1918. His father was a chief, but once, when he was summoned to an English court, he refused to appear and thus lost his land, his cattle, and his position. Nelson was called Buti then, and he learned that his father stood by his beliefs. His family lived with relatives after that. When Buti was seven, he went to school, the first person in his family to do so. The teacher there gave all of the children English names, and that is how he got the name Nelson.

Mandela was proud to be South African, but as he grew older he realized how unjust the whole South African system, called apartheid, was. He vowed that he would dedicate his life to changing it. And, in spite of many, many setbacks, including 27 years spent in a terrible prison, Mandela succeeded.

If you know anything at all about the history of the Crusades, you have heard of Saladin, the great Muslim leader. He was the man who defeated King Richard the Lion-hearted. He was the man who often treated his enemies kindly, even though his own subjects were mistreated by his foes. He yearned to win Jerusalem back from the European Crusaders.

Diane Stanley reminds us in *Saladin: Noble Prince of Islam* that in 1095, the Muslims had ruled Jerusalem for more than 400 years. But four years later, the First Crusaders conquered the city. Saladin had not been born yet, and was not to be born until 1138. His father became the governor of Damascus, working for the great Turkish sultan Nur al-Din. Saladin became an aide to the sultan himself. When Nur al-Din died, Saladin took over the kingdom, but not without nine years of fighting. By 1185, the fighting was over. The Muslims united to drive out the crusaders. And two years later they succeeded.

"Immediately the kings of Germany and France took the cross. So did King Richard I of England, the most fearsome opponent Saladin would ever face. To finance this mighty effort, Richard levied a 10 percent tax on the possessions of all persons, called the 'Saladin tithe.' Elevating his fund-raising to a new level, Richard fired his public officers, and then made them buy their jobs back. 'I would sell London,' he said, 'if I could find a buyer for it' " (n.p.).

What happened on that disastrous, expensive crusade, and what happened to its leaders makes for an excellent true story. Stanley's book is illustrated with dozens of beautiful pictures, which resemble medieval Persian miniatures.

Islam's mighty founder finds a terrific introduction in *Muhammad,* written and illustrated by Demi. According to the introduction, this "is the first, long-awaited biography of Prophet Muhammad for children in a western language." Demi, the author, is also a skilled illustrator, and she has worked out a brilliant way of depicting the prophet, for Islamic tradition does not allow images of him or his family. So where he would appear in any picture, there is instead a gold outline of his body. Like Stanley's book on Saladin, this fascinating biography is filled with illustrations based on Persian miniatures. It is a fine introduction to the man and to the world religion he founded.

After showing Demi's book to your booktalk group, reach for Diane Hoyt-Goldsmith's *Celebrating Ramadan*. Her book depicts how modern-day Muslims celebrate one of their most famous holidays.

Figure 3.7. *Celebrating Ramadan* by Diane Hoyt-Goldsmith.

Ibraheem lives near Princeton, New Jersey, and is nine years old and in the fourth grade. He is a Muslim. So are five million other Americans. And this book tells us about what he and other Muslims believe, how they practice their faith, and how they celebrate the holiest time of the year, Ramadan.

Muslims believe that there is only one God, whom they call Allah, and that Muhammad was the last and most important prophet. Other prophets are Abraham, Moses, David, and Jesus. Observant Muslims pray to Allah, facing the holy city of Mecca, five times a day.

Many people have become more interested in the Muslim religion in the last few years, and this book tells us something about that religion. There are five pillars of Islam, five major beliefs, which are clearly described on page 4.

Ibraheem is, in many ways, a good and ordinary American kid, but, in other ways, he is different. He has been able to fast every day during Ramadan since he was six years old—no eating or drinking after breakfast and before dinner. Ask your booktalk kids if any of them think they could be as disciplined as Ibraheem. Would it be hard not to eat throughout a full school day when they see their classmates having lunch? Then show the pictures of Ibraheem praying on pages 12–13.

Nothando lives in South Africa, "where yellow pumpkins grow all summer long" (n.p.). A lovely text and beautiful photographs of Kathryn Cave's *One Child, One Seed: A South African Counting Book* form a counting book about the seeds, and include information about Nothando's life. It all ends with a feast of the traditional Zulu dish "ishijingi," a recipe for which is included at the back of the book.

World history is full of stories about people who have had to go without food. What would it be like to starve to death? Have you ever been terribly hungry but could not find anything to eat? Have you ever been so hungry you tried to eat grass? The potato famine was one of the worst disasters in history, and Susan Campbell Bartoletti tells its story with poignant horror in *Black Potatoes: The Story of the Great Irish Famine, 1845–1850.*

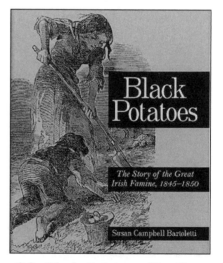

Figure 3.8. *Black Potatoes: The Story of the Great Irish Famine, 1845–1850* **by Susan Campbell Bartoletti.**

In Ireland in the 1840s, there were a lot of poor farmers. In fact, most of the people lived on tiny farms. They got by with hard work, few possessions, and no luxuries. But one thing they had in abundance was potatoes. They ate potatoes for breakfast, lunch, and dinner. They stored potatoes when they were harvested and ate them until the next harvest. With enough potatoes, and low expectations, life was fairly good and the people were fairly happy.

In 1845, disaster stuck: A terrible blight infected the potatoes. They turned black and rotten. People nearly starved to death, but they knew if they could make it through the winter, fresh new potatoes could be planted. But when the new crop was planted and harvested, it rotted too.

Most of the poor Irish farmers were Catholic, and the British government, which did not care for Catholics, turned its back on the starving population. What drove the starving Irish crazy was that there was a lot of food in Ireland—livestock and grains, for instance—but all of that food was exported to other countries. Although their own citizens were starving, the wealthy British landlords let them die rather than stop making money on the food they exported. The landlords tore down their huts and cottages, leaving many to wander homeless and starving on the roads. Some took shelter in ditches.

To relieve some of their misery, the Irish were faced with two equally horrible choices. They could go to either the workhouse or the poorhouse, where families were separated and humiliated and did boring, sometimes meaningless work. Or, if they had saved enough money or the landlord could pay their way, a family might emigrate to the United States or Canada. This book is sad and interesting to read—the story of one of the worst disasters in history.

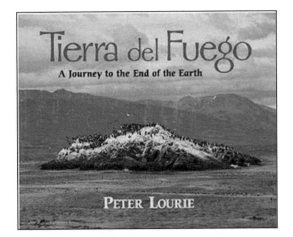

Figure 3.9. *Tierra Del Fuego: A Journey to the End of the Earth* by Peter Lourie.

Peter Lourie must love to have adventures, because he certainly goes to a lot of exciting places. His *Tierra Del Fuego: A Journey to the End of the Earth* describes his journey to Tierra del Fuego, which is about as close to Antarctica as you can get without being in Antarctica. It lies at the very tip of South America and is famous for its terrible weather and dangerous, difficult, almost unnavigable waters. Many ships have been wrecked in them, and many of their remains can still be seen.

Tierra del Fuego had been inhabited by natives for thousands of years, but the first European to see the area was Magellan, who believed he could get from the Atlantic to the Pacific Ocean by going through it—and he was right. He gave the place its name, which means "Land of Fire," probably because of the native campfires that he could see along the shores. Whaling ships had to sail around it; gold seekers on the way to California did too. In fact, the only way to get from the Atlantic Ocean to the Pacific Ocean before the Panama Canal was built was to go around Tierra del Fuego or to go overland. Charles Darwin sailed around it too, in one of the most famous sea journeys of all time, the voyage of the *Beagle*.

Tierra del Fuego has changed a lot in the last 150 years or so. Now the people who originally lived on the land are almost extinct, killed by European diseases and by new settlers.

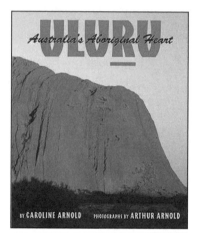

Figure 3.10. *Uluru: Australia's Aboriginal Heart* **by Caroline Arnold.**

Caroline Arnold guides us to another far-flung locale in *Uluru: Australia's Aboriginal Heart* (photographs by Arthur Arnold). Uluru (OOL-ol-roo) is the correct name, the original name, for what many people still know as Ayer's Rock, in the middle of the Australian desert. It is the biggest single rock in the world! If you walk around it, you will walk 5.8 miles, and the rock is over 1,000 feet high. The enormous rock lies now in a national park, one owned by the aboriginal people, to whom it has always been a sacred place.

Beautiful photographs highlight this respectful look at the park and the living things that flourish there, both animal and vegetable. One amazing fact: There are more wild camels in Australia than in any other place. Even than the Sahara! The mammals were brought there by European settlers. Before roads and railroads, riding camels was the most reliable way to cross the Australian deserts. In the 1920s, many were just released, and the outback and the region around Uluru still suits their descendants fine.

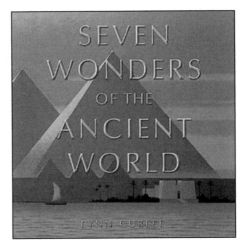

Figure 3.11. *Seven Wonders of the Ancient World* **by Lynn Curlee.**

Have you ever heard of the Seven Wonders of the Ancient World? If you like history, maybe you can name some of them. One of them is still a wonder of the world! But only one—the rest are long gone. We learn in Lynn Curlee's *Seven Wonders of the Ancient World* that the oldest of the ancient seven wonders is the only one that still exists: the Great Pyramid in Egypt. It was built in around 2580 BC—about 4,500 years ago. It is still one of the most stupendous structures ever made. Until just a little over 100 years ago, it was the tallest structure ever built. It is about 50 stories high and about two-thirds of a mile around its base.

What is incredible is how much archaeologists have learned about these structures in the last decades. Many of the sites where the structures stood have been excavated and we now know much more about them than we did even a few years ago. But many mysteries remain. For example, no one is certain of the original location of the Hanging Gardens of Babylon. And there are several theories as to what the original Mausoleum, which was the tomb of King Mausolus, looked like. A 16th-century Dutch artist drew pictures of the seven wonders, but he was really just guessing. We are almost certain that the Colossus of Rhodes did not stand with its legs so far apart that warships could pass between them. We know more about the Pharos, or lighthouse, at Alexandria, partially because its appearance is depicted on many ancient coins. And also because divers have found remnants of it in the harbor of modern-day Alexandria.

The pictures here are great. Show your audience the one of the diver finding the statue on page 31—and then ask them what they consider to be the seven wonders of the *modern* world! The two-page spread on pages 34–35 is also great to show. Even the U.S. Capitol looks small compared to the Great Pyramid!

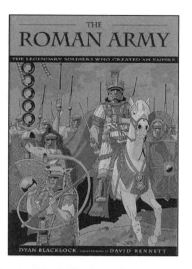

Figure 3.12. *The Roman Army: The Legendary Soldiers Who Created an Empire* **by Dyan Blacklock.**

Another wonder of the ancient world was the Roman Empire. It was monstrously huge! For almost 500 years, it was by far the greatest, mightiest empire in the world. It covered much of Europe, northern Africa, eastern Asia, and what is now Great Britain. And as Dyan Blacklock tells us in *The Roman Army: The Legendary Soldiers Who Created an Empire*, it took one of the greatest armies the world has ever seen to run the massive empire.

Roman soldiers were paid for their trouble. In early times, they may have been paid with salt, which was highly valued in the ancient world. The word "salary" that we use today comes from the Latin word for "salt."

The armies lived mostly in forts, organized to keep their subjects from being too far away from the main authorities. The Roman army was unmatched for efficiency and organization. Each soldier carried around about 66 pounds of gear, and, when on campaign, marched as much as 22 miles a day. They had the best arms and armor around, and many people who saw them coming simply surrendered on the spot. When they camped, even their tents were highly organized, and were set up very quickly. Each tent held eight men, and those eight men "slept, ate, trained and fought together for the entire twenty years of their service, and it was little wonder that they were so easily able to construct a camp—even in the dark! Soldiers went to bed fully dressed so that they were ready for action in case of enemy attack" (page 28).

In cartoon-style illustrations, we learn what Roman soldiers wore, what weapons they used, how they treated their enemies (you wouldn't want to be a defeated enemy), even what they ate. These were tough guys. You'll enjoy reading about them.

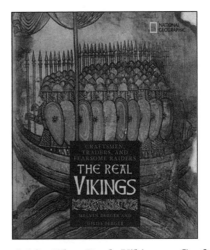

Figure 3.13. *The Real Vikings: Craftsmen, Traders, and Fearsome Raiders* **by Melvin Berger and Gilda Berger.**

Want to read about some more rough customers? Turn to Melvin Berger and Gilda Berger's *The Real Vikings: Craftsmen, Traders, and Fearsome Raiders.*

In AD 793, Vikings attacked a monastery on the island of Lindisfarne, off the northeast coast of England. The raiders completely destroyed it, killing many of the monks and capturing the rest to be sold into slavery. Historians now say that attack was the beginning of the Viking era, which lasted for the next 300 years.

The mental picture most of us conjure up about Vikings sees them sailing on ships, braving fierce weather, and raiding as much as they could. But the truth is that most of them were craftsmen, merchants, farmers, hunters, and fishermen. The Vikings were also amazing shipbuilders. Due to their skill, and their seafaring ways, one of them, Leif Eriksson, is now credited with being the first European to land on the coast of North America. Europeans and Russians, however, lived in terror of Viking raids for many, many years. The warrior crews that did the fighting and raiding were not gentle conquerors.

Today we are learning a great deal about how they lived. Viking artifacts and sites are being excavated, not only in Scandinavia, but also in Iceland, Greenland, and even North America. The Bergers have great pictures of some reconstructed buildings.

The influence of the Vikings is still felt in the words we use. For example, the early Vikings believed in several gods. The king of the gods was Odin, sometimes called Woden. He plucked out his own eye to gain wisdom. Today we honor him whenever we say "Wednesday," which mean's Woden's Day. Friday was named after Frigg, his wife, and Thursday after Thor, the god of thunder. Other words we borrowed from the Vikings are "husband," "ugly," and "happy." Even our system of having a jury of 12 people comes from the Vikings!

This book is loaded with grand pictures. Show the one of one-eyed Woden on page 16.

If you enjoy learning about ancient mysteries, turn to *Secrets in Stone: All About Maya Hieroglyphs* by Laurie Coulter with illustrations by Sarah Jane English. If you enjoy codes and mysteries, this is the book for you. In 1839, one English and one American explorer traveled through Central America searching for ruins. The men had quite a time of it, but their journey was wildly successful. There were more Mayan ruins than anyone had possibly guessed (even more were found a few decades later when chewing gum became popular and its manufacturers looked for more of the sapodilla trees from which it was made).

The local natives, however, knew only that the ruins existed. They did not know the names of the grown-over cities or much about the civilization that had produced them. Nor did they understand the hieroglyphs that covered many of the statues and the crumbling buildings.

Finding and deciphering hieroglyphs was an exciting thing to do. In 1922, a Frenchman, Jean Champollion, deciphered the Rosetta Stone, and, after that, ancient Egyptian writing could be decoded. Now a very different hieroglyph needed deciphering. But the complete secret of the Maya hieroglyphs was not discovered until the 1970s. Now we know a great deal about the Maya, although there is much to be learned still. We know some wonderful things:

- They built elaborate structures without metal tools

- Until the invention of the telescope in the 1600s, Mayan calendars were more accurate than the calendars of any other civilization.

- They were the first people to make rubber balls!

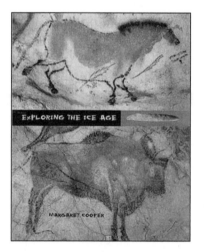

Figure 3.14. *Exploring the Ice Age* **by Margaret Cooper.**

Margaret Cooper takes us back to the fringes of human history in her marvelous *Exploring the Ice Age.* We have all seen cartoons of cavemen. They usually wear animal skins and carry a club and may be dragging a woman around with them. But these, of course, are just comic stereotypes. Scientists are learning more and more about the people who lived in the Ice Age, starting about 35,000 years ago.

One of the first clues that tipped off scientists that cave people were more intelligent than many of us give them credit for is that, in the skeletons of extinct mammals, many of the bones show signs of having been cut with a tool. It seems that some of the cavemen were pretty inventive people.

During the Ice Age, much of the world was indeed covered with ice. The whole island of Manhattan lay under a 1,000-foot-thick sheet of ice, which would reach as high as the Empire State Building. Human beings could not survive in that much ice, but in regions closer to the equator, people managed pretty well. We know that rock ledges on cliffs gave them shelter and that some of them really did live in caves.

But a lot of the time it was cold, and they wore animal skins, resembling what the Inuit, or Eskimo, people wear today. Some brilliant person thousands of years ago invented the needle, and its design has not changed since! The device enabled people to make clothes that fit well. Animal skins were softened with handmade scrapers and with teeth. This was not so good for their teeth, but Ice Age humans did not have sugar either, which means they had no cavities.

Some of the early humans also created incredible art, and Mrs. Cooper takes a good look at that. Show any of the art pictures in the color insert. This is a fascinating look at the habits and culture of our cool long ago ancestors.

BIBLIOGRAPHY

Adler, David A. *A Hero and the Holocaust: The Story of Janusz Korczak and His Children.* Illustrated by Bill Farnsworth. Holiday House, 2002. ISBN 0823415481. Unpaged. Grades 1–4.

Amis, Nancy. *The Orphans of Normandy: A True Story of World War II Told Through Drawings by Children.* Atheneum Books for Young Readers, 2003. ISBN 0689841434. Unpaged. Grades 1–4.

Andronik, Catherine M. *Hatshepsut: His Majesty, Herself.* Illustrated by Joseph Daniel Fiedler. Atheneum Books for Young Readers, 2001. ISBN 0689825625. 40 p. Grades 4–7.

Anne Frank in the World 1929–1945. Compiled by the Anne Frank House. Alfred A. Knopf, 2001. ISBN 037581177X. 144 p. Grades 5–up.

Arnold, Caroline. *Uluru: Australia's Aboriginal Heart.* Photographs by Arthur Arnold. Clarion Books, 2003. ISBN 0618181814. 64 p. Grades 4–7.

Bartoletti, Susan Campbell. *Black Potatoes: The Story of the Great Irish Famine, 1845–1850.* Houghton Mifflin, 2001. ISBN 0618002715. 184 p. Grades 5–up.

Berger, Melvin, and Gilda Berger. *The Real Vikings: Craftsmen, Traders, and Fearsome Raiders.* National Geographic, 2003. ISBN 0792251326. 60 p. Grades 4–9.

Blacklock, Dyan. *The Roman Army: The Legendary Soldiers Who Created an Empire.* Illustrations by David Kennett. Walker, 2004. ISBN 0802788963. 48 p. Grades 4–9.

Cave, Kathryn. *One Child, One Seed: A South African Counting Book.* Photography by Gisele Wulfsohn. Henry Holt in Association with Oxfam, 2003. ISBN 0805072047. Unpaged. Grades K–3.

Colman, Penny. *Where the Action Was: Women War Correspondents in World War II.* Crown, 2002. ISBN 0517800756. 118 p. Grades 4–8.

Cooper, Margaret. *Exploring the Ice Age.* Atheneum Books for Young Readers, 2001. ISBN 0689825560. 93 p. Grades 4–8.

Coulter,Laurie. *Secrets in Stone: All About Maya Hieroglyphs.* Illustrations by Sarah Jane English. Historical consultation by Dr. Elizabeth Graham and Simon Martin. A Madison Press Book produced for Little, Brown, 2002. ISBN 0316158836. 48 p. Grades 4–8.

Curlee, Lynn. *Seven Wonders of the Ancient World.* Atheneum Books for Young Readers, 2002. ISBN 068983182x. 36 p. Grades 3–6.

Demi. *Muhammad.* Written and illustrated by Demi. Margaret K. McElderry Books, 2003. ISBN 0689852649. Unpaged. Grades 3–6.

Drez, Ronald. J. *Remember D-Day: The Plan, The Invasion, Survivor Stories.* National Geographic,2004. ISBN 079226668. 60 p. Grades 4–9.

Filer, Joyce. *The Mystery of the Egyptian Mummy.* Oxford University Press in association with the British Museum, 2003. ISBN 0195219899. 48 p. Grades 4–8.

Freedman, Russell. *Confucius: The Golden Rule.* Illustrated by Frederic Clement. Arthur A. Levine Books/An Imprint of Scholastic Press, 2002. ISBN 0439139570. 48 p. Grades 4–8.

Gibbons, Gail. *Mummies, Pyramids, and Pharaohs. A Book about Ancient Egypt.* Little, Brown, 2004. ISBN 0316309281. 32 p. Grades K–3.

Giblin, James Cross. *The Life and Death of Adolf Hitler.* Clarion Books, 2002. ISBN 0395903718. 256 p. Grades 5–up.

———. *Secrets of the Sphinx.* Illustrated by Bagram Ibatoulline. Scholastic Press, 2004. ISBN 0590098470. Unpaged. Grades 4–8.

Goldman, Susan Rubin. *Searching for Anne Frank: Letters from Amsterdam to Iowa.* In collaboration with the Simon Wiesenthal Center—Museum of Tolerance Library and Archives. Harry N. Abrams, 2003. ISBN 0810945142. 144 p. Grades 4–8.

Hoyt-Goldsmith, Diane. *Celebrating Ramadan.* Photographs by Lawrence. Migdale. Holiday House, 2001. ISBN 0823415813. 32 p. Grades 3–6.

Lawton, Clive. *Auschwitz.* Candlewick Press, 2002. ISBN 0763615951. 48 p. Grades 4–8

Lewin, Ted. *Lost City: The Discovery of Machu Picchu.* Philomel Books, 2003. ISBN 0399233024. Unpaged. Grades K–3.

Lourie, Peter. *Tierra del Fuego: A Journey to the End of the Earth.* Boyds Mills Press, 2002. ISBN 156397973X. 48 p. Grades 4–8.

MacDonald, Fiona. *You Wouldn't Want to Be an Aztec Sacrifice! Gruesome Things You'd Rather Not Know.* Illustrated by David Antram. Created and designed by David Salariya. Franklin Watts, a division of Scholastic, 2001. ISBN 0531162095. 32 p. Grades 4–8.

Mann, Elizabeth. *Tikal: A Wonders of the World Book.* With illustrations by Tom McNeely. Mikaya Press, 2002. ISBN 193141405x. 48 p. Grades 4–7.

McDonough, Yona Zeldis. *Peaceful Protest: The Life of Nelson Mandela.* Illustrations by Malcah Zeldis. Walker & Company, 2002. ISBN 0802788211. Unpaged. Grades 2–4.

Nir, Yehuda. *The Lost Childhood: A World War II Memoir.* Scholastic Press, 2002. ISBN 0439163897. 284 p. Grades 5–up.

O'Connor, Jane. *The Emperor's Silent: Terracotta Warriors of Ancient China.* Viking, 2002. ISBN 0670035122. 48 p. Grades 3–6.

Preston, Diana. *Remember the* Lusitania! Walker & Company, 2003. ISBN 0802788467. 95 p. Grades 4–8.

Stanley, Diane. *Saladin: Noble Prince of Islam.* HarperCollins, 2002. ISBN 0688171354. Unpaged. Grades 4–8.

Tanaka, Shelley. *D-Day: They Fought to Free Europe from Hitler's Tyranny: A Day That Changed America.* Paintings by David Craig. Historical Consultation by Joseph Balkoski. Hyperion Books for Children/A Hyperion/Madison Press Book, 2003. ISBN 0786818816. 48 p. Grades 4–8.

CHAPTER

American Voices

4

MAKING A NEW COUNTRY

The Boston Massacre. The Boston Tea Party. Thomas Paine's pamphlet, *Common Sense*. The Stamp Act. The shot heard round the world. One if by land and two if by sea. "Give me liberty or give me death!" The Declaration of Independence. You've heard the names and phrases, but how do they fit together? How did it all happen? Natalie S. Bober does an amazing and concise job of putting the pieces together in *Countdown to Independence: A Revolution of Ideas in England and the American Colonies: 1760–1776.* What made it possible for a group of delegates from all 13 American colonies to unite in hot, humid Philadelphia, put their lives on the line, and declare themselves traitors to their country? Their country was England. The British authorities could have had them hanged, disemboweled, and cut into four parts for what they did. The revolutionaries could have lost their homes, their families, and their fortunes. Some of them did.

Natalie Bober's wonderful book shows us what led up to that amazing declaration. And it was not only citizens of the 13 colonies who made it happen. The colonies had friends, such as the great William Pitt, back in England itself, who felt that the colonists' rights were being violated. In Parliament, arguing with someone who felt that Americans must obey British tax laws, for they had not been emancipated from Britain, Pitt stated, " The gentleman asks, when were the colonies emancipated? But I desire to know, when were they made slaves?" (page 92). Most Britons, of course, did not agree with Pitt. Most believed that since Britain protected the colonists, the colonies should pay for that protection. Some even felt that the colonials were hypocrites, since they clamored for freedom, yet kept slaves.

People and ideas eventually came together to create the glorious experiment that was the Declaration of Independence. Natalie Bober shines the light on them in a brilliant, exciting read.

Rosalyn Schanzer reminds us that there are two sides to the story in *George vs. George: The American Revolution as Seen from Both Sides.*

> There were once two enemies who were both named George. George Washington was the man who freed the American colonies from the British, and George III was the British king who lost them. Was King George a "Royal Brute?" American patriots said so. But others hailed him as "the Father of the People." Was George Washington a traitor? The king's supporters thought so. But many celebrated Washington as 'the father of his country.' Who was right? There are two sides to every story. (page 7)

George Washington and King George had a lot in common. They were both tall with light blue eyes and reddish-brown hair. They loved farming and horses and hunting—and their families.

George Washington was a good and loyal subject of King George, even though he lived an ocean away in the American colonies. He fought in the king's army during the French and Indian War. But, by the 1760s, many thoughtful American colonials, including Washington, were wondering whether they were being treated fairly by their king and his government. They were being taxed on all sorts of things, and they had no say in the matter. No one cared what Americans thought—until they started fighting back.

The first really big crisis was the Boston Tea Party. A group of patriots, protesting an unfair tea tax, dumped costly tea into Boston Harbor. As punishment, the British government closed the harbor down. Bostonians were afraid they would starve, but soon the other colonies pitched in to provide food and clothing and even animals. More and more people were considering war with King George. Americans wanted independence from the unjust British government, and, as we all know, with Washington's help, they won it. This is the story of the Revolution as seen through the eyes of two men who had more in common than just their names.

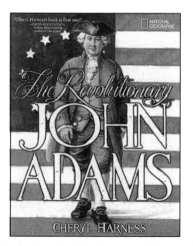

Figure 4.1. *The Revolutionary John Adams* **by Cheryl Harness.**

Cheryl Harness makes the amazing claim in *The Revolutionary John Adams* that if John Adams had never existed, the United States of America would not have turned out the way it did. Adams, she points out, had an incredible influence on the beginnings of our country. He truly believed in the equality of men affirmed in the Declaration of Independence. As Harness says

> There stands John Adams, the stout, stubborn New Englander eternally bookended and overshadowed by tall, glamorous Virginians. On one side, the reserved, heroic General George Washington, "first in the hearts of his countrymen." Imagine having to take up the Presidency—and keep a fragile republic in business—after that fellow! On the other is the cool, complicated genius of Monticello, Thomas Jefferson. (page 3)

John was the son of a Massachusetts farmer, and he expected he would be a farmer, too. His father had different ideas, however, and packed him off to Harvard College. After he graduated, John became a teacher. Law and history interested him more, however, and eventually John studied to become a lawyer. He had the good fortune to meet and marry an intelligent young woman named Abigail. Their mutual love and respect lasted the rest of their lives. They wrote long letters to each other, and we can learn a lot about them and the times they lived in from those letters.

When the king and Parliament started taxing the colonies, John was one of the first to lead the protests. He sided with the colonists who were against taxation without representation, and eventually he went to the Continental Congress in Philadelphia. He became one of the prime movers behind the Declaration of Independence. And when the United States Constitution was written a few years later, it was partially based on one that John had written earlier for Massachusetts.

And, of course, John Adams became the second president of the United States. He was an incredible man. Show the double-page spread on pages 28–29 of Adams along with Thomas Jefferson, George Washington, and Alexander Hamilton.

Every early American patriot risked his or her life in the battle against England. Shannon Zemlicka tells about one of the men who faced death for his country in *Nathan Hale: Patriot Spy* (On My Own Biography).

Nathan Hale lived in interesting times. He grew up on a farm in Connecticut but was lucky enough to be able to go to college at Yale when he was almost 14 years old. Times were troubled. In 1769, Connecticut was a colony, and people were talking about how unfair their British rulers were. Taxes were way too high, and no one in the American colonies had any right to protest.

Hale started teaching school when he was 18 years old. He did something highly unusual for the time: He held classes for girls. He became a popular teacher, but when war broke out in 1775, Hale joined the army. And then he found out that George Washington needed a spy.

> But spying was dangerous!
> Spying meant sneaking and lying.
> It meant lurking and hiding.
> If a man was caught spying, the best he could expect was a quick death.
> (page 29)

Despite the danger, Hale volunteered. And because of what he did, and because of the famous phrase he uttered, he is considered one of the greatest heroes in American history.

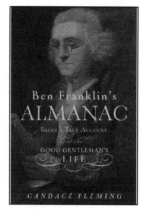

Figure 4.2 *Ben Franklin's Almanac: Being a True Account of the Good Gentleman's Life* **by Candace Fleming.**

One of Nathan Hale's most famous contemporaries is the star of Candace Fleming's unusual biography, *Ben Franklin's Almanac: Being a True Account of the Good Gentleman's Life.* Ben Franklin was born in Boston in 1706, the youngest in a large family. He had only two years of formal schooling, but he pretty much educated himself, and he later gained fame as one of the world's most brilliant thinkers. Franklin loved to read, was very curious, and enjoyed figuring things out for himself. When he was a teenager, he was apprenticed to his brother. He became a fine printer, learning the craft that would make him a wealthy man. But he and his brother quarreled once too often, so Franklin left Boston to move to the biggest city in the American colonies, Philadelphia.

When Franklin arrived in Philadelphia, a girl standing in a doorway laughed at the sight of him. He ended up marrying her!

Fleming's book is organized almost like a scrapbook; you can dip into it the way you might look at a scrapbook, or you can read it straight through. Along the way you will pick up some great information, such as:

- Ben read the book *The Pilgrim's Progress* by John Bunyan when he was only eight years old. It became his favorite book for the rest of his life.

- Ben never legally married his wife.

- Somewhere around the time he got married, he also acquired a son, William. He seems to have had a relationship outside of his marriage, but his wife raised his illegitimate son—although she never liked him very much.

- Every day Ben asked himself, "What good shall I do today?" (page 34)

- Ben had a great sense of humor and told a lot of funny stories.

Ben made a lot of money being a printer, but more than anything else, he wanted to help people lead better lives. He retired from printing when still relatively young, and he started doing scientific experiments. Throughout his life, he was interested in the relationship of the American colonies with their ruler in Great Britain. This is a good introduction to a great American innovator.

Maybe your booktalk audience would like to hear more about the actual fighting that took place during the Revolution. Turn to Anne Rockwell's *They Called Her Molly Pitcher.*

When William Hays closed up his barbershop and set off for Valley Forge to join the Colonial Army under George Washington, his wife Mary, who was nicknamed Molly, came along too. Conditions were horrifying. The soldiers had worn-out, inadequate clothing, and not enough food or supplies of any sort. Molly and the other women tried their best to tend to the men, but many died anyway.

At the end of June, the army engaged in battle with the British forces at Monmouth. The weather was blazing hot! Molly made herself extremely useful by bringing a pitcher of water to anyone who needed it. Then her husband was shot by a British sniper. So Molly made herself even more useful by taking over her husband's cannon. She became a beloved American legend.

If you know one thing about Benedict Arnold, it is that he was a traitor. A bad guy. And, basically, he got away unpunished. The very name "Benedict Arnold" has come to describe in American English any one guilty of treason and treachery. But we learn in Susan R. Gregson's *Benedict Arnold* that Arnold did not start out to be a turncoat. Originally he was a patriot and spent his own money to help raise a fighting force in the American colonies. Arnold won some dazzling victories, but he never felt he received the proper credit for his hard work and ingenuity.

Arnold eventually asked George Washington for the command of the American fort at West Point in New York. Then Arnold contacted the British and offered to turn it over to them for the sum of £20,000 British, which would be roughly $1 million today. Arnold met with Major John Andre to turn over the plans for West Point.

Andre was captured by the Americans and hanged. Benedict Arnold escaped, and, after leading British troops on fierce raids against his fellow colonists, he lived out the rest of his life peacefully in Britain. In his new home, however, Arnold was neither successful nor happy.

No one really knows why Arnold made such a life-changing decision. But surely that proud military man would hate the way we remember him today. Show the picture on page 5, of Arnold as a young officer.

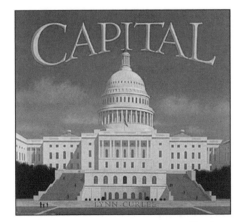

Figure 4.3. *Capital* by Lynn Curlee.

The capital of the United States of America is a city, Washington, District of Columbia. The Constitution of our country authorized the building of a capital city, one that would not belong to any state but to the entire country. A site was chosen between a northern state and a southern state, Maryland and Virginia, on the Potomac River.

The first president, George Washington, for whom the city was named, appointed an engineer and architect named Pierre-Charles L'Enfant to lay out the city. L'Enfant laid out a grid, which included many spaces for public monuments, but the entire city could not be more than 10 miles square.

Lynn Curlee tells us the stories behind the city and many of the famous monuments in her book *Capital.* For instance, Thomas Jefferson entered a contest to design what turned out to be the White House. He lost. And the British burned down most of the buildings during the War of 1812.

George Washington laid the cornerstone for the Capitol although it was not finished until 36 years later. The first dome was replaced, and a statue of Freedom was placed on the new dome on December 2, 1863, during the Civil War.

Over the years, many monuments have been built in Washington, D.C. Perhaps the most famous is the George Washington Monument, the shining obelisk in the National Mall. But the memorials to Thomas Jefferson and Abraham Lincoln are also successful and memorable. Curlee says, "Many visitors are profoundly moved by the Lincoln Memorial. Its architecture is severe, its mood grave and somber. Here we seem to be at the heart of America's conscience. If our nation has a soul, this is the one place where it may be felt" (page 34).

Laura Krauss Melmed is a lucky lady, for she lives in Washington, D.C., the capital of the United States of America. Her home is the setting for *Capital! Washington, D.C. from A to Z.* But as she tells us right away on her "Welcome!" page, "since our government is a democracy, each of us plays an important part in it. So whether you live in Anchorage, or Detroit, on a farm in Nebraska or a small town in Mississippi, Washington is yours to be proud of."

There is a lot there to be proud of. What a fun place to visit!

In Washington, D.C., you can see buildings and items that played an important part in American history: the Declaration of Independence, the real one signed by all of those famous people; the first airplane that had a controlled flight built by the Wright Brothers in 1903; a spacesuit that was worn on the moon; memorials to our greatest presidents; the White House, where our presidents have lived for about 200 years; memorials to soldiers and wars; monuments to famous people; and great museums filled with the work of the world's greatest artists and scientists.

You can even touch a piece of the moon.

Show the picture of the Lincoln Memorial. We've all seen the picture of Lincoln sitting in his famous pose, but how many of us have looked closely at his hands? "One hand is clenched to show his strong will in keeping the nation together during the Civil War. The other hand is open to show that he was warm and caring"(n.p.).

Have you ever read the Declaration of Independence all the way through? Do you know what the words say? Do you know what they mean? Sam Fink wasn't always sure that he did, and he decided it would be a good thing to find out. He takes all of the words in the famous document and shows us with neat illustrations in *The Declaration of Independence* exactly what those words mean.

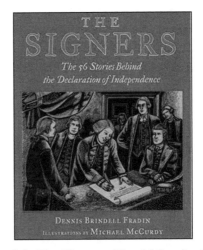

Figure 4.4. *The Signers: The 56 Stories Behind the Declaration of Independence* **by Dennis Brindell Fradin.**

What about all those names signed at the bottom of the Declaration? Dennis Brindell Fradin had a terrific idea. In *The Signers: The 56 Stories Behind the Declaration of Independence,* he introduces us, one by one, to the 56 men who took their lives and their fortunes in their hands and risked it all to sign the Declaration of Independence in 1776. If the colonial Americans had lost the Revolution, they probably all would have been executed as traitors to Great Britain. As it was, many of them suffered mightily. These are some of their stories:

- Richard Henry Lee and Francis Lightfoot Lee, both of Virginia, were the only signers who were brothers. Richard went down in history for being the one to make the first resolution, " that these United Colonies are, and of right ought to be, free and independent States" (page 19). Richard had had a bad accident a few years before that in which he blew off four of his fingers while hunting.

- Robert Morris of Pennsylvania, who spent as much as a million dollars of his own money to help the Revolution, spent three and a half years in prison because he could not pay his debts. He ended his life in poverty.

- George Taylor of Pennsylvania came to America as an indentured servant. He worked for a Mr. Savage. When Savage died, George married his widow. They had two children, but George also had five children by his housekeeper.

- Several signers were caught by the British and sent to prison.

- Francis Hopkinson of New Jersey was the first American colonist to write a nonreligious song.

- The signer with the most unusual name was Button Gwinnett of Georgia. In 1777, he got involved in a duel, was shot, and died three days later.

Fradin's book is jam-packed with interesting information about the people who were present at the creation of our country. It includes a picture of each of them and a reproduction of their signature on the declaration. This book is a must-have for any fan of American history!

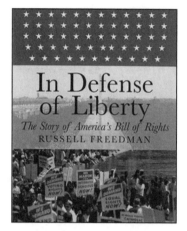

Figure 4.5. *In Defense of Liberty: The Story of America's Bill of Rights* **by Russell Freedman.**

Where did the fight for American freedom begin? In *In Defense of Liberty: The Story of America's Bill of Rights*, Russell Freedman answers that question by taking the long view. In 1215, something incredible happened in England. King John signed an agreement. His barons were sick of not having any rights, and they decided to do something about it at long last. The Magna Carta "placed legal limits on the king's power. Nothing like that had ever happened before. The king was no longer free to do anything he wanted. He was no longer above the law, but had promised to obey those written rules like any other Englishman" (page 6).

The Magna Carta was just a start, but it had a powerful effect on history. As time went on it wasn't only the barons or nobility who wanted rights; ordinary people started demanding their own fair share. And by the time the colonials in America had won their Revolution, most of their leaders believed that ordinary citizens had basic rights that no government could legally take away.

In 1787 in America, 55 delegates from every state except Rhode Island met in Philadelphia to write a national constitution. That document started with the words many of us know by heart: "We, the people." The people gave the government rights. This was a world-shaking concept at the time. It still is. But the Constitution was not a perfect document. Slaves were not treated as people with equal rights. Neither were many other groups, including women. There were other problems, and these prompted James Madison to bring a list of amendments for the Constitution to the first Congress held in 1789. Ten of those amendments were adopted and became known as the Bill of Rights.

Russell Freedman tells us the fascinating story behind each of the original 10 amendments and the later amendments that also became a part of the ever-expanding Bill of Rights. He takes us through some of the controversy that certain amendments have caused. For instance, the Second Amendment has been called "the embarrassing Second Amendment." It is known as the right to bear arms. Many people are certain that what our nation's founders meant over 200 years ago is not how that amendment is interpreted today. Do all of the kids in your booktalk audience know what rights they have just by being born in this country?

This is an amazing book, and it is so interesting to read you will have a hard time putting it down. Give it a try!

Many children learn that the story of the United States begins with the Pilgrims. Judy Donnelly takes a cool spin on the idea in her *The Pilgrims and Me* (Smart about History). Carrie Rosen has an assignment to write about events from the past. She has a fairly easy time choosing, for her family went on a vacation to Plimoth Plantation, in Massachusetts. Plimoth Plantation is a re-creation of the settlement where the Mayflower pilgrims lived, complete with costumed guides to show people around.

The pilgrims who came to Massachusetts in 1620 had a hard time getting there, and an even harder time after they arrived. The *Mayflower* was a tiny ship, and the travelers slept on the floor. No one took a bath or washed clothes, and there was no bathroom. They had very little to eat, and the voyage lasted 66 days!

It was November 11 when the *Mayflower* arrived, and the new land looked cold, wild, and forbidding. Half of the pilgrims died that first winter.

This is an interesting look at some important people in American history, and it may just give you some ideas for your next school report.

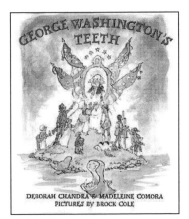

Figure 4.6. *George Washington's Teeth* **by Deborah Chandra and Madeleine Comora.**

After a booktalk full of serious history, it's fun to pull out a copy of Deborah Chandra and Madeleine Comora's delightful *George Washington's Teeth* as a tasty treat.

You may have heard that George Washington had a set of wooden teeth. This is not true! He never ever did. But he did have teeth made of hippopotamus and walrus and elephant ivory, and of cow, elk, and human teeth. George Washington was definitely a man who had a lot of trouble with his teeth. And Brock Cole's bright, breezy illustrations are funny without making fun of our first president's painful predicament.

This book has two separate parts. One is a snazzy poem about George and all of the teeth he lost (it does have a happy ending), and the other is a chronology of George's life, telling about *how* the teeth were lost and how they affected the way he looked. You better believe that if you do not have any teeth, your face looks really different than it does when you have teeth. Show the photo of George's false teeth on the second-to-the-last page.

Next, show your booktalk audience George's face on the $1 bill. Now they'll know why he wasn't smiling. He didn't want to show he was missing some teeth. Besides, his mouth hurt. It hurt him during the entire American Revolution! You will feel very sorry for George when you read this, and you might even wonder how on earth he won a war when his teeth were almost always aching.

AMERICA KEEPS GROWING

No one knows for certain how the first immigrants came to America. But Patricia Lauber describes the search for those early travelers in *Who Came First? New Clues to Prehistoric Americans.*

Figure 4.7. *Who Came First? New Clues to Prehistoric Americans* **by Patricia Lauber.**

For many years, scientists felt that the first Americans crossed a land bridge connecting what is now Russia to what is now North America. But new evidence is accumulating that this may not be the case. Besides, ask some experts, why would a group of people, who did not even know what a wheel looked like, travel so far south when there were plenty of places to stop and settle along the way?

In 1996, a skull (and later a lot more bones that went with it) was discovered along the edge of the Columbia River in Kennewick, Washington. The young men who found it called the police, and the police gave it to a medical examiner. The medical examiner was sure the bones were ancient. Carbon-14 dating proved that the bones were at least 6,000 years old. And the skull did not look like the skull of a Native American. It resembled the skulls of Europeans.

Scientists were excited and bewildered. What was going on?

We really do not know. What we do know is that the old theories are being shattered by new discoveries, even though not all of the new information is reliable. Current historians are wondering if ancient people came in ships from places so far away that we never guessed they could make it. Scientists are studying DNA patterns and speech and language to try to find other ways of figuring out where the first Americans came from.

This is a fascinating book loaded with terrific photographs.

Show the picture of the skull discovered in the Columbia River on page 4 and its reconstruction on page 53.

Grown-ups are not the only ones who ever did anything historically interesting. Kids were there too, from the very beginnings of recorded American history. Some of them fought in wars, often illegally, for they were not really old enough to enlist. Some of them fought for their rights and the rights of their people. Some of them took big chances. Some of them just happened to be in the right place at the right time. *We Were There Too!: Young People in U.S. History* by Philip Hoose tells many of their stories.

Recorded history in what is now the United States pretty much started with the voyage of Columbus. Did you know there were children on his famous ships? Diego Bernardez, age 12, was one of about 20 teenagers or younger who sailed with Columbus. Bernardez was a page and did a lot of grunt work. Other boys were apprentice seamen. They often had to do dangerous things, like climbing up high into the rigging of the ship. "Captains hired teenagers partly because they showed little fear and partly because, unlike many of the old sailors, most boys still had both arms and legs" (page 3). In those days the concept of "teenager" did not exist—anyone over 12 was pretty much considered an adult because life expectancy was so short.

Caroline Pickersgill was 13 when she helped her mother and grandmother sew the enormous flag that became the most famous flag in American history. It was the same flag Francis Scott Keyes saw and that became the subject of his song, "The Star Spangled Banner." Pickershill's flag was 42 feet wide by 30 feet long, and it weighed over 200 pounds. She helped make many of the 1.7 million stitches sewn in the flag, and this was before the invention of the sewing machine. The gigantic flag was made in 1813, and you can still see it today in Washington, D.C.

Charles Denby was 17 when he moved north from Alabama, joining thousands of other African Americans in what is called "The Great Migration." He was sick of being treated as though he had no rights and hoped that his life would be better in Detroit. Another young man who migrated summed up his reasons for going to his father, a black minister: "When a young white man talks rough to me, I can't talk rough to him. You can stand that; I can't. I have some education and inside I have the feelings of a white man. I'm going" (p. 185).

All through history, children have had to work. Young people fought for their own rights and for the rights of other workers and, whenever workers united for better pay and better working conditions, kids were there. And sometimes kids were the leaders! Susan Campbell Bartoletti describes the kind of work young people had to do in *Kids on Strike!*

Figure 4.8. *Kids on Strike!* **by Susan Campbell Bartoletti.**

In the 1800s, many young women worked in textile mills. The 1828 strike in Paterson, New Jersey, is one of the first on record. The girls wanted their workday reduced from 13 1/2 hours to 10, and to have their dinner time restored. They won only the second demand, and the leaders of the strike were fired.

Factory owners liked hiring kids because legally they didn't have to pay them as much as they paid adults. Of course, the kids worked long, hard hours and had no time to go to school. Conditions were often horrifying. There was frequently no heat in the winter, and windows were kept closed in the summer, making the temperatures inside stiflingly hot. Kids had to work fast, and sometimes, if they made mistakes, they lost fingers, or even arms, in the factory machinery. Children as young as four years old were hired and had almost no time to play.

Other kids worked in coal mines or lived on the streets and sold newspapers in New York City. Even kids who lived with their families often suffered dire poverty. But wherever kids worked and were treated unfairly, some of them fought back. And some of them won! Conditions gradually improved for most child laborers.

Read this book, loaded with photographs, to find out the true stories.

When settlers originally from Europe came to what is now the United States, they wanted land. They wanted to treat the land as property, and they did not feel that the Native Americans, who were already living on the land, had any rights to it. Although there were more settlers than there were Native Americans, many Native Americans wanted to protect their own rights, and to try to drive the settlers away.

The Legend of Blue Jacket by Michael P. Spradlin tells us that in the 1700s, Duke Swearingen was 16 years old and living in Virginia when he was captured by a small war group of Shawnee. Duke volunteered to go with them if they would leave his brother Charlie at home. So they took him, and they left Charlie.

Duke never returned. He had many adventures in the Shawnee camp, and he decided to become a Shawnee himself. Eventually he became friends with Daniel Boone, but always, for the remainder of his life, he considered himself a Shawnee.

Show the picture of the two boys being confronted by the Shawnee near the beginning of the book.

Many people celebrated the bicentennial of the famous Lewis and Clark expedition by getting reacquainted with the story, or by reading about that heroic journey for the first time. A good place to start is Rosalyn Schanzer's *How We Crossed the West: The Adventures of Lewis and Clark.*

Figure 4.9. *How We Crossed the West: The Adventures of Lewis & Clark* **by Rosalyn Schanzer.**

Before 1804, very few people who were not Native Americans had seen any of America west of the Mississippi River. No one knew what it was like, or what might be found there, but it became a part of the United States after the Louisiana Purchase from France, and someone needed to go and take a look.

President Thomas Jefferson had a good friend whom he asked to take charge of the "Corps of Discovery," the group that would explore the land and report back to Washington. That friend was Meriweather Lewis, and Lewis had a good friend, William Clark, whom he asked to accompany him. The two men hired several other people and set out from Missouri. They explored the great Missouri River and hoped that it flowed all the way to the Pacific Ocean, so that people could traverse the entire United States east to west by boat.

No such luck. But what the explorers did find and how they made their journey is one of the most wonderful stories in American history. Someone has remarked that Lewis and Clark were like the space voyagers on *Star Trek.* They had no idea what they would find!

Rosalyn Schanzer has painted some wonderful illustrations and included actual words from the diaries of the men who made the journey.

Continue with Lewis and Clark in Dorothy Hinshaw Patent's *The Lewis and Clark Trail: Then and Now.* The mission of the Corps of Discovery was to explore the Louisiana Purchase. This included much of the land west of the Mississippi River, all the way to the Continental Divide in the Rocky Mountains. Jefferson wanted Lewis and his colleague, William Clark, to map the territory, make friends with the natives, describe of the animals and plants living there, and, hopefully, find a water passage that went all the way through to the Pacific Ocean.

The mission, with the exception of finding a single water passage, was a huge success. For a time, however, people back in Washington thought the expedition had failed. The trip was taking so long that people assumed the explorers had died!

The official starting point of the expedition was Saint Louis, Missouri. Twenty-seven men were listed as members of the expedition, plus Clark's African-American slave, York, and Lewis's dog Seaman. Along the way others joined, such as the French trader Charbonneau and his young wife, Sacagawea.

This book describes their journey. Patent does a great service for the modern reader by describing what happened and what the land looked like, and then comparing it with the modern U.S. landscape. The Corps of Discovery probably wouldn't have a clue that this was the same land they explored. Wildlife has disappeared. Rivers have changed course. Other waterways, like the formerly breathtaking Great Falls of Montana, have been dammed for irrigation purposes. A number of the places important to the journey, including former campsites, are now under water. You will be amazed at how much our country has changed since Lewis and Clark journeyed through it.

One thing has not changed much. Clark carved his name in a stone, and that is still there! Show its picture on page 53.

David A. Adler guides younger readers over the same territory in *A Picture Book of Lewis and Clark*. Meriweather Lewis was born in 1774 and grew up in Virginia and on the frontier in Georgia. When he joined the army, he made a new friend, William Clark, who was born in Virginia in 1770 and grew up on the frontier in Kentucky. Adler shows how the two friends led more than 30 men and eventually one woman, Sacagawea, through the new Louisiana Purchase that had doubled the size of the United States.

Show the double-page spread of the grizzly bear threatening the expedition.

Figure 4.10. *On the Trail of Lewis and Clark: A Journey up the Missouri River* **by Peter Lourie.**

Peter Lourie's adventures always make for a good read. *On the Trail of Lewis and Clark: A Journey up the Missouri River* recounts how Lourie and three friends decided to travel up the Missouri River, following the trail that Lewis and Clark took about 200 years ago.

The Missouri is nicknamed by some "The Big Muddy" because it is indeed a dirty, muddy river. Steamboat captains used to call it "Old Misery" because it was so hard to navigate. The river is 2,450 miles long, but when Thomas Jefferson bought the Louisiana Territory in 1803, he wanted someone to explore it, and hopefully, find a good path, a navigable waterway all the way to the Pacific Ocean.

Lewis and Clark could not have been better chosen. They traveled over 8,000 miles in two and a half years and saw things no white person had ever seen before.

You will learn a lot about this fascinating piece of American history and see some beautiful photographs of a new journey of discovery. Show your audience the photo on page 32 of the lovely White Cliffs Region of the Missouri.

It's a great idea to take the story of one participant in the Lewis and Clark expedition and tell the story from his point of view, while sticking to the facts as we know them. Judith Edwards uses this idea to great advantage in *The Great Expedition of Lewis and Clark by Private Reubin Field, Member of the Corps of Discovery*. Reubin and his brother Joseph were recruited by William Clark and were promised a farm when they returned. Lewis and Clark wanted "able woodsmen and hunters." Boy, did they need them! This picture book for older readers is a great introduction to the tale.

Lise Erdrich's *Sacagawea* starts out by trying to answer the question most readers have about this heroine: How do you pronounce her name? One thing the author tells us in the foreword, before the book even really begins, is that it most likely was pronounced sa-KA-ga-WEE-ah, judging by the way the Hidatsa word would have been pronounced.

However her name was pronounced, the person who bore that name is one of the most famous women in American history. Sacagawea would never have guessed that her name would still be remembered two centuries after she took her most famous trip.

For Sacagawea, life must have been very hard. When she was about 11 years old, she was captured by the enemies of her Shoshone people and taken far away from her home to the earth lodge villages of the Hidatsa and Mandan people in what is now North Dakota. There she worked hard, until a few years later when she was given in marriage to a fur trapper named Toussaint Charbonneau.

Charbonneau managed to get a job as a guide and interpreter for the Corps of Discovery led by Meriweather Lewis and William Clark, and Sacagawea accompanied them to do most of the interpreting.

She had two new jobs, being a mother and being an interpreter, and she performed them both brilliantly. This is the story of the contributions she made to the great journey of the Corps.

If your booktalk audience would like to examine a side of African-American history that is also part of a great adventure story, turn to Rhoda Blumberg's *York's Adventures with Lewis and Clark: An African-American's Part in the Great Expedition*. We really don't know much about the young man named York, but we do know more about him than about other African Americans who were slaves in the early 1800s. We know that York went on a grand and glorious adventure; that he became an integral, important part of that adventure; and that he was the first African American who ever got to vote. All of these things make York a fascinating man, someone we wish we knew more about.

York was born a slave, and by the time he was 12 or 13 years old, he had a new master. That new master was William Clark, who was himself only 14 years old. The two were friends as boys, but York was never treated as an equal. William always had rights over him and could tell him what to do. Historians know a fair amount about how slaves lived and were treated in 1784, so Blumberg can make some educated guesses as to what York's life was like. She knows for sure that York moved west with his owner's family to Kentucky and grew up on the frontier there.

In Kentucky, York fell in love with another slave, who belonged to a neighbor of the Clark family. York married her in the only way that slaves were allowed to marry, and we know that he loved her, although they never got to spend much time together.

York leapt into history in 1803 when his owner, William Clark, brought him along on the famous expedition that he and his partner Meriwether Lewis undertook to explore the Missouri River and the West.

This is the story of their adventures, of how the Native Americans who met York were very impressed with him, and how York helped make that incredible journey a success.

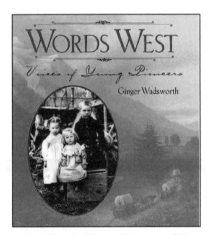

Figure 4.11. *Words West: Voices of Young Pioneers* by Ginger Wadsworth.

Years after the Louisiana Purchase had first been explored, large numbers of people started moving west. They headed toward California and Oregon and Utah, and other places, in about 1848. They went to find gold, to get free good land, to find adventure, or to settle in an area where they could freely practice their religion. A lot of pioneers took their kids. What Ginger Wadsworth has done in *Words West: Voices of Young Pioneers* is to allow those young people to tell us about their journeys, using diaries and reminiscences that the kids left behind. Many great photographs help clarify the story. This is a rousing good read. Young readers will learn that:

- The early mountain men often served as guides, forging the way and finding the paths the settlers used.

- One child and his father, living in Missouri, heard a speaker brag that "in Oregon, the pigs are running about under the great acorn trees, round and fat, and already cooked, with knives and forks sticking in them so you can cut off a slice whenever you are hungry" (page 44).

- More people were killed by disease than anything else. There were thousands of graves along the trails. Lack of sanitation was a horrible problem that caused many deaths.

- Many kids played America's first popular board game, called *The Mansion of Happiness.*

- Traveling with a wagon train was dangerous, and people often got badly injured. Amputations were performed without any anesthetic.

- Although less than 10 percent of the wagons had any unfriendly incidents whatsoever with the Native Americans, there were problems. Some children, such as Olive Oatman, were captured and taken as slaves.

- Brigham Young, the Mormon leader, asked his people to treat the Indians with kindness. The Mormons thus had fewer problems than anyone else.

- Crossing rivers and mountains and deserts was dicey; many people died en route.

- Fresh drinking water became harder and harder to find as more people traveled the same trails. So pioneers learned to drink coffee, which disguised the bad taste of the water and killed the bugs!

- The seven Sager children, orphaned when both of their parents died during travel, were taken in at the Whitman mission in Oregon. Marcus and Narcissa Whitman basically adopted them for the next three years. But two of the children and both Whitmans were killed in a massacre in 1847.

- The big migration west lasted only 30 years. By 1869, railroads crossed the country, and people preferred trains to covered wagons.

Just a few years ago, a salvage worker unearthed a tin box in a California dump. It contained the diary of a 16-year-old girl who had traveled west in 1866. Ginger Wadsworth confidently expects more such diaries and reminiscences to be found—allowing more and more young voices from our nation's past to be heard.

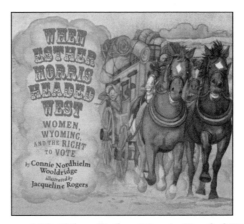

Figure 4.12. *When Esther Morris Headed West: Women, Wyoming, and the Right to Vote* **by Connie Nordhielm Wooldridge.**

That same year the major migration stopped, one of America's more colorful characters took her own trip. Connie Nordhielm Wooldridge tells the story in *When Esther Morris Headed West: Women, Wyoming, and the Right to Vote*. Esther Mae Hobart McQuigg Slack Morris was 55 years old when she trekked to the Wyoming Territory in 1869. Esther had a big name, and even bigger ideas. One of her most outrageous ideas was that women should be allowed to vote and hold office. A lot of Esther's neighbors thought she was completely crazy. No woman anywhere in the world was allowed to vote. Why should American females be any different?

But then a miracle happened. The Wyoming Legislature passed a law that same year allowing women to vote and hold office the same as men. Before long, Esther herself was holding public office. This is an amazing and fun true story. It took years for the rest of the country to catch up with Wyoming.

Show the picture of Esther, who had just cast her vote for the first time, with her physician, who is taking her pulse to find out if voting has a bad effect on a woman's health!

All through European and American history, women were not treated as equal to men, and they did not enjoy the same rights. African Americans had the same problem. Many people who observed the struggles of both groups felt that it was wrong, and many of the women described in Cheryl Harness's *Rabble Rousers: 20 Women Who Made a Difference* fought hard for equal rights for women and for African Americans.

Although Ann Lee was born in 1736 in England, and Dolores Huerta was born in 1930 in New Mexico, they, like all the other women in this book, had several things in common. They were either born Americans or became Americans. They were intelligent and determined. And they wanted to change the way things were. Ann Lee led the first colony of the "Shaker" religion in America. Huerta co-founded the United Farm Workers of America.

Emma Willard created a school for advanced women students in Troy, New York, in 1818—the first in the United States. Some men could not believe she was bothering with it. " 'They'll be educating the cows next,' a farmer was heard to say" (page 13).

Sojourner Truth born a slave, traveled the country talking to people about her beliefs. Women like Susan B. Anthony, Annie Paul, and Elizabeth Cady Stanton fought for women's rights, particularly the right to vote.

These women risked danger and opposition, but they made a huge difference in our country. Pick up the book and start reading about any one of them. You will be hooked!

Show the two-page spread on pages 44–45 of the women celebrating the passage of the 19th Amendment, which gave them the right to vote.

Figure 4.13. *In the Days of the Vacqueros: America's First True Cowboys* **by Russell Freedman.**

Even before the Pilgrims landed on Plymouth Rock, there were cowboys in Mexico, and there were parts of Mexico that are now the United States. In *In the Days of the Vaqueros: America's First True Cowboys* by Russell Freedman we learn that those cowboys were called *vaqueros*, from *vaca,* the Spanish word for "cow."

Modern-day Americans still use many of the words the cowboys invented.

When you talk about a bronco, a mustang, chaps, a lasso, a lariat, or rodeo, you are using the same words the vaqueros used. Even the word *buckaroo,* which is another word for "cowboy," is just a version of *vaquero.*

When Spain conquered much of the Americas, it needed cheap labor. A source was already here, the natives of the land they had conquered. Over the years, many of those native families acquired Spanish blood, but the men of those families were still treated as second-class citizens. The same men who became exceptionally skilled horse riders and cattle herders were uneducated, underpaid, and never attained the glamorous image that Anglo cowboys still have today, although cowboys copied much of what the earlier vaqueros did first.

This book is full of great illustrations and wonderful, sometimes horrible, stories. Read about the grizzly bear hunts starting on page 39, and show the picture on page 26. You might wish to read the last two paragraphs, on pages 58–59:

> Born to the saddle, he had always worked cattle much as his father, grandfather, great-grandfather, and even great-great-grandfather had done. And yet the Spanish, and later the Mexicans, had never glorified the figure of the vaquero in the same way that North Americans came to romanticize the image of the cowboy. No matter how skilled the vaquero was, how courageous, colorful or proud, he continued to be regarded as just a poor laborer on horseback—a peon.
>
> Even so, his legacy endures. Today, whenever a man chooses to call himself a cowboy, whenever he puts on a wide-brimmed hat, pulls on a pair of chaps, swings a lariat, brands a calf, rides a bucking bronco, or strums a guitar and sings a love song to his favorite horses, he is paying tribute to those barefoot Indian cow herders who started it all nearly five hundred years ago.

Almost every American knows we need to "remember the Alamo." But why? What happened there? There are movies and books about it, and a lot of legends about the men who fought there, but the reality, according to Jim Murphy's *Inside the Alamo*, is that historians do not really *know* a lot of what may have actually happened.

The people in the Alamo were Texicans, mostly Americans who had been granted land in Texas on the condition that they become Catholics and remain loyal to the Mexican government. This did not work out very well. The Texicans felt they were being treated unfairly and decided to stand up for their rights. They were poorly trained, badly organized, and lacked adequate ammunition. But they did have a lot of guts and some good leaders, including Colonel William Travis, who died early on in the battle.

On March 6, 1836, the Alamo fell. No one even knows how many people were inside. Estimates range from 182 to 257. Not very many, compared to the thousands of soldiers in the Mexican army storming the fortress. There were women and children there, and some of them were killed too. One thing we are sure of is that it was a blood-bath. The battle was a horrible nightmare for everyone involved. Among the famous people who died were Davy Crockett and Jim Bowie, names that were to go down in American history.

Jim Bowie was sick and had been so for weeks. He died in his sickroom. Some historians wonder if he killed himself or if he was even conscious when the Mexican soldiers attacked him. Or whether, as happens in the movies, Bowie fought off the soldiers from his sickbed. Some experts say that David Crockett was executed after he was captured and thus did not die fighting. No one really knows the answers to these questions, but Mr. Murphy gives us a great deal of fascinating information.

Another Alamo title, *A Day That Changed America: The Alamo: Surrounded and Outnumbered, They Chose to Make a Defiant Last Stand* by Shelley Tanaka has some fine color paintings by David Craig and some great dramatic stories about the last stand.

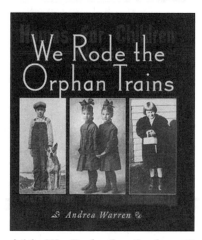

Figure 4.14. *We Rode the Orphan Trains* **by Andrea Warren.**

Andrea Warren wrote a wonderful book in 1998 called *Orphan Train Rider,* and many people asked her for more. Her new book, *We Rode the Orphan Trains,* is another fascinating look at what life was like for poor children not all that long ago.

The Children's Aid Society was founded in 1883 with a marvelous goal. They looked for good new homes for homeless, abandoned, abused children, and for children whose parents could no longer afford to keep them or did not want them. Many of these children would have died at a very early age if the Society had not stepped in to save them.

But how the Children's Aid Society accomplished its goal seems very cruel to us today. The Society shipped groups of children on trains headed west from New York City. The trains stopped at random towns, where people could pick the children they wanted to take home. These new families were supposed to treat the children as though they were their own, and many did. Others did not. Some children were neglected or abused. Some were used as free labor. A worker from the Society came through the same towns to check on the children each year and sometimes took them back. Then the process would begin all over again.

Can you imagine life as one of the train orphans? One survivor says it was like being sold in a slave market. People would check their teeth and feel their muscles. One little girl was locked in a basement all night because she was scared and kept crying the first night she went to her new home.

Warren tells the true stories of seven kids who were taken in by strangers. In many cases, the care they received was wonderful. In others, it was awful. Their stories are riveting.

Show the picture on page 81 of Howard and Fred Engert, two brothers who rode the train to Nebraska in 1925. Then show the photo on page 94 of the two of them, adopted by different families, and now with different last names, together at the same tree nearly 75 years later!

Deborah Hopkinson describes unbearable living conditions in *Shutting Out the Sky: Life in the Tenements of New York 1880–1924*. Immigrants came to America from the time of the Jamestown settlement in 1607 on—more than five million people before 1880. But historians figure that between 1880 and 1919, 23 *million* arrived, and 19 million of those entered through New York City. The foreword notes that "the majority of these immigrants came from eastern and southern Europe," unlike most of the previous immigrants. Many of them stayed in New York. And many moved to the lower east side of the city, living in horribly crowded, unsanitary conditions, in buildings called tenements. These buildings had little light and were frequently unsafe. Toilet facilities were horrible. The immigrants had to work almost all the time just to make enough money to eat and live, and they often took in "boarders" who slept in any available space in the room.

Hopkinson focuses on five young immigrants and the lives they lived and tried to make for themselves in this strange new country, where, at the beginning at least, there was hope for the future, if not much happiness in the present.

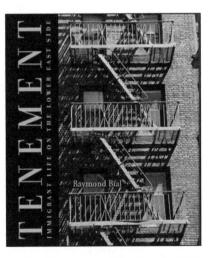

Figure 4.15. *Tenement: Immigrant Life on the Lower East Side* **by Raymond Bial.**

For a good book on the same subject for younger readers, take a look at Raymond Bial's *Tenement: Immigrant Life on the Lower East Side*. Find out what it was like to come to a new land and live in an exciting but horrible place.

THE AFRICAN-AMERICAN EXPERIENCE

Many African Americans loved the sea so much that they made it a part of their lives—or, in fact, their life's work. Eloise Greenfield profiles seven men and women at some length in *How They Got Over: African Americans and the Call of the Sea,* and gives us snapshots of a few others.

Paul Cuffe's father was kidnapped when he was only 10 years old and lived in Ghana. He came to America as a slave. He had at least some good fortune: He was sold to a Quaker family who became opposed to slavery and released him years later. Paul was born free.

When Paul was only 13, his father died, and Paul signed on as part of the crew of a whaling ship. That was the beginning of a career that included a spell in a British prison (he had not done anything wrong except to be an American) and eventually led to huge success with his own shipping company. Paul also became involved with the abolitionist movement and the movement to take freed slaves back to Liberia in Africa.

His story is amazing, but even more amazing are the adventures of Robert Smalls, who was a slave himself. Smalls was the wheelman on a Confederate ship, and he took charge of the operation to hijack it and deliver it to the Yankees, while it was still in Charleston Harbor! He received a monetary reward and became a pilot on several ships and eventually the captain of the *Planter,* the very ship he stole. Smalls ended up buying the home where he had been a slave and living there for the rest of his life; a real-life adventure with a true happy ending. There are some fine stories here.

From the beginning of slavery, slaves rebelled against the terrible things that were happening to them. Doreen Rappaport reminds us in *No More! Stories and Songs of Slave Resistance* that resistance took place in Africa, on board ship, and on America's shores. Olaudah Equiano was captured when he was only 10 years old. He lived as a slave for 20 years before he was able to purchase his freedom. When he saw the ship that was going to take him to America, he thought it was a ship from hell—but then he asked another captive what was happening. That man told him, "We are going to their country to work for them" (page 13), and Olaudah was soothed, knowing that, at least for the moment, he was not going to die.

Some slaves were certain that drowning at sea would be better than living as a slave. One of the most famous ex-slaves was Frederick Douglass, whose life changed on the day he fought back.

Some sang songs of resistance and of hope. Some ran away. But all of their stories are incredible, and the paintings by Shane W. Evans are terrific. Show your audience the one of the boy in the ocean on page 17.

If you know students who are interested in learning about the Underground Railroad, or are a history and research buff yourself, an excellent source is Joyce Hansen and Gary McGowan's *Freedom Roads: Searching for the Underground Railroad.* Almost everyone has heard of the Underground Railroad. Its story is a wonderful one, full of adventure and danger and excitement. But the truth is, we know more stories about the Underground Railroad than we know hard facts. As Hansen and McGowan point out:

Over time some of the stories about the Railroad have become romantic adventures with elements of myth and legend, and it is difficult to separate fact from fiction. How can we possibly find proof and evidence of activities that were purposely clandestine? Is there a way to recover a secret past? Perhaps. (page ix)

Archaeologists are searching for the truth behind the fiction. Historians and scientists hope to get as much accurate information as possible. But we don't even know how many slaves actually escaped, or how many people helped them. Sometimes the Railroad was effectively organized, with groups of people, such as Quakers, acting and working together. (By 1776, if you were a Quaker who owned slaves and you wanted to remain a Quaker, you had to free them.) At other times, individuals might unexpectedly encounter a runaway slave in need of help, and they acted selflessly and alone.

Historians examine old buildings that were supposedly hiding places for runaway slaves. Oral tradition plays a big part in pointing to the right locations. If people have heard stories over time that nearby buildings hid runaways, historians check them out. Sometimes their efforts are rewarded by fascinating treasures, such as the clay faces hidden in the basement in a church in Syracuse, New York.

Historians also examine books, such as William Still's *The Underground Railroad*. Still was a free African American whose parents had been runaway slaves. He became an abolitionist who helped many runaways and then quickly recorded their stories. In the 1930s, many ex-slaves were interviewed as part of a government project, and their stories also contain much information. But these were elderly people, and the events they described had taken place decades before. Still's work was important because it is more likely that stories are accurate when they are written down close to the time in which they took place. If you are interested in history and historical research, this is a fascinating book.

Figure 4.16. *A Picture Book of Harriet Beecher Stowe* by David A. Adler.

Ask your booktalk audience what they would do if they saw slaves. How would they help them? The last thing your kids would think of doing would be to write a book. David A. Adler provides a great introduction for children ages six through eight about the antislavery movement and the work of one famous American in *A Picture Book of Harriet Beecher Stowe.* Not many women in history have been called "the little lady who made this big war," but Harriet Beecher Stowe was. And the person who called her that was President Abraham Lincoln.

Harriet was born in Connecticut, and she did not see many slaves until her father got a job in Ohio and the family moved west. Ohio was a free state without slaves, but it was across the river from Kentucky, where many slaves lived and labored. Young Harriet was stunned. She saw slaves herded onto boats, separated from their homes and families, and working and being treated like animals by cruel slave owners.

Harriet decided she had to do something to help them. She wrote a book called *Uncle Tom's Cabin* that electrified the American public and helped change the course of history.

Linda Lowery introduces us to a woman born into slavery in *One More Valley, One More Hill: The Story of Aunt Clara Brown.* Clara Brown was a slave for over half of her life. By some standards, she was lucky, for she had fairly decent working conditions, and her final owner set her free in his will. She figured she was about 56 years old at the time.

But by anybody's standards today, Brown's life as a slave was awful. When she was a young woman, her family was taken away from her and sold. She knew her husband and her son had probably been worked to an early death, but she yearned to be reunited with her daughter, Eliza Jane, who had been sold as a small child. Brown made it her life's work to find Eliza Jane, and she was lucky. The owner who freed her also left her $300, a huge sum of money in the 1850s.

Brown took her small fortune and headed west. Gold had been discovered in Colorado, and gold seekers were streaming into the territory. It was a long and difficult journey for a single woman to make alone, but Brown hired herself out as a cook with a wagon train. Brown, who became known as "Aunt Clara," cooked and walked her way to the distant gold camps. She made more money. She gave most of it to her church or other African Americans who were in need, but she always kept her hopes up for finding Eliza Jane. Then one day Brown received a life-changing letter.

Read the book to find out what happened to this amazing woman.

One of the first African-American writers was named after the slave ship that brought her to this country. In *A Voice of Her Own: The Story of Phillis Wheatley, Slave Poet,* Kathryn Lasky tells us that Phillis came to America half-starved and nearly naked except for a piece of carpet she had wrapped around herself before she was sold as a slave.

It was 1761, and the little girl looked to be about seven years old. Boston Harbor was cold, and she was shivering. Her luck was about to change in a small way, however, for the Wheatleys, who purchased her, were kind and considerate. Susannah Wheatley, her new owner, saw quickly that Phillis was highly intelligent and quick to learn. So Susannah started teaching the young girl to read and write.

Phillis loved to write, particularly poetry. People who read her wonderful and elegant poems found it hard to believe they were really written by a black person. A group of 18 men, led by John Hancock, questioned Phillis and declared she really had written those poems.

Phillis had a sad life and died young, but she was the first African-American woman to have her work published, and her story is a fine one. Show the first double-page spread, the picture of Phillis in the slave ship.

There was not just one Day of Jubilee, as the slaves in the United States called it, when they were freed. There were a lot of those days, and *Days of Jubilee: The End of Slavery in the United States* by Patricia C. and Fredrick L. McKissack shows what happened at different times and places.

Slaves who helped their masters celebrate freedom on the Fourth of July wondered why that freedom didn't apply to them. The Declaration of Independence, which proclaimed "all men are created equal," did not include African-American men, and it certainly didn't apply to women and children.

So they waited. And when the Civil War broke out, since slavery was one of the reasons for war, they hoped and prayed.

Slaves in Washington, D.C., were freed on April 16, 1862, when Congress passed a vote to abolish slavery. The government also voted to compensate loyal slave owners for their loss of property. The next year, on January 1, 1863, many more slaves celebrated with the signing of the Emancipation Proclamation. Although that proclamation was basically unenforceable, it gave slaves great hope. As the McKissacks say, "It didn't matter whether slaves lived in a rebel state or a loyal state, once they got word that *some* of them were free, they counted themselves in that number and left from wherever they were and headed toward Union lines. They fled in droves" (page 57).

For some, freedom from slavery came with the arrival of General William Tecumseh Sherman, who marched from Atlanta to the sea, treating the slaves with great courtesy and informing them of their freedom. Some people thought that Sherman should be compared to Moses.

In Texas, slaves learned about their freedom on June 19, 1865, two months after the war ended. Ever since that day, African Americans have celebrated "Juneteenth." In many other places all over the South, slaveholders did not tell their slaves they were free until much later.

The official, absolute Day of Jubilee came six months later on December 18, 1865, when Congress ratified the 13th Amendment, abolishing slavery everywhere in the United States. This book is full of the joys and the disappointments that the slaves faced both before and after gaining their freedom.

Dennis Brindell Fradin paints an unforgettable portrait of slavery and freedom in *My Family Shall Be Free: The Life of Peter Still.* Peter Still must have been one of the most determined and stubborn men who ever lived. He knew what he wanted and tried everything he could to get his heart's desire. And he succeeded, against almost impossible odds.

Peter was born a slave around 1800. Like most slaves he did not know the exact date of his birth. One day when he was about six years old, he and his older brother Levin awoke to find the rest of their family gone. In the middle of the night, while Peter and Levin were sleeping, the rest of their family had escaped. Their mother made the horrible choice of leaving the boys behind because she could not take care of everyone. But the boys' parents knew they would have to try to find their young sons later. Later, it turned out, was a long, long time.

A white man came along and offered to help Levin and Peter find their family. But it was all a trick. The boys were taken and sold to another owner. Peter and Levin spent most of their captivity together, suffered together, worked together, and talked about their family, wondering where they could have gone. Levin was beaten so savagely when he married against the wishes of his owner that his health was damaged beyond repair, and he died young.

Peter, now married with children of his own, wanted more than anything to be free and to secure freedom for his family as well. He developed a plan. He would somehow save the money and find a way to purchase his own freedom, a very complicated matter in the South at that time, and then he would figure out a way to buy them as well or steal them.

He did exactly what he set out to do, and he needed and received help from some sympathetic and brave white people. How Peter Still rescued his own wife and children, and how he found his family, which had escaped without him almost 40 years earlier, is a story that will stick with you for years to come.

Figure 4.17. *Fight On! Mary Church Terrell's Battle for Integration* by Dennis Brindell Fradin and Judith Bloom Fradin.

Dennis Brindell Fradin and his wife Judith Bloom Fradin team up, as they have for a number of award-winning books, to tell the story of another freedom fighter in *Fight On! Mary Church Terrell's Battle for Integration.* Mary Church Terrell, who fought hard for civil rights and integration for African Americans in the 1950s, may have been a slave once herself. She was born on September 23, 1863, and her parents were slaves for much of their lives. What we do not know is whether they had been freed by the time Mary was born. Her father, Robert Church, was the son of a white steamboat captain named Charles B. Church and a slave named Emmeline. His father treated him well, and may have even freed him. By any standards, Robert Church was an extraordinary man. Shortly after the Civil War, he made a lot of money and spent most of his life as a wealthy man, who could afford to give his family the best of everything.

And that is how Mary got a fine education, including a college degree.

Mary started teaching at a school for African Americans in Washington, D.C., and fell in love with another teacher there, Robert Terrell. Eventually they married.

Both of them were extremely interested in promoting the rights of African Americans and ending segregation.

But Mary's true moment of glory came when she was close to 86 years old. She and about 25 other people decided to form an organization dedicated to ending segregation in Washington, D.C. The group had uncovered two old laws, written in the 1870s, that made it illegal to discriminate, but the laws had been forgotten and were not honored any more. The goal of Mary's group was to reestablish the old laws. Although they suffered setback after setback, they ended up in the Supreme Court of the United States of America, and they eventually won.

This is a little-known story in the long battle for racial equality, but it is a riveting one. Read it and hope you can do as much for the world as Mary Church Terrell did. Turn to page 138 and read aloud the typed-in words on the hate letter that was nailed to Mrs. Terrell's front door in 1950.

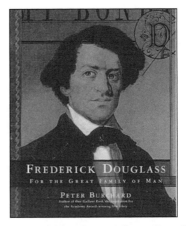

Figure 4.18. *Frederick Douglass: For the Great Family of Man* **by Peter Burchard.**

America's most famous ex-slave is the subject of Peter Burchard's *Frederick Douglass: For the Great Family of Man*. Frederick Douglass must be one of the most amazing people who ever lived. He was born in 1818 in a terrible situation, as a slave in Maryland. He was smart, and he took advantage of every opportunity that came his way. He pretty much figured out by himself how to read, with some help, but he was treated badly by many of the people who were in charge of him, and he was beaten and bore scars on his back all his life. But one day he fought back, and he was never beaten again.

Most people born into slavery had little chance to escape its clutches, but Frederick did just that when he was about 20 years old. By then he was married to a free African American, five years his senior, who helped him in his struggle. Douglass took a train to freedom, and he never looked back.

Frederick Douglass traveled extensively, became well-known as a great speaker, supported the women's suffrage movement, became friends with Abraham Lincoln, helped support John Brown in his efforts to free the slaves before the Civil War, and saw two of his children join the Massachusetts 54th Regiment. Women loved him, and he loved them right back. His second wife was 20 years younger than he and white, which was scandalous to most people at the time. Douglass died many years later in the mansion he owned in Washington, D.C. He was rich and he was famous. How he made the journey from slave to wealthy man makes for an incredible story.

Figure 4.19. *My Brother Martin: A Sister Re-members: Growing up with the Rev. Dr. Martin Luther King Jr.* **told by Christine King Farris.**

A modern-day counterpart of Douglass comes to life in *My Brother Martin: A Sister Remembers: Growing up with the Rev. Dr. Martin Luther King Jr.* told by Christine King Farris. This is a marvelous introduction to King for young readers, told from a perspective they can all appreciate: the childhood memories of a sister.

Christine and Martin, or M. L. as she called him, grew up, with their other brother, Alfred Daniel, in Atlanta, Georgia. Their father was a minister and their mother was a musician. Their grandmother brought them up and told them all sorts of stories.

Like kids everywhere, they got into trouble sometimes. "Our best prank involved a fur piece that belonged to our grandmother. It looked almost alive with its tiny feet and little head and gleaming glass eyes. So, every once in a while, in the waning light of evening, we'd tie that fur piece to a stick, and, hiding behind the hedge in front of our house, we would dangle it in front of unsuspecting passersby. Boy! You could hear the screams of fright all across the neighborhood!" (n.p.). (Show the picture that goes with the fur piece story.)

But the Kings were African American, and they learned at a young age that not everyone in their country looked favorably on its darker-skinned citizens. When Christine and M. L. were children there were many laws that made it easy for people to not treat them fairly. M. L. determined to change all of that. Christine's little brother became so famous and so honored that there is now a national holiday named after him.

What was it like to live as a kid under Jim Crow laws, laws that almost ensured that no black Americans were ever treated fairly? What was it like to live in terror that the Ku Klux Klan might come after your father or burn your home or even kill you? Tanya Bolden answers these terrible questions in *Tell All the Children Our Story: Memories and Mementoes of Being Young and Black in America.* This book will haunt your dreams.

The first black child born in America was in Virginia, only four years after the Pilgrims landed. His parents were not slaves, and neither was he. They were indentured servants and had to work for the person who had paid their passage for a set period of time; then they would be free. That first child, William, thus had it better than many of the black children who came later, for they had no way out. Born into slavery, most of them would remain slaves, frequently dressed in rags with very little to eat, always working hard from the time they were small children until, with little or no medical care, they died.

Black children's lives did not improve much after the slaves were freed at the end of the Civil War. Many children remained virtual slaves, at least until they were 18, and most who did not lived in terrible poverty.

Only within the last 50 years have the lives of black Americans improved in a major way, and we still have a long way to go. But these are some amazing stories, with many great photographs and illustrations to accompany them.

Chris Crowe tells young readers a story that no one should forget in *Getting Away with Murder: The True Story of the Emmett Till Case.* Emmett Till had just turned 14 in the summer of 1955, and although he was African-American in a time in the United States when African Americans were treated unfairly, he had a pretty good life. He was a popular kid, and he lived in Chicago, where racial discrimination was not nearly as blatant as it was in the Deep South, where his mother had grown up.

But that fateful summer, Emmett decided to visit his relatives in Mississippi. His mother warned him before he left that things were different outside Chicago, but Emmett was a kid, a kid who liked to show off and loved jokes. He certainly did not take what she told him seriously enough.

No one is exactly sure what happened that night in the general store in the tiny town of Money, Mississippi, but the evidence is that Emmett talked to and whistled at a young white woman, and that was absolutely unacceptable behavior in that time and place.

Within the week, two white men came in the middle of the night and took Emmett out of his uncle's home, and he never came back. A few days later his horribly mutilated body was found in a river.

His mother wanted that body back in Chicago. When she saw what had been done to her son, Mamie Till Mobley decided to fight back, in the only way she could think of. During the funeral, she made the decision to leave the casket open. She allowed photographers to view the body. A picture of Emmett's face was printed on the front page of a newspaper. Later, his killers confessed to their crime in *Look* magazine. The murder of a black teenager meant nothing to them. Emmett Till's death was the catalyst for the civil rights movement, which began growing by leaps and bounds. It changed the way African Americans and white people have interacted with each other ever since.

When American pioneers headed west, a number of them were black. But some African Americans headed east, looking across the Atlantic to their ancient homeland of Africa. Bringing Africans to the United States to live in slavery had been a terrible thing, so would it not be a good thing to take them back to Africa and let them set up their own land there? What seemed like a brilliant, well-thought-out idea at the time turned out to be just the opposite. Catherine Reef describes the outcome of this bold enterprise in *This Our Dark Country: The American Settlers of Liberia.*

The experiment started in 1820, and it was a failure from the beginning. The new colony was called Liberia, for liberty. But many of the African Americans and ex-slaves had little in common except the color of their skin. Some slaves in America were deported across the ocean against their will. While many well-meaning Americans looked at Liberia as a promising new world, others in the United States saw it as a way of getting rid of troublesome African Americans. A lack of planning and organization doomed the small colony to dependency on their former homeland, in many cases on their former masters. This is an interesting look at a country that may be unfamiliar to your booktalk audience, but that still has strong ties to America and is in today's headlines.

AMERICA REMEMBERS

Boys who lived during the Civil War who were too young to enlist would put a slip of paper with the number 18 on it in their shoe. Then, when asked their age, they would say they were "over 18."

James M. McPherson's *Fields of Fury: The American Civil War* is filled with fascinating information about the Civil War. Use some of these fun facts to intrigue your audience:

- In the battle of Antietam alone, in one day, over four times as many were killed as were killed invading the Normandy Beaches on D-Day in World War II.

- At the battle of Gettysburg, one Confederate general saw and heard another get hit by a bullet, and asked if he was hurt. "No, no," replied the other. "It don't hurt a bit to be shot in a wooden leg" (page 54).

- A law was passed in 1808 making it illegal to import slaves—so owners had to breed them to produce more.

- "Joseph and Willie Breckinridge were brothers from a prominent Kentucky family. Joseph fought for the Union and Willie for the Confederacy during the Battle of Atlanta. When Willie heard that his brother had been captured, he rode all night to where his brother was being held. Willie then gave Joseph some gold coins so he'd have money while a prisoner of war" (page 22).

- Several women fought in the Army as men—and got away with it!

- During Sherman's march from Atlanta to the sea, "Union troops would rip up the iron rails from Southern railroad beds and bend them almost double so they couldn't be reused. These bent rails were called 'Sherman's neckties' " (page 76).

- Wilmer McLean owned a house in Manassas, Virginia. It was struck by fire in the first battle of the Civil War. He moved away to get away from the fighting—to Appomattox—and Lee surrendered to Grant in McLean's parlor!

Loaded with photographs and illustrations, this book is a pleasure to read.

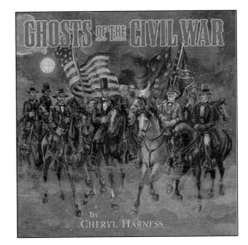

Figure 4.20. *Ghosts of the Civil War* **by Cheryl Harness.**

What Judy Donnelly's book did for the Pilgrims, Cheryl Harness does for *Ghosts of the Civil War,* giving us a modern-day kid's viewpoint on a slice of American history. When Lindsey's parents take her to a Civil War reenactment, she thinks it is a really stupid way to spend a day—until she runs into a ghost. It is the ghost of Willie Lincoln, and he gives her a tour of the main events of the Civil War, starting in 1619 with the arrival of slaves in the colony of Virginia, on to Willie's own death in 1862, and climaxing with the assassination of his father Abraham Lincoln in 1865.

Harness loads her book with colorful pictures and fascinating information about the war and the people who fought in it. Did you know that many Civil War battles have two names? This was because the Union armies named them after some *landmark* in the area, such as Antietam Creek, and the Confederates named them after the nearest *town.* You'll be surprised at all of the facts you will learn in these colorful pages.

Show any of the spreads, but perhaps the most moving is the one near the end of the book showing Abraham Lincoln moving among the newly freed slaves.

President Abraham Lincoln, however, was not universally loved and admired. The country he led was divided by the Civil War even after the cannons stopped roaring. Thousands of his fellow countrymen had died in bloody, horrible conflict. More people suffered in the South than in the North, for most of the battles were fought there, and the North had blockaded Southern ports. Supplies like medicine, paper, cloth, and other goods were no longer available in the South. Southerners were starving, and many of them hated Abraham Lincoln, blaming him for the war and holding him responsible for their sufferings. Harold Holzer tells what happened next in *The President Is Shot!: The Assassination of Abraham Lincoln.*

Figure 4.21. *The President Is Shot!: The Assassination of Abraham Lincoln* **by Harold Holzer.**

President Lincoln himself suffered mightily as well. Although he rejoiced when Robert E. Lee, the Confederate leader, surrendered, he knew how much work it would take to put his country back together. Five days after the war officially ended, Lincoln decided to give himself and his wife a treat. They went to the theater, which was his favorite pastime after reading.

Lincoln had a bad dream that week. He dreamed that a funeral was taking place in the White House. When he asked who was dead, a guard told him, "The President. . . . He was killed by an assassin!" (page 55). This scared Lincoln so much that he woke up and could not stop thinking about it. Lincoln had known for a long time that if someone really wanted to kill him, it could be done.

And someone did want to kill him.

That someone was John Wilkes Booth, a young, good-looking actor in love with the Confederate cause. With two of his oldest friends, Booth began planning to assassinate the president. As time went on, he recruited more conspirators. His goal was to kill several top officials in the U.S. government along with the president. How Booth half-succeeded in his plans is the subject of this compelling book, loaded with photographs. This is a true story filled with incredible information. Booth was clearly insane, believing that "he would be able to enter the presidential box [at Ford's Theatre], tie up Lincoln with a rope, lower him to the stage, and drag him away without anyone trying to stop him" (page 72).

Show the pictures of "The Gang That Killed Lincoln" on pages 68–69.

Right smack in the middle of the Civil War, in April and May 1863, something incredible happened. The Yankees sent out a secret mission to travel through Mississippi. One amazing thing about it is that there were *1,700* men on the mission. How do you keep that many men secret? Learn how it was done in Tom Lalicki's *Grierson's Raid: A Daring Cavalry Strike Through the Heart of the Confederacy*.

There were several reasons for the mission. One was that the Union soldiers wanted to do major damage to Southern railway lines so that much-needed Confederate supplies could not get through. Another was to destroy any enemy supplies they found along the way. And a third was to provide distraction. General Ulysses S. Grant was about to attack the major Confederate stronghold and transportation depot at Vicksburg, Mississippi, and that was going to be tricky. He needed a lot of help, and he thought one great plan would be to send out Colonel Benjamin H. Grierson to lead this secret raid. Grierson and his men would confuse the Confederate leaders, alarm the people, and, in general, just divert attention away from Vicksburg. Confederate soldiers who might have been guarding Vicksburg were instead chasing around the country looking for those mysterious Yankee soldiers.

It worked! It worked unbelievably well. Grant could not have found a better leader for the raid that Grierson, and this is one of the most amazing stories you can imagine. Here are a few interesting facts:

- Colonel Grierson, who had to ride a horse for 16 days, didn't like horses! He didn't trust them either. When he was eight years old, he was kicked in the head by a horse, and he nearly died. He was in a coma for weeks. He wasn't a professional soldier, either, but rather a musician.

- None of the men in the unit got to change clothes during the entire 16-day raid. After a few days, you could not even tell what color their uniforms were. At one school, the teacher thought the whole group were Confederates and gave the kids a recess so they could go out and cheer for the troops!

- They carried almost no supplies and had to live off the land, eating whatever they could find. They liked to locate large plantations, which often had a lot of food stored. They never knew what they were going to have to eat—or if they were going to get to eat at all.

- The group was given many tips by runaway slaves, some of whom joined them (but it was hard to keep up on foot with men on horseback).

If you enjoy war stories and reading about history, this is a great read!

Figure 4.22. *Remember Pearl Harbor: American and Japanese Survivors Tell Their Stories* **by Thomas B. Allen.**

War and violence, it seems, are an inevitable part of American history. Nowadays, almost all Americans can tell you where they were on September 11, 2001. Middle-aged Americans will say that they cannot forget what happened on November 22,

1963, the day John F. Kennedy was assassinated. And an older generation of Americans will remember another day that clings to their memories, December 7, 1941.

Thomas B. Allen asks us all to *Remember Pearl Harbor: American and Japanese Survivors Tell Their Stories.* He remembers what he was doing that day. He came home from a Boy Scout meeting and found his parents strangely quiet, listening to the radio. When asked what was going on, they told him the Japanese had bombed Pearl Harbor. Where was Pearl Harbor? Allen asked. Then he found out that America had become involved in World War II.

Allen lived in a duplex. Another family lived upstairs. Allen heard his neighbor's son, who wore an Army Air Corps patch on his uniform, walk away from the house. He never came back. Lots of soldiers never came back, because of Pearl Harbor and the battles that followed it.

No one believed that Japan would attack the United States. Japan was attacking a lot of other, weaker countries. President Franklin Roosevelt moved his fleet of battleships from California to Pearl Harbor in Hawaii, which was nearer Japan, to make the Japanese forces nervous. What that move did, instead, was make it easier for Japan to attack U.S. battleships. They planned to bomb, torpedo, and destroy our fleet, thus making it impossible for us to win against them in the Pacific Ocean.

What happened that day was a nightmare for everyone who lived and worked on the base. U.S. battleships capsized, trapping sailors inside them. Airplanes were destroyed. The harbor was filled with blood and oil. One Japanese submarine navigator was captured, becoming the first U.S. prisoner of that war. This book tells us the story of what happened, as told by both American and Japanese survivors. Show the picture on page 40 of the capsized ship.

Figure 4.23. *Remembering Manzanar: Life in a Japanese Relocation Camp* **by Michael L. Cooper.**

After Pearl Harbor was attacked on December 7, 1941, all of the people whose ancestral background was Japanese were under grave suspicion. The U.S. government thought many of them were likely to be Japanese spies. The fact that many of them had never been to Japan and were children and grandchildren of immigrants made no difference. In *Remembering Manzanar: Life in a Japanese Relocation Camp* Michael L. Cooper tells us that the Japanese Americans who lived in the West Coast states of

Washington, Oregon, and California were transported, detained, and imprisoned in camps in the mountains and the desert, away from the shore and from possible contact with America's overseas enemies.

The Japanese-American families were ordered to report to the camps, but they did not have much time. Many received a 48-hour notice to leave their homes and their possessions and move into a barracks. Some of them quickly sold their belongings for whatever they could get. Kids had to leave their schools and their friends. Families were loaded onto trucks and moved to camps.

This is the story of one of those camps, Manzanar, what it was like to live there, and how the children went to school there, in rooms without furniture and textbooks.

On September 11, 2001, America was attacked again. But this time we tried hard not to accuse every Muslim person of being a spy or terrorist. America learned a lot from imprisoning its own citizens during World War II.

The photos are small and black-and-white, but if you can make a transparency or a PowerPoint slide, the one on page 42 will show your audience how desolate the camp was.

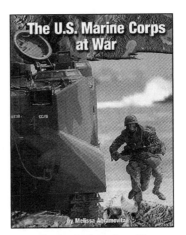

Figure 4.24. *The U.S. Marine Corps at War* **by Melissa Abramovitz.**

Whenever there is a major emergency, the U.S. government sends in the Marines! They were even there when America was young and needed them, during the Revolutionary War. That's why some call them the military's "911" force. But as Melissa Abramovitz shows us in *The U.S. Marine Corps at War*, the Marines do a lot of things besides fighting battles. They help out during disasters such as earthquakes and forest fires. They assist in evacuating dangerous areas. They even track down drug dealers. No wonder people are proud to be Marines!

A nickname for this branch of the armed forces is "Leathernecks." The first Marines used to wear thick leather collars to protect their necks from sword injuries when they were fighting. Swordsmanship was a necessary skill when the Marine Corps was founded in 1775!

You will be amazed at the many different duties these special men and women perform. Show the picture on page 19 of the Marines wearing haz-mat gear "to protect themselves against biological and chemical weapons" (page 18).

Figure 4.25. *Hana's Suitcase: A True Story* **by Karen Levine.**

The Japanese are as intrigued with the events of World War II as Americans are. In Karen Levine's moving book, *Hana's Suitcase: A True Story,* we meet Fumiko Ishioka, the coordinator of a small museum in Tokyo called the Tokyo Holocaust Center. The museum's purpose is to teach Japanese children about the Holocaust, and Fumiko wrote to museums all over the world asking them to loan her items to display in the museum.

The museum at the former Auschwitz Concentration Camp in Poland sent her a suitcase. There was a name on it: Hana Brady, a date of birth, May 16, 1931, and the word *Waisenkind*, which means, "orphan."

Who was Hana Brady? Is she still alive? Did she die at Auschwitz? What did she look like? And how could Fumiko find out? The young schoolchildren who came to the museum were as curious as she was.

This is the story of what Fumiko discovered and how she met Hana's brother George, who had grown up with her in Czechoslovakia. George also knew what had happened to his sister in Auschwitz. The book is full of the many photographs he shared with Fumiko, including one on page 23 of Hana and George. This is an amazing story.

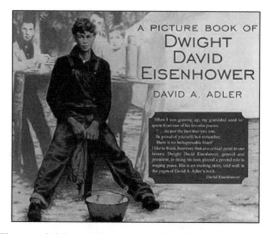

Figure 4.26. *A Picture Book of Dwight David Eisenhower* **by David A. Adler.**

In David A. Adler's *A Picture Book of Dwight David Eisenhower,* the young Eisenhower seems the typical all-American boy. He grew up in the Midwest in Abilene, Kansas, and his large family did not have much money. To help out, Dwight went door to door and sold their homegrown vegetables. When Dwight was older, he said, "I have found out in later years we were very poor . . . but the glory of America is that we didn't know it" (n.p.).

A lot of people called him "Ike," and the name stuck. Ike knew he did not have enough money to go to college, so he set his sights on getting into a military academy, which was free. He made it into West Point. And that was just the beginning of a wonderful career, in which Ike became first a five-star general and then the president of the United States. Kids will like seeing the photo of our former president as a football player.

Which one of America's presidents got into big trouble, almost being expelled, in high school? Which one never seemed to be as good as his elder brother? Which one was sick much of the time but never let it stop him from being fun and funny, charming and adventurous? Which one was a war hero who saved the lives of his men?

Ilene Cooper tells us about the man who was all these things in *Jack: The Early Years of John F. Kennedy.* Jack Kennedy was the second son of Joseph and Rose Kennedy, Irish Americans who were discriminated against at the turn of the last century. Although they were an intelligent and successful couple, they wanted even more for their kids. Joe wanted his eldest son, also named Joseph, to become president of the United States, and he did everything he could to make that happen.

Joe did not expect much of his second son Jack. Yes, he wanted Jack to do well, but Joe Jr. was the family star. Jack did not like that.

This is a good story, a true one, about the man many people consider to have been one of our most charming and beloved presidents. He was a special kid, but like kids everywhere, he got into a lot of trouble.

Show the picture of Joe Jr. with Jack on page 55.

Figure 4.27. *High Hopes: A Photobiography of John F. Kennedy* **by Deborah Heiligman.**

For another look at our 35th president, Deborah Heiligman gives us *High Hopes: A Photobiography of John F. Kennedy.* She reminds us that while Jack lived much of his childhood in the shadow of his charming older brother, Joe Jr., John (called Jack) was also sick a lot. He suffered from bronchitis, whooping cough, ear infections and more serious illnesses. He spent a lot of time in bed.

Jack came from a large, wealthy Irish-American family in Massachusetts. When Joe was killed in World War II, the boys' father wanted Jack to step into his brother's shoes, with the long-range goal of becoming the first Catholic president of the United States.

Jack had already made a promising start, despite his continuing frail health. He had become a war hero himself. He was the commander of a small boat, called a PT boat, which was rammed by a Japanese ship. Two of the thirteen men on board were killed immediately, but Jack did everything he could, in spite of being in terrible pain, to make sure that the others survived.

Jack began his political career by running for the House of Representatives. And then he ran for the Senate. Along the way, he married a beautiful, fascinating woman. In 1960, when he was only 42 years old, Jack became the youngest person ever elected president of the United States. And three years later he was assassinated. His shocking death is still surrounded by mystery and unanswered questions.

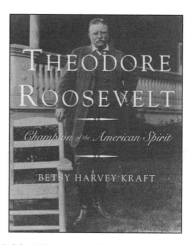

Figure 4.28. *Theodore Roosevelt: Champion of the American Spirit* **by Betsy Harvey Kraft.**

Theodore Roosevelt was another president who began life as a sickly child. As a small boy he suffered from asthma. But he never let his weak health stop him from enjoying life to the fullest. He strode through the world with a great zest and curiosity. As Betsy Harvey Kraft points out in *Theodore Roosevelt: Champion of the American Spirit*, Roosevelt was one of those men people could not help liking, even if they hated him!

Theodore Roosevelt was born in 1858, and he lived in New York City. There is an amazing picture in the book of President Lincoln's funeral procession going by Theodore's grandfather's house, and, if you look very closely, you can see two little boys leaning out a top window looking down. One of them is Theodore. He was seven years old.

When he was a boy Theodore's father told him he would have to strengthen and take care of his body, and Theodore took the advice to heart. He was full of energy and strength and worked hard at exercising his body. He did everything enthusiastically. "He once chopped down a tree with such vigor that an observer 'felt sorry for the tree' " (photo caption opposite page ix).

- Roosevelt worried that America was losing its beautiful scenery and trees and wild animals, and as president he made millions of acres of land into national parks and forests—even though he himself loved to hunt.

- He graduated from Harvard University, fell in love and got married, and had the horrible tragedy of losing his wife (during childbirth) and his mother in the same day.

- He loved to laugh and have fun, and he married for a second time and had six children in all. He was elected vice president and became president a few months later when the president, William McKinley, was assassinated. He was the first president to call his new home the White House, and his kids treated the place like a gigantic playground.

- He tried to help poor people and people in minority groups. He was the first president of the United States to invite an African American, Booker T. Washington, to dinner in the White House. He got in so much trouble with people criticizing him for it that he never did it again.

- He loved to be the center of attention. His daughter Alice said "he always had to be the bride at every wedding and the corpse at every funeral" (page 127).

Roosevelt loved his family, his children, his country, and its citizens. You'll enjoy getting to know him.

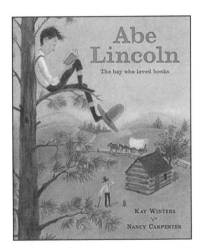

Figure 4.29. *Abe Lincoln: The Boy Who Loved Books* **by Kay Winters.**

You'll also enjoy getting to know our 16th president in Kay Winters's *Abe Lincoln: The Boy Who Loved Books*. The artwork is lovely and charming, and the text as clean as a Midwestern spring breeze. Abe Lincoln grew up in a log cabin. He was born in Kentucky and moved to Indiana when he was seven years old. Abe loved to go to school, he loved to learn, and above all, he loved to read.

But he had to work hard, and there was not much time for books. When he was nine years old, his mother died. Abe had loved her very much, and he missed her so much!

When Abe's father married a new wife a year later, she brought books with her into their home—and she let Abe read. And read. And read. The poor boy, with little formal education, eventually traded his log cabin for the White House.

This is a beautiful book and a good one for children ages five through eight. Show the picture of Abe as a baby in his diapers.

Lincoln seems to inspire great books! Look at Amy L. Cohn and Suzy Schmidt's *Abraham Lincoln*. Lincoln has probably never been more lovingly depicted than he is in this charming book. Read your audience a couple of the pages while showing them the accompanying pictures by David Johnson. The picture of Abraham reading is great, as is the quote, "My friend's the one who has a book I ain't read yet" (n.p.). Lincoln would walk miles for the chance to borrow something new to read. Show the picture of him going to bed, exhausted, after a day of riding the county courthouse circuit. He could make everybody laugh! "That puts me in mind of the time I was walking along a dusty road and a farmer in his wagon passed by," Lincoln once said. 'Would you be good enough to take my overcoat to town for me?' I asked. The farmer agreed. 'But how will you get it back?' 'No trouble at all,' I said. 'I'm going to stay right inside!' "(n.p.).

Many people consider Abraham Lincoln to be our greatest president. Read this and find out why.

Using all sorts of different and unlikely materials, Hanoch Piven has constructed portraits of several of our most famous presidents and given us some interesting and often little-known information about each of them in *What Presidents Are Made of*. Take a look at each picture and try to figure out what he used in these hilarious illustrations. Then check out the information:

- Andrew Jackson, who liked to fight duels, was shot once in the chest. Doctors could not remove the bullet, which was too close to his heart, so it stayed there for the rest of his life.

- Ulysses S. Grant got fined for speeding in the streets of Washington, D.C. He was driving his one-horse carriage! He paid the fine and wrote a letter praising the policeman for doing a good job.

- During World War II, John F. Kennedy saved a man's life by towing a man to safety after his PT boat was sank. He towed the man's life jacket with his teeth!

Show any of these great pictures to your students.

Kids enjoy hearing about real-life men and women who devoted their lives to helping others. Kathleen Krull brings a hero to life for younger readers in *Harvesting Hope: The Story of Cesar Chavez*. If Cesar Chavez was poor when he was a kid, he didn't know it. His family owned a ranch in Arizona. He had cousins to play with all around him, and there was plenty of food to eat. Cesar's best friend was his brother Richard.

But when Cesar was 10 years old, in 1937, his life changed in a horrible way. A terrible drought struck the country. Food became scarce. His family lost their ranch. So, like millions of others, the Chavez family moved to California, hoping to find work.

Cesar's new life was a nightmare. The family lived in filthy old sheds and shared outdoor toilets with many other people. Nothing was clean. They had no legal rights or protection. For working a full day of hard work, they were paid almost nothing. Some days the entire family working together might make only 30 cents.

Cesar attended 35 different schools. In one of the schools, the teacher made him wear a sign around his neck that said, "I am a clown. I speak Spanish." His friend and neighbors, all the Hispanic workers, were treated brutally and unfairly. By the time Cesar entered his early twenties, he believed it was time for a change.

The illustrations by Yuyi Morales are beautiful. Any of the two-page spreads would be good to show, but the one showing Cesar with the sign around his neck will touch even a casual reader.

Besides slavery and the Civil War and discrimination against ethnic groups, there are other dark sides to America's history. For older readers interested in themes of justice and innocence, open up *Witch Hunt: Mysteries of the Salem Witch Trials* by Marc Aronson. In the late 1600s, the town of Salem, Massachusetts, was suffering growing pains. Formerly a small farming community, Salem was growing and changing and a new, prosperous merchant class was rising. Change created conflict. There was, in fact, so much tension and disagreement that some residents wanted to split away and form a new town of their own. They called it "Salem Village" (today it is the city of Danvers), and it would have its own church and minister and its own rules.

It was in Salem Village, not the tourist town of Salem that we see today, that the famous troubles began. A few young girls claimed that they "seemed to be 'pinched and bitten by invisible agents; their arms, necks, and backs turned this way and that, and returned back again . . . . Sometimes they were taken dumb, their mouths stopped, their throats choked, their limbs wracked and tormented' " (page 80).

The author points out that the girls could easily have been influenced by a witchcraft accusation a few years earlier in Boston, an account of which was published by one of the participants, the influential Puritan leader Cotton Mather. The girls would have had access to this powerful and disturbing account.

The girls of Salem Village were convinced they had been bewitched by evil witches under the power of Satan. The first person accused of witchcraft was a slave, Tituba. Tituba, who was not an African-American slave, as she is usually depicted, but a Native American, was smart, and she knew the best way to protect herself. She confessed, and because of that confession she was never executed. In fact, as the witchcraft mania grew more frenzied, it became very clear that Tituba's example was the surest method of survival

What Marc Aronson does in his unusual book is to not only tell us the facts but also share the various theories surrounding the witch trials, and how the story, over the years, has been told and retold with new relevance for its fascinated hearers.

Another famous American city, Philadelphia, was struck by a different kind of evil in the stifling summer of 1793. Open sewers and rotting garbage were everywhere, and the city streets stank to high heaven. Sanitation was unheard of. No one knew about bacteria. That summer Philadelphia was a disaster waiting to happen.

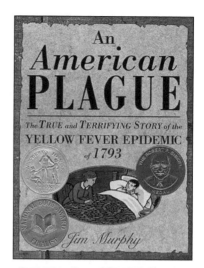

Figure 4.30. *An American Plague: The True and Terrifying Story of the Yellow Fever Epidemic of 1793* **by Jim Murphy.**

Jim Murphy, in *An American Plague: The True and Terrifying Story of the Yellow Fever Epidemic of 1793,* describes how the disaster struck. A terrible epidemic erupted. As far as we know, the first person died on August 3, 1793, and we do not know his name. Within a week, eight people died in two houses on the same street. No one paid much attention at first; fevers and diseases were common. But before the end of the month, *everyone* was paying attention. Lots of people became ill, and most of them were dying. They became deathly sick, their pulse slowed, their eyes grew bloodshot, and their skin took on a yellowish color. They vomited horrible-smelling black stuff.

The most famous doctor in America at the time was a Philadelphian, Benjamin Rush, one of the signers of the Declaration of Independence. He believed he recognized the disease—yellow fever. Years earlier Rush had worked with yellow fever patients, and he was positive this was the same thing. Other doctors disagreed. Tempers flared, and the deaths increased. Dozens of people were now dying every day. No one knew what to do.

In 1793, Philadelphia was the capital of the United States of America, and the epidemic virtually closed down the government. Many wealthy people fled the city. President George Washington stayed longer than most, but in the end he also left.

Who was left? A few caring people, a lot of poor people, and an incredible group of African Americans who did all that they could to help.

How Philadelphia survived (after 5,000 people died), how this crisis helped shape our government, and how long it took the world to find out what really caused yellow fever are just parts of this amazing story.

Figure 4.31. *Thank You, Sarah: The Woman Who Saved Thanksgiving* **by Laurie Halse Anderson.**

The name Sarah Josepha Hale may be a new one to your listeners, but we all reap the benefit of her enthusiasm. *Thank You, Sarah: The Woman Who Saved Thanksgiving* by Laurie Halse Anderson introduces us to an incredible lady. For one thing, Sarah wrote a verse that absolutely everybody knows—"Mary Had a Little Lamb"—as well as children's books and poetry, novels, and biographies. And this was in the 1800s, before women were allowed to vote. But Sarah is even more famous for spearheading a huge campaign to make Thanksgiving a national holiday. She published articles in her magazine. She wrote letters to president after president until, finally, Abraham Lincoln, said yes. Americans celebrate Thanksgiving because of Sarah Hale's unflagging efforts.

Katherine Lee Bates used her talents to enhance American life. In Wendell Minor's *America the Beautiful,* we learn that Katharine Lee Bates took a train trip in 1893 from her home in Cape Cod, Massachusetts, to Colorado. What she saw on the journey delighted, impressed, and amazed her. She was proud to be a citizen of such a beautiful country. Katherine wrote a poem about it, and that poem was eventually set to a song, one that almost all of us can sing today.

Famous illustrator Wendell Minor has created stunning pictures of some of the sights he thinks of when he sings the song. See if you would pick the same ones, or if you think of others!

Mark Twain was a young man who viewed America from the windows and decks of a riverboat. But in fact, Mark Twain wasn't his real name. William Anderson's *River Boy: The Story of Mark Twain* tells young readers that the real Twain was Sam Clemens, a boy who grew up in Hannibal, Missouri, a town on the Mississippi River, which he loved dearly. Clemens wanted more than anything to be a steamboat pilot on the Mississippi, and he got his wish. Boatmen measured the depth of the river, shouting out the measurements, or "marks" to the pilot. Twelve feet deep was "mark twain." Sam liked the sound of that, and when he started writing stories, that was the name he used.

Sam was always getting into trouble when he was kid, and this book tells us how his mischief and adventures made their way into his books. You'll enjoy learning about one of America's favorite writers. A fun picture book.

Twain was a colorful and outspoken figure, but he pales next to the star of *Jesse Ventura Tells It Like It Is: America's Most Outspoken Governor Speaks out About Our Government* by Ventura himself with Heron Marquez. Jesse Ventura isn't the governor of Minnesota anymore, but a lot of people still like him and like the way he thinks and talks. Not every governor first became famous as a pro wrestler!

In this book, Jesse tells us what he thinks about a lot of things, specifically, about government. He does think that the United States has the best government in the world, and for that he thanks the men who wrote the Constitution back in 1787. He especially appreciates James Madison, who was primarily responsible for writing the Bill of Rights, which ensures that all Americans have rights as individuals. Jesse thinks that today's government has become way too big, and that a lot of people who work for and are elected to government offices don't always care what the people who elected them want. Jesse also tells us how and why he decided to run for office and how he was able to win.

Jesse Ventura is never short on opinions. If you are one of his fans, you will enjoy this for sure. Show the picture of Jesse wrestling on page 6.

Figure 4.32. *Vote!* by Eileen Christelow.

Once you talk about Jesse Ventura, it might be a good idea to talk about the idea of voting. Pick up Eileen Christelow's *Vote!* Elmer and Sparky are two dogs belonging to the Smith family, and Chris Smith, the mom, is running for mayor. This gives the dogs a great opportunity to tell us how democracy and voting actually work. In fact, Elmer is a member of the family only because the Smiths voted to pick him out at the dog pound. This book tells what candidates have to do to win, how they must raise funds, and how sometimes candidates are not completely truthful. Christelow includes information on the history of voting and voter eligibility in the United States. Fun pictures enliven this basic, much-needed look at elections.

A light, breezy book about how things used to be, maybe how life was for your audience's great-grandparents, is the brilliant William Steig's *When Everybody Wore a Hat.* Younger readers will enjoy hearing how different American life was when Steig was eight years old. For example, in 1916 every man and woman wore a hat whenever they went outside. Men even wore their hats at work.

People then did not have all of the things we take for granted today—television, computers, cell phones—but they got along just fine. Mr. Steig paints a wonderful picture of the way life was when he was a kid. Be sure to look at the picture of him today at the end of the book.

Peter Ganci wasn't sure what he wanted to do for a living when he was a young man. All he knew was that he "wanted to be where the action was." In 1965 the action was in Vietnam, so Ganci joined the army. He joined the airborne division mostly because he would be able to jump out of planes.

As his son Chris Ganci notes in *Chief: The Life of Peter J. Ganci, a New York City Firefighter,* military service didn't work out so well. Ganci spent his entire time in the army in North Carolina and never got to Vietnam. He felt guilty about that. After he left the army, he signed up as a volunteer fireman and realized that fighting fires was where the action was. Ganci joined the fire department of New York.

He loved being a firefighter. He helped people and saved lives. And he had a lot of fun with his buddies in the firehouse. He was always joking and thinking up pranks.

Along the way, Ganci learned a lot about fires and how to fight them. He studied hard and passed the test to become a lieutenant. He kept earning promotions, until, finally, in October 1999, he became chief of the New York Fire Department. He was in charge of 15,000 firefighters. And he worked hard and was a popular chief.

And then, less than two years later, two planes flew directly into the two towers of the World Trade Center. Ganci rushed to the site to direct the operations there. And the the hard-working, popular fire chief was one of the 343 firefighters who died that day.

This terrific, real-life hero is remembered by his son. Wonderful photographs.

Figure 4.33. *Safely to Shore: America's Lighthouses* **by Iris Van Rynbach.**

Have any of your listeners visited a lighthouse? America has hundreds of lighthouses, all over the country. Iris Van Rynbach tells us about some of the most famous in her colorful *Safely to Shore: America's Lighthouses.*

- The oldest original light tower is the Sandy Hook Lighthouse, built in 1764 in New Jersey.

- The Scotch Cap Lighthouse in Alaska was built in 1903. In 1946, a tsunami struck the lighthouse and all five keepers were swept out to sea.

- "In 1822 French physicist Augustin Jean Fresnel designed a new kind of reflector that used a series a glass circles to bend and concentrate light in a single, bright beam" (page 12). Fresnel's design and variations of it are still in use.

- In 1856, Abbie Burgess worked with her father, the keeper of the Matinicus Rock Lighthouse in Maine. When she was 17, her father left one day to buy supplies and she was left in charge of her family. A terrible storm blew up, and she had to keep the lighthouse going all by herself. Abbie's gravestone looks like a miniature lighthouse.

The tallest lighthouse in the United States is the Cape Hatteras Lighthouse in North Carolina. It is 210 feet high and is striped like an old-fashioned barber pole. In 1999 it was moved half a mile inland to protect it from the eroding landscape and prevent it from falling into the ocean.

Figure 4.34. *Red, White, Blue, and Uncle Who?: The Stories Behind Some of America's Patriotic Symbols* **by Teresa Bateman.**

Americans see them all the time: our flag, pictures of our White House, the Liberty Bell, Uncle Sam, the Statue of Liberty, Mount Rushmore, and famous buildings and monuments in Washington, D.C. But what are the stories behind them? Teresa Bateman tells us in *Red, White, Blue, and Uncle Who?: The Stories Behind Some of America's Patriotic Symbols.* Did you know that the American flag has 13 stripes because there is one for each colony, or for the first 13 states? At first, every time a new state joined, another stripe was added to the flag. But by 1817, it was beginning to look pretty messy. A law was passed determining that there would only be 13 stripes, but that there would be a star added for every new state.

There are many great stories here. Mount Rushmore was built to help bring tourists to South Dakota, and it certainly did. The Vietnam Memorial on the Mall in Washington, D.C., which makes almost everyone cry, was designed by a 21-year-old architecture student. She originally did it as a class assignment—and only got a B! A lot of people wanted our national bird to be the turkey. Do you think the eagle is a better idea?

BIBLIOGRAPHY

Abramovitz, Melissa. *The U.S. Marine Corps At War* (On the Front Lines). Capstone High-Interest Books, 2002. ISBN 0736809231. 32 p. Grades 4–up.

Adler, David A. *A Picture Book of Dwight David Eisenhower.* Holiday House, 2002. ISBN 0823417026. Unpaged. Grades 1–3.

————. *A Picture Book of Harriet Beecher Stowe.* Illustrated by Colin Bootman. Holiday House, 2003. ISBN 0823416461. Unpaged. Grades 1–3.

————. *A Picture Book of Lewis and Clark.* Illustrated by Ronald Himler. Holiday House, 2003. ISBN 0823417352. Unpaged. Grades 1–3.

Allen, Thomas B. *Remember Pearl Harbor: American and Japanese Survivors Tell Their Stories.* National Geographic Society, 2001 ISBN 0792266900 57 p. Grades 4–8

Anderson, Laurie Halse. *Thank You, Sarah: The Woman Who Saved Thanksgiving.* Illustrated by Matt Faulkner. Simon & Schuster Books for Young Readers, 2002. ISBN 0689847874. Unpaged. Grades 1–3.

Anderson, William. *River Boy: The Story of Mark Twain.* Illustrated by Dan Andreasen. HarperCollins, 2003. ISBN 0060284005. Unpaged. Grades 1–4.

Aronson, Marc. *Witch Hunt: Mysteries of the Salem Witch Trials.* Atheneum Books for Young Readers, 2003. ISBN 0689848641. 288 p. Grades 6-up.

Bartoletti, Susan Campbell. *Kids on Strike!* Houghton Mifflin, 1999. ISBN 0618369236. 208 p. Grades 4–up.

Bateman, Teresa. *Red, White, Blue, and Uncle Who?: The Stories Behind Some of America's Patriotic Symbols.* Illustrated by John O'Brien. Holiday House, 2001. ISBN 0823412857. 64 p. Grades 3–8.

Bial, Raymond. *Tenement: Immigrant Life on the Lower East Side.* Houghton Mifflin, 2002. ISBN 0618138498. 48 p. Grades 3–6.

Blumberg, Rhoda. *York's Adventures with Lewis and Clark: An African-American Part in the Great Expedition.* HarperCollins, 2003. ISBN 0060091118. 88 p. Grades 4–9.

Bober, Natalie S. *Countdown to Independence: A Revolution of Ideas in England and the American Colonies: 1760–1776.* Atheneum Books for Young Readers, 2001. ISBN 0689813295. 342 p. Grades 5–up.

Bolden, Tanya. *Tell All the Children Our Story: Memories and Mementos of Being Young and Black in America.* Henry N. Abrams, 2001. ISBN 0810944960. 128 p. Grades 5–up.

Burchard, Peter. *Frederick Douglass: For the Great Family of Man.* Atheneum Books for Young Readers, 2003. ISBN 0689832400. 226 p. Grades 5–8.

Chandra, Deborah, and Madeleine Comora. *George Washington's Teeth*. Pictures by Brock Cole. Farrar, Straus & Giroux, 2003. ISBN 0374325340. Unpaged. Grades 1–3.

Christelow, Eileen. *Vote!* Clarion Books, 2003. ISBN 0618247548. 48 p. Grades 1–4.

Cohn, Amy L., and Suzy Schmidt. *Abraham Lincoln*. Pictures by David Johnson Scholastic Press, 2002. ISBN 0590935666. Unpaged. Grades 1–4.

Cooper, Ilene. *Jack: The Early Years of John F. Kennedy*. Dutton Children's Books, 2002. ISBN 0525469230. 176 p. Grades 4–up.

Cooper, Michael L. *Remembering Manzanar: Life in a Japanese Relocation Camp*. Clarion Books, 2002. ISBN 0618067787. 68 p. Grades 4–8.

Crowe, Chris. *Getting Away with Murder: The True Story of the Emmett Till Case*. Phyllis Fogelman Books, 2003. ISBN 0803728042. 128 p. Grades 5–8.

Curlee, Lynn. *Capital*. Atheneum Books for Young Readers, 2003. ISBN 0689849478. 44 p. Grades 3–6.

Donnelly, Judy. *The Pilgrims and Me* (Smart about History). Illustrated by Maryann Cocca-Leffler. Grosset & Dunlap, 2002. ISBN 0448428830. Unpaged. Grades 1–3.

Edwards, Judith. *The Great Expedition of Lewis and Clark by Reubin Field, Member of the Corps of Discovery*. Pictures by Sally Wern Comfort. Farrar, Straus & Giroux, 2003. ISBN 0374380392. Unpaged. Grades 2–5.

Erdrich, Lise. *Sacagawea*. Artwork by Julie Buffalohead. Carolrhoda Books, 2003. ISBN 0876146469. Unpaged. Grades 2–5.

Farris, Christine King. *My Brother Martin: A Sister Remembers: Growing up with the Rev. Dr. Martin Luther King Jr.* Illustrated by Chris Soentpiet. Simon & Schuster Books for Young Readers, 2003. ISBN 0689843879. Unpaged. Grades K–4.

Fink, Sam. *The Declaration of Independence*. Illustrated and inscribed by Sam Fink. Scholastic Nonfiction, 2002. ISBN 0439407001. 160 p. Grades 4–up.

Fleming, Candace. *Ben Franklin's Almanac: Being a True Account of the Good Gentleman's Life*. An Anne Schwartz Book/Atheneum Books for Young Readers, 2003. ISBN 0689835493. 120 p. Grades 4–up.

Fradin, Dennis Brindell. *My Family Shall Be Free: The Life of Peter Still*. HarperCollins, 2001. ISBN 0060295953. 190 p. Grades 4–up.

———. *The Signers: The 56 Stories Behind the Declaration of Independence*. Illustrations by Michael McCurdy. Walker & Company, 2002. ISBN 0802788491. 160 p. Grades 4–9.

Fradin, Dennis Brindell, and Judith Bloom Fradin. *Fight on! Mary Church Terrell's Battle for Integration*. Clarion Books, 2003. ISBN 0618133496. 181 p. Grades 4–up.

Freedman, Russell. *In Defense of Liberty: The Story of America's Bill of Rights*. Holiday House, 2003. ISBN 0823415856. 196 p. Grades 5–8.

———. *In the Days of the Vaqueros: America's First True Cowboys.* Clarion Books, 2001. ISBN 0395967880. 70 p. Gr. 5–up.

Ganci, Chris. *Chief: The Life of Peter J. Ganci, a New York City Firefighter.* Orchard Books, 2003. ISBN 0439443865. Unpaged. Grades 3–5.

Greenfield, Eloise. *How They Got Over: African Americans and the Call of the Sea.* Illustrated by Jan Spivey Gilchrist. HarperCollins/Amistad, 2002. ISBN 0060289910. 104 p. Grades 4–7.

Gregson, Susan R. *Benedict Arnold* (Let Freedom Ring). Bridgestone Books, 2002. ISBN 0736810323. 48 p. Grades 3–9.

Hansen, Joyce, and Gary McGowan. *Freedom Roads: Searching for the Underground Railroad.* Illustrations by James Ransome. Cricket Books: A Marcato Book, 2003. ISBN 0812626737. 164 p. Grades 4–8.

Harness, Cheryl. *Ghosts of the Civil War.* Simon & Schuster Books for Young Readers, 2002. ISBN 0689831358. Unpaged. Grades 3–7.

———. *Rabble Rousers: 20 Women Who Made a Difference.* Dutton Children's Books, 2003. ISBN 0525470352. 64 p. Grades 4–7.

———. *The Revolutionary John Adams.* National Geographic, 2003. ISBN 0792269705. 40 p. Grades 3–5.

Heiligman, Deborah. *High Hopes: A Photobiography of John F. Kennedy.* National Geographic, 2003. ISBN 0792261410. 64 p. Grades 4–8.

Holzer, Harold. *The President Is Shot!: The Assassination of Abraham Lincoln.* Boyds Mills, 2004. ISBN 1563979853. 181 p. Grades 5–up.

Hoose, Philip. *We Were There Too!: Young People in U.S. History.* Melanie Kroupa Books/Farrar, Straus & Giroux, 2001. ISBN 0374382522. 264 p. Grades 4–up.

Hopkinson, Deborah. *Shutting out the Sky: Life in the Tenements of New York 1880–1924.* Orchard Books, an imprint of Scholastic, 2003. ISBN 0439375908. 134 p. Grades 4–8.

Kraft, Betsy Harvey. *Theodore Roosevelt: Champion of the American Spirit.* HE Clarion Books, 2003. ISBN 0618142649. 180 p. Grades 5–8.

Krull, Kathleen. *Harvesting Hope: The Story of Cesar Chavez.* Illustrated by Yuyi Morales. Harcourt, 2003. ISBN 0152014373. Unpaged. Grades 1–4.

Lalicki, Tom. *Grierson's Raid: A Daring Cavalry Strike Through the Heart of the Confederacy.* Original maps by David Cain. Farrar Straus Giroux, 2004. ISBN 0374327874. 200 p. Grades 5–up.

Lasky, Kathryn. *A Voice of Her Own: The Story of Phillis Wheatley, Slave Poet.* Illustrated by Paul Lee. Candlewick Press, 2003. ISBN 0763602523. Unpaged. Grades 3–5.

Lauber, Patricia. *Who Came First? New Clues to Prehistoric Americans.* National Geographic, 2003. ISBN 0792282280. 64 p. Grades 4–6.

Levine, Karen. *Hana's Suitcase: A True Story.* Albert Whitman, 2003. ISBN 0807531499. 120 pp. Grades 4–7.

Lourie, Peter. *On the Trail of Lewis and Clark: A Journey up the Missouri River.* Boyds Mills Press, 2002. ISBN 1563979365. 48 p. Grades 4–8.

Lowery, Linda. *One More Valley, One More Hill: The Story of Aunt Clara Brown.* Landmark Books/Random House, 2002. ISBN 0375810927. 223 p. Grades 5–8.

McKissack, Patricia C., and Fredrick L. McKissack. *Days of Jubilee: The End of Slavery in the United States.* Scholastic Press, 2003. ISBN 059010764x. 134 p. Grades 4–up.

McPherson, James M. *Fields of Fury: The American Civil War.* A Byron Press Visual Publications, Inc. Book, Atheneum Books for Young Readers, 2002 ISBN 0689848331 96 p. Grades 5–8

Melmed, Laura Krauss. *Capital! Washington D.C. From A to Z.* Illustrated by Frane Lessac. HarperCollins Publishers, 2002. ISBN 0688175619. Unpaged. Grades 1–4.

Minor, Wendell. *America the Beautiful.* Poem by Katharine Lee Bates. G. P. Putnam's Sons, 2003. ISBN 0399238859. Unpaged. Grades K–5.

Murphy, Jim. *An American Plague: The True and Terrifying Story of the Yellow Fever Epidemic of 1793.* Clarion Books, 2003. ISBN 0395776082. 165 p. Grades 4–8.

———. *Inside the Alamo.* Delacorte Press, 2003. ISBN 0385900929. 122 p. Grades 4–8.

Patent, Dorothy Hinshaw. *The Lewis and Clark Trail: Then and Now.* Photographs by William MuZoz. Dutton Children's Books, 2002. ISBN 0525469125. 59 p. Grades 4–up.

Piven, Hanoch. *What Presidents Are Made of.* Atheneum Books for Young Readers, 2004. ISBN 0689868804. Unpaged. Grades 1–6.

Rappaport, Doreen. *No More! Stories and Songs of Slave Resistance.* Illustrated by Shane W. Evans. Candlewick Press, 2002. ISBN 0763609846. 60 p. Grades 3–6.

Reef, Catherine. *This Our Dark Country: The American Settlers of Liberia.* Clarion Books, 2002. ISBN 0618147853. 136 p. Grades 5–up.

Rockwell, Anne. *They Called Her Molly Pitcher.* Illustrated by Cynthia von Buhler. Alfred A. Knopf, 2002. ISBN 0679991875. Unpaged. Grades 4–8.

Schanzer, Rosalyn *George vs. George: The American Revolution as Seen from Both Sides.* National Geographic, 2004. ISBN 0792273494. 60 p. Grades 3–5.

———. *How We Crossed the West: The Adventures of Lewis and Clark.* National Geographic Society, 1997. ISBN 0792237382. Unpaged. Grades 1–4.

Spradlin, Michael P. *The Legend of Blue Jacket.* Illustrated by Ronald P. Himler. HarperCollins, 2002. ISBN 0688158358. Unpaged. Grades K–3.

Steig, William. *When Everybody Wore a Hat.* Joanna Cotler Books, an imprint of HarperCollins, 2003. ISBN 0060097000. Unpaged. Grades K–4.

Tanaka, Shelley. A *Day That Changed America: The Alamo: Surrounded and Outnumbered, They Choose to Make a Defiant Last Stand.* Paintings by David Craig. Historical Consultation by Dr. Bruce Winders. Hyperion Books for Children/A Hyperion/Madison Press Book, 2003. ISBN 0786819235. 48 p. Grades 4–8.

Van Rynbach, Iris. *Safely to Shore: America's Lighthouses.* Written and Illustrated by Iris Van Rynbach. Charlesbridge, 2003. ISBN 1570914346. 32 p. Grades 2–5.

Ventura, Jesse, with Heron Marquez. *Jesse Ventura Tells It Like It Is: America's Most Outspoken Governor Speaks out About Our Government.* Lerner Publications, 2002. ISBN 0822503859. 64 p. Grades 4–8.

Wadsworth, Ginger. *Words West: Voices of Young Pioneers.* Clarion Books, 2003. ISBN 0618234756. 208 p. Grades 4–up.

Warren, Andrea. *We Rode the Orphan Trains.* Houghton Mifflin, 2001. ISBN 0618117121. 144 p. Grades 4–6.

Winters, Kay. *Abe Lincoln: The Boy Who Loved Books.* Illustrated by Nancy Carpenter. Simon & Schuster Books for Young Readers, 2003. ISBN 0689825544. Unpaged. Grades K–3.

Wooldridge, Connie Nordhielm. *When Esther Morris Headed West: Women, Wyoming, and the Right to Vote.* Illustrated by Jacqueline Rogers. Holiday House, 2001. ISBN 082341597x. Unpaged. Grades 1–3.

Zemlicka, Shannon. *Nathan Hale: Patriot Spy* (On My Own Biography). Illustrations by Craig Orback. Carolrhoda Books, 2002. ISBN 0876145977. 48 p. Grades 1–3.

CHAPTER ———————— 5

Dreamers, Flyers, and Innovators

ARTISTS AND MUSICIANS

The gorgeous pottery of Juan Quezada is made with a special twist. In *The Pot That Juan Built*, Nancy Andrews-Goebel follows Juan from the tiny village of Mata Ortiz in northern Mexico, where he grew up, to the surrounding hills and towns where he learned his craft. During his wanderings, Juan found the same natural materials used by craftsmen in ancient times. He closely studied the potshards he found and developed a way to create new pots in the old styles. Juan now lives in a village of over 400 people, and they all make pots in the old way. Many of Juan's pots are in museums.

Take a look at this beautiful book with its colorful, vibrant pictures. A poem on the left-hand side (it will remind you of "The House That Jack Built") is a bouncy accompaniment to the left-hand side's nitty-gritty on Juan's art and pottery technique. This is truly an amazing and exciting story.

Show the picture of Juan shoveling cow manure to feed the flames that fire the pots.

Grandma Prisbey lived in an even tinier village than Juan Quezada did, a bottle village. And if you don't know what that is, maybe that's because Prisbey lived in the *only* bottle village in the world. And she invented it.

Melissa Eskridge Slaymaker tells us in *Bottle Houses: The Creative World of Grandma Prisbey* that Grandma P. always liked collecting things, and she wanted a place to display all of the pencils she had collected. She decided to drive down to the local garbage dump to see what was there—and, heavens, there were all sorts of wonderful things in that dump! She hauled a lot of junk home, and eventually she brought back enough bottles to build a house.

Grandma stacked the bottles together to form walls and stuck them together with cement. In fact, the cement was the only thing she had to buy.

You won't believe how her incredible house turned out! Then she went on to recycle all her newfound treasures into a village. She worked 25 years on her amazing art project.

Kids will be fascinated by and maybe even inspired by Grandma Prisbey's passion of her unusual vision. After all, it was her childlike enthusiasm that led to the building of the bottle houses that still catch the sunlight in Simi Valley, California.

Figure 5.1. *Grandma Moses* **by Alexandra Wallner.**

Another woman artist who was famous as a "grandma" is remembered in Alexandra Wallner's *Grandma Moses.* Born Anna Mary Robertson in upstate New York in 1860, she had a happy childhood, but when she was 12 years old she left home to work as a hired girl. Although she loved to paint pictures, there was no time for it—and not much time for school, either.

At age 26 years of age, she met a hired man, Thomas Moses. They fell in love and were married. She had ten babies, but only five lived. She and Thomas had a happy marriage, but when he died, Anna was 67 years old. That's when her new life began: She painted the pictures she had never had time for. Those pictures were so new and fresh and so exciting to people that she became one of America's most famous artists!

Artists seem to thrive on the impossible. Tell them they can't do something, and the next thing you know, they've whipped up a masterpiece out of thin air. In *Hokusai: The Man Who Painted a Mountain,* Deborah Kogan Ray introduces your booktalk audience to a painter who was told he could not paint.

Figure 5.2. *Hokusai: The Man Who Painted a Mountain* **by Deborah Kogan Ray.**

Hokusai was born in what is now Tokyo in 1760. His poor, unmarried mother died when he was only six. From the drab house in which he lived, he could see something beautiful—Fuji, the most sacred mountain in Japan. Hokusai fell in love with the mountain. He loved to draw its shape with a stick in the dirt. And above everything else, Hokusai wanted to be an artist.

Hokusai, however, as well as everyone else in Japan at that time, was strictly regulated by law and custom. No one with Hokusai's background and upbringing was allowed to be an artist. Instead, he did menial work, polishing mirrors for his uncle. But when he could find discarded scraps of paper and snatch a few minutes of time alone, Hokusai drew.

How Hokusai achieved his heart's desire and became the most famous artist in the history of Japan makes a terrific story. Almost any of the paintings is great to show.

For an interesting booktalk, pair this book with *Shipwrecked* by Rhoda Blumberg (in Chapter 1). Both books feature young men who achieved what seemed unachievable in Japan before it opened up to the world. Plus a painting by Hokusai is on the cover of *Shipwrecked*.

For a biography of another world-famous painter, turn to Susan Goldman Rubin's *Degas and the Dance: The Painter and the Petits Rats, Perfecting Their Art.* Edgar Degas was one of the greatest painters who ever lived. He especially loved to portray the hard-working young ballet dancers who were still learning their craft. Show the pictures of the dancers on page 19. Degas himself said, "People call me the painter of dancing girls" (page 3).

This intriguing book tells us his story, as well as a few stories about the young women he painted. Reproductions of his beautiful paintings dance on the pages. If you like the arts of ballet or painting, you will enjoy reading this.

Matisse was a contemporary of Degas and is the subject of Jane O'Connor's *Henri Matisse: Drawing with Scissors* (Smart about Art). Have you ever met someone through a booktalk who needed to do a report about a famous person? If you ever do, this book will help them with it!

Henri Matisse was born in 1869 in a small town in France. Although his father wanted him to become a lawyer, Henri preferred to be a painter. His father predicted that he would starve to death, but Henri ignored him and moved to Paris to study art. Henri started by painting pictures in the then-current, socially acceptable styles. But he was dazzled and turned on by the bold new creations of Cezanne and Monet. In fact, he once he sold his wedding ring so he could purchase one of Cezanne's paintings. Henri was inspired to paint pictures in his own way. By the time he was 40 years old, his art had made him a wealthy man. And when Henri grew older, his art took an even bolder, wilder turn.

The coolest element of this book is that it is told as a kid's book report, with the narrator/kid's handwriting and artwork. This is a good introduction to Matisse—a great story of a man who never stopped learning. Show the two-page spread of the books and the snail, two distinct, and dissimilar, pieces of art created by Henri at different times in his life. Matisse's creative collages may also inspire some young artists to take up colored paper and scissors.

Vincent Van Gogh is another great name in the world of art, and most of us have seen at least one of his paintings (they're reproduced so often in television commercials and magazines), but he certainly wasn't world-famous when he was alive. Then he was a poor artist who dressed shabbily, behaved strangely, and would rather buy oil paints than eat. Van Gogh sold only one painting during his lifetime. In his heart, however, he knew with absolute certainty that he would be famous and that his paintings would be priceless.

Jan Greenberg and Sandra Jordan tell us in *Vincent Van Gogh: Portrait of an Artist* that the Dutch Van Gogh was born in 1853 and was named after his elder brother, who died in infancy. Vincent was very close to his family and knew he could rely on them, especially on his younger brother, Theo. Throughout his life, when things were not going well, Vincent could always count on Theo to rescue him by supplying him with money or even sharing Theo's home. He wrote Theo hundreds of letters, and through his own words, Vincent tells us what he thought and felt and wanted to paint. We know that young people made fun of him because of his shabby, unusual appearance. We also know few people thought his paintings were any good. This is a compelling read about a compelling man who never gave up.

Show the picture of *Vase with Sunflowers* in the color insert. "A hundred years after his death [in 1991, *Still Life with Sunflowers* sold at auction for $29.9 million. The poster of Vincent's sunflowers is one of the most popular reproductions in the world, thus making Vincent's wish come true that it might 'brighten the rooms of working people' " (page 106).

Winfred Rembert is an artist who may not be well known to your booktalk audience, but his story is unforgettable. Rembert tells us in *Don't Hold Me Back: My Life and Art,* along with Charles and Rosalie Baker, that he grew up in the Deep South during the time of Jim Crow laws, which were designed specifically to keep African Americans from having equal rights with white people. As a child, Rembert was horribly poor. He was nearly lynched when he was only 19 years old. He fought for civil rights, got arrested, and ended up spending years in jail. During some of those years, he was a prisoner on a chain gang.

Rembert says he learned a lot in prison, and he learned a skill that would one day make him famous. Another prisoner taught him how to work with leather. Several years ago, Winfred started making pictures on leather. This book shows us several of those pictures, and they show what his life was like growing up and in prison. Show the picture of the chain gang on pages 28–29. How many of your booktalk audience have seen an artist in chains?

Marian Anderson was a little girl with a big voice. She could sing like no one in her family or neighborhood had ever heard before. She sang, most of the time, with her eyes closed, just as she's pictured on the lovely cover of Pam Muñoz Ryan's *When Marian Sang: The True Recital of Marian Anderson, the Voice of a Century*. It was as if Marian were watching and hearing what was going on inside of her.

But Marian was African American, at a difficult time in American history. Even later, after Marian had performed in operas in Europe and was in demand for her amazing singing voice, she learned first-hand how common it was for African Americans to be mistreated back home. Most hotels were closed to them; they had to ride in separate, dirty railroad cars; and often they could not even attend her concerts, at least not the ones that were also attended by white people.

Marian wanted to give a concert in Washington, D.C., but the best concert hall was owned by the Daughters of the American Revolution. These women would not allow a black singer to perform in their building. Eleanor Roosevelt was so incensed at their decision that she dissolved her membership in DAR. With the pulling of a few strings, and the help of friends, Marian was able to give a concert in the capital, at the Lincoln Memorial. It was standing room only. That concert was a landmark in American history. There are people still living who remember that night. Show the double-page spread of the crowd in front of the Lincoln Memorial.

Ryan's book is given an extra element of drama by the design of Brian Selznick, her partner in their previous *Amelia and Eleanor Go for a Ride*. Selznick illustrates Marian's life story as if it were a concert, complete with painted backdrops, spotlights, and velvet curtains. It's a terrific touch that would be distracting in less sure hands, but Selznick pulls it off magnificently. A great tribute to a great lady.

Here's another queen of American music. *Mahalia: A Life in Gospel Music* by Roxanne Orgill opens when the girl called Mahala was only six years old, in 1917. Her mother died and Mahala was taken in by an aunt. The girl worked hard, cleaning and doing laundry. She was lonely, unhappy, and felt unloved. Her aunt kicked her out of the house when Mahala was 16 years old. She was what they called a Negro back then in New Orleans, and her future did not look bright.

Another of Mahala's aunts, her beloved Aunt Bell, had told the girl when she was only nine that she would be famous someday and meet queens and kings. Aunt Bell was right. Mahala changed her name to Mahalia and moved north to Chicago, where she worked at more menial jobs and always went to church. Church was where Mahalia could be herself and sing. Mahalia became famous for her performances of gospel music.

Mahalia also became friendly with another famous person, Doctor Martin Luther King Jr., who often ate at her home. She sang on the day King delivered his "I Have a Dream" speech at the Lincoln Memorial, and she sang at his funeral. Sick or well, Mahalia fought for what she thought was right. She fought for her people and always expressed her love for Jesus. The story of her life makes a great read. Show the photo of Mahalia riding the bus with Dr. King and Reverend Ralph Abernathy on the first integrated bus in Montgomery, Alabama, on page 82.

Where would American music be today without Woody Guthrie? Woody Guthrie wrote at least one song that almost everyone knows: "This Land Is Your Land" (in your booktalk, sing it!). Most people probably don't know too much about him, or that he led a sad life and died of a horrible disease.

Open up Elizabeth Partridge's *This Land Was Made for You and Me: The Life & Songs of Woody Guthrie.* We learn that right after Woody was born, a lot of things started going wrong in his life. For one thing, his mother was strange. Some people thought she was insane. She seemed to have a lot of trouble with fire, and more than one of their homes burned down. When Woody was only seven years old, his beloved older sister Clara burned to death, and no one ever knew exactly what happened, although people claimed that Clara and her mother had had a fight. Mrs. Guthrie was eventually hauled off to an insane asylum.

Woody ended up living wherever he could. He was a survivor, but very self-absorbed. He did not seem to think much about how his behavior affected other people, especially the young girl he married or his family.

He went around the country singing, drawing, doing odd jobs, and eventually he started making a little bit of money as a singer and songwriter. He rode the rails, jumping on trains, and spent time in jail. He stood up for the rights of the little guy when not too many people seemed to be doing that. He stood up for African Americans when not too many people were doing that, either. He sometimes went back to his wife and kid, and sometimes not. And he had a lot more trouble with fire. This is a fine read about an intriguing, interesting man who influenced an entire strain of American music and singers, including Bob Dylan.

Another singer we *think* we may know a lot about but probably don't is the subject of Candice F. Ransom's *Maria Von Trapp: Beyond the Sound of Music.* Maria von Trapp was not just a character in a film. She was a real person whose own life was as good as any movie. Maria's mother died when she was very young, and her father left her in the care of an elderly cousin who made her life miserable. Maria finally ran away from home and worked hard at saving money so she could get an education and become a teacher.

Maria's life changed completely when she decided that it was the will of God that she should enter a convent and become a nun. She was a very determined young lady and decided to enter the strictest, severest convent of them all. And in real life, as in the movie, she drove a lot of the other nuns crazy! Maria's mother superior asked her to leave the convent for nine months to go to work as a governess for a widowed baron who had seven children.

Anyone who has seen *The Sound of Music* knows what happened next. But movies don't always tell the exact truth. A lot of things happened after the von Trapp family fled the Nazis, left Austria, and eventually traveled to America. Along the way, they became the Trapp Family Singers and made an exciting new life for themselves. Music would be a great addition to this booktalk. Play a song from the famous film soundtrack, or sing, "Do, Re, Mi."

Kathleen Krull begins *The Book of Rock Stars: 24 Musical Icons That Shine Through History* with the undisputed king of American pop and rock, Elvis. We don't even need to add his last name. "At concerts, crowds went insane, breaking through

police barriers to try to touch him or even rip his clothes off" (page 6). Even though Elvis wasn't a good guitar player and didn't write his own music, people couldn't get
enough of him. The way the King sang and moved was heart-pounding, crowd-pleas-
ing, and controversial. Elvis became one of the greatest stars who ever sang into a
microphone.

The next blazing superstars, the Beatles, followed only a few years later. They
just *loved* Elvis. The four of them, whose band started in Liverpool, England, not only
sang well but were able to write smart, catchy, clever music. When the Fab Four came
to America and appeared on the *Ed Sullivan Show* in 1964, it was the start of
"Beatlemania."

Krull's book is filled with colorful, amazing illustrations of the performers. It
also includes much fascinating information, such as the folllowing:

- *The Guinness Book of World Records* says that The Who gave the loudest
  performance ever by a rock group.

- Eric Clapton is the only person ever inducted into the Rock and Roll Hall of
  Fame for three separate contributions: as a member of the Yardbirds, as a
  member of the supergroup Cream, and as himself.

- Davie Bowie started out as a mime.

- Bono of the band U2 was the son of a Catholic father and a Protestant
  mother in Dublin, Ireland—so he knows about political conflict. Helping
  others in the world has been one of his major causes.

What is your favorite classic rock singer or group? See if you can find their picture.

As the King, Elvis surely demands his own book. And Barry Denenberg does the
honors in *All Shook Up: The Life and Death of Elvis Presley.* At the beginning Elvis
had nothing, and he came out of nowhere. Born in a shack, he was what some folks
called "poor white trash." And when he began his singing career, he faced a strange
obstacle. Critics said that Elvis Presley was a white boy whose singing sounded like he
was African-American. Not everyone liked his music. His sound was new and raw and
exciting, and before he was even 20 years old, teenage girls across the Southern states
were screaming at the very sight of him.

Elvis found himself a manager. Colonel Tom Parker was not a colonel and not a
gentleman, but he knew that Elvis was his ticket to fame and fortune. By the time Elvis
died at the age of 42, however, he was fat, drugged out, and had ceased to make new or
real music for years. But what a ride he had at the beginning, and what a fall he had at the
end! This is one heck of an amazing story, about a man who is still considered the King.

For a complete change of tempo, read M. T. Anderson's two companion books
about marvelous musicians of orchestral music. In the *Strange Mr. Satie* we read that.
Eric Satie "was always a child with an old man's face" (n.p.). All of his life. And he was
considered a strange person. For example, he did not take baths. Instead, he rubbed his
body with a stone! This weird fact alone will charm your booktalk audiences.

Satie wanted above all other things to make music—but not the kind of music that
most people were making. He had new ideas about how music should be put together
and about how it should sound, and he followed his own rules no matter how hard it
was when people made fun of him. He lived his life in a strange and unusual way, but
now he is considered one of the greatest composers. Show Petra Mathers's colorful

picture of Eric playing music (the first two-page spread) and his listeners' response. Mathers's delightful, quirky illustrations perfectly match Satie's eccentric lifestyle and unusual music.

Anderson reveals that the youngster George Frederic Handel knew with a kidlike stubbornness what he wanted to do with his life: make music. In fact, we learn in *Handel: Who Knew What He Liked* that the determined boy somehow smuggled a clavichord, an early version of the piano, into his parent's attic without their knowing. Late at night, Handel taught himself how to play. (They must have had a huge house!)

Another example of the famous musician's persistence: Handel's father decided to go visit another one of his sons, who was a servant in a castle. George, who was almost seven at the time, wanted to go, but his father refused. A few miles after leaving, Handel's father glanced out the coach window and saw Handel running right alongside. His father had to let him come.

Would anyone in your booktalk audience be able to sneak a piano into their parent's house? Would any of them wear a wig like Handel's? You will enjoy Anderson's fun angle on the creator of the "Hallelujah Chorus."

Figure 5.3. *What Charlie Heard* by Mordicai Gerstein.

Sometimes it takes a genius to write about another genius. And in this case, Mordicai Gerstein and Charles Ives are perfectly matched. Open the first page of *What Charlie Heard* and read a great dedication: "For my parents, who filled my childhood with that mysterious, invisible, magical stuff—music." And isn't that a wonderful way to define music?

"Charles Ives was born with his ears wide open. The very first sound he might have heard might have been his father's trumpet announcing his birth to the town of Danbury, Connecticut" (n.p.).

Charles Ives was an American who grew up loving music and heard it absolutely everywhere. His father was a music teacher, led the town's brass band, and loved noises and sounds and music of all kinds. So did Charlie. But when Charlie tried to write his music down, he found that most people did not get it or understand it. No one wanted to pay for his music, so he made a living as an insurance salesman until he was very old. And then someone very important heard his music and wanted others to hear it, too. Read this to find out what happened, and be delighted by the glorious illustrations.

Show the children the picture of Charlie listening to the notes of his father's trumpet. And then show the amazing page when, for the first time in his life, Charlie hears nothing! We can all relate to that picture. It is unforgettable.

A hundred years before Charlie Ives was born, James Audubon was prowling the forests near his home. The young man had an incredible idea and a bold goal. He wanted to paint all of the birds of America, in full color—and life size. Did you know that this most famous of American nature painters was born in the West Indies, and later lived in France? Turn to Jennifer Armstrong's *Audubon: Painter of Birds in the Wild Frontier.* She tells us that Audubon later moved to America. In the early 1800s, if a young man wanted adventure, there was no better place to be than the wilds west of Pennsylvania. Audubon decided to travel to Kentucky with a business partner and open a general store. During their journey down the Ohio River, he drew pictures. One day he saw thousands and thousands of passenger pigeons, so many that the sky turned black.

In Kentucky, Audubon followed the birds called swifts as they flew into a giant sycamore tree. He figured 9,000 swifts made their home in that tree. Audubon witnessed a flock of trumpeter swans scaring away a pack of wolves. He even said he met Daniel Boone, who showed him how to kill an animal without damaging its body.

And always, always, Audubon painted what he saw.

Figure 5.4. *Into the Woods: John James Audubon Lives His Dreams* by Robert Burleigh.

For more about Audubon, grab Robert Burleigh's *Into the Woods: John James Audubon Lives His Dreams.* Burleigh tells us the young painter wanted to draw pictures of America and its creatures before they really changed. Audubon wrote: "Who can imagine my dear country's dark woods, its great forests, its vast Atlantic bays, its thousands of streams, lakes and magnificent rivers. I wish that I could draw it all!" (n.p.).

Audubon could not draw it all, but he did paint magnificent pictures of the birds of America, and his record of them is now a national treasure. This book has some beautiful illustrations by Wendell Minor.

Don Brown has one of the greatest opening lines of a book in *Mack Made Movies*: "In 1900, twenty-year-old Mack Sennett was a horse's rear end" (n.p.). And look at that great picture of Mack peeking out from the middle of a clumsy stage horse.

Mack yearned to be a stage star, but he wasn't very good at acting. But he loved show business, and he found a fine way to be involved in it. He came along at the right time to start making movies, and he did something different from what other people were doing—he made comedies. He wanted to make people laugh!

And he did, with the help of the crazy Keystone Cops and Charlie Chaplin. Ask your booktalk audience if they've ever seen a silent movie. This book tells you about a great American character who made his mark when the pictures started to move. Without Mack, we'd never have seen someone throwing a pie in someone else's face. What a loss that would have been!

ATHLETES AND DAREDEVILS

When Annie Oakley shot game for food, people liked to buy the meat she sold. She shot the animals right in the head, and people did not have to pick the buckshot out of their food like they normally did. That's just one of the facts you learn in Stephen Krensky's *Shooting for the Moon: The Amazing Life and Times of Annie Oakley.*

Annie Mozee was only a little girl when her father died, and her family had never had any money. Living in a small cabin in Ohio, they found it hard to get enough food to eat. Annie did what she could to help, setting traps for animals, and eventually using her father's Kentucky rifle.

When she was 20, Annie entered a shooting contest with a man named Frank Butler. He was considered a great shot, but Annie beat him. He didn't seem to care. The two shooters fell in love, got married, and performed tricks as a duo. Finally they joined Buffalo Bill's Wild West Show.

No one knows why the little girl from Ohio decided to call herself Annie Oakley, but she is certainly the most famous woman shooter of them all, and an American legend. Show the picture of Annie and her rifle in the woods.

Bessie Coleman did unbelievably difficult things. *Talkin' About Bessie: the Story of Aviator Elizabeth Coleman* by poet Nikki Grimes is Bessie's story, told by her family and her friends, who are gathered together at her funeral and share their memories. In the early 1900s, when Bessie was 23, she moved north to Chicago, where she had heard African Americans had more opportunities. And there she found what she wanted to do. She wanted to fly planes! But no flying school in the United States would teach her. She had to figure out where she could get flying lessons and how she could become a pilot.

Bessie Coleman did all of this, in an amazing way, but she also died in a plane. This is her story, and it has great illustrations!

On the first page of Bonnie Christensen's *The Daring Nellie Bly: America's Star Reporter,* the excitement of real-life adventure lures us onward: "In 1899, a twenty-five year old newspaper reporter had a daring idea. She would travel around the world in less than eighty days." That reporter was Nellie Bly. Bly's idea was daring for several reasons. First, *no one* had ever traveled around the world so quickly except for a fictitious character, Phileas Fogg, in Jules Verne's novel, *Around the World in Eighty Days.* Everyone thought it was impossible. Second, because Bly was a woman. And women just did not do things like that in 1889.

How many trunks would a woman have had to bring for an 80-day trip? Nellie packed one satchel, wore her only dress and coat, and set out on the adventure of a lifetime. Could she do it? There were no planes at that time, and ships and trains were often delayed by unforeseen disasters. Would she make it? A lot of people were rooting for her.

Bly had started her unlikely career as a newspaper reporter by writing about the hard lives of working girls and women. Once she was voluntarily locked up in a lunatic asylum so she could report on the conditions there. It seemed this tough young cookie would dare and do anything. Find out if Bly truly succeeded in circumnavigating the globe in this colorful look at a piece of American history.

In 1998, *Maclean's,* the famous Canadian magazine, saluted the "100 Most Important Canadians in History" (page 97). In the 10-person category called stars. Wayne Gretzky came in third. Celine Dion came in ninth. But Tom Longboat came in first. And hardly anyone has ever heard of him. But, in his day, he was an incredible star.

Jack Batten reminds us of this great athlete in *The Man Who Ran Faster Than Everyone: The Story of Tom Longboat.* He was a racer, a runner who specialized in long-distance racing and in the marathon racing that became popular at the turn of the last century. He could outrun anyone else, and this was at a time when athletic shoes hadn't been invented.

Longboat was a Canadian Indian, belonging to the Onondaga Nation, raised on a reserve in dire poverty. When he was 12 years old, he was taken from his home and sent to a mission school for Indians. He hated it. He ran away, and although the authorities brought him back the first time, they never found him the second time, which basically meant that Tom received no further formal education. But could he run! People who saw him used him, exploited him, and made fun of him, but many fans loved him. He was a victim of racism and discrimination, but he prevailed. In World War I, Tom met the king of England and told him he would like to go home to his mother!

Longboat spent much of the war as a runner carrying messages. Show the photo of him on page 84. Tom's story is fascinating, as well as sad. He spent much of his life as a garbage collector for the city of Toronto, the city that had once voted to give him $500 but did not actually do it until more than 30 years *after* he died.

Figure 5.5. *Major Taylor: Champion Cyclist* **by Lesa Cline-Ransome.**

Know some younger readers who can't get enough books about young athletes? Then breeze through Lesa Cline-Ransome's *Major Taylor: Champion Cyclist*. Marshall Taylor was only 13 years old when his life changed completely. He was getting his bike repaired in a shop in his hometown of Indianapolis, and while he waited he practiced doing bicycle stunts. The owner of the shop was wowed. He offered Marshall a job cleaning and sweeping and doing those stunts. People walking by stopped to watch Marshall's stunts, and that created more business traffic for the bike shop. The owner paid Marshall more than he was making for his current job on a paper route, and threw in a free bicycle as a bonus.

Marshall was African American, and, in 1891, there were not a lot of good jobs or opportunities for young African Americans. But there was almost no one better than he was at riding a bicycle or doing stunts on it, and this is the story of how he became famous doing something he loved. Show the page that has four pictures of Marshall doing stunts.

Pair up Cline-Ransome's book with Charles R. Smith Jr.'s *Hoop Kings*. Read aloud any of the poems in this graphically fascinating look at a few of the current top pro basketball players. Be sure to show the life-sized photograph of Shaquille O'Neal's footwear. Size 20! Kids who love basketball and sports but not poetry will be pleasantly surprised.

If you need a good book for younger kids about figure skating, Jane Feldman's *I Am a Skater* is the one. Sarah Hughes won the Olympic Gold Medal in 2002, but she is not the only skater in her family. In fact, all six of the kids in the family skate, and their father got them all interested in it. He once tried out for the Toronto Maple Leafs after playing hockey at Cornell University. Feldman includes great photographs of a kid who is working very hard at what she does but also has a great deal of talent and obviously a great deal of family support.

The book is so loaded with great pictures that almost any of them would be good to show. A keeper: the page with the two photos of Emily Hughes, age 12, falling down. Who can't relate?

INVENTORS AND INVENTIONS

The one thing that all of the buildings in Susan Goldman Rubin's *There Goes the Neighborhood: Ten Buildings People Loved to Hate* have in common is that almost everyone hated them, *despised* them, before they were completely built. Lots of people hated them afterward, too.

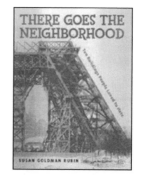

Figure 5.6. *There Goes the Neighborhood: Ten Buildings People Loved to Hate* by Susan Goldman Rubin.

The oldest building in Rubin's list is one we all recognize, the Washington Monument in Washington, D.C. Some people thought it was a national disgrace to build a monument that looked like "a stalk of asparagus." It did not help that it took almost 60 years to complete. The majority of Americans at the time thought it was a disgusting way to honor our first president.

Other buildings met similar opposition. The Eiffel Tower is considered the most famous building in the world. Gustave Eiffel planned his building to be the world's tallest (it beat the Washington Monument for that honor), and entered his design in a competition celebrating the 100th anniversary of the French Revolution. There were dozens of entries. One applicant offered to build a giant guillotine! But when people saw Eiffel's plan they were convinced his tower would sink, topple over, or maybe even cause fires.

Buildings that still drive some people crazy include the Eiffel Tower's neighbor, the Pompidou Center, an underground library in Minneapolis, McDonald's golden arches, and a glass house in Connecticut built by famed architect Philip Johnson. And you won't believe the house Frank Gehry created for himself. Show the picture of the glass house on page 30 or the Washington Monument on page 6.

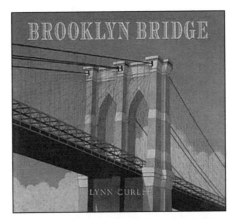

Figure 5.7. *Brooklyn Bridge* **by Lynn Curlee.**

A structure everyone seems to love is the *Brooklyn Bridge,* highlighted in Lynn Curlee's book. Have you ever walked across it? Lynn Curlee says that the Brooklyn Bridge is the "grandest, and perhaps the most important, structure built in America during the nineteenth century" (page 2).

Although Brooklyn and New York, which were separate cities at that time, were only half a mile apart, that half-mile was full of water. The only way across was by ferry. John Roebling, an engineer who had immigrated to New York from Germany, set his sights on constructing a bridge between the two shorelines. He came up with a meticulous plan, and then disaster struck. In a freak accident, he developed lockjaw when his foot was caught in a dock struck by a ferry. He died in horrible pain, and his son Washington, only 32 years old, took over the project.

Roebling's bridge was to be a suspension bridge, hanging between two stone towers. The bridge had to be anchored firmly below the water. Roebling had figured out a method for builders to work below water, but the conditions were not good. One of the foremen described it as a scene from hell. It was hot, filthy, and scary. As they went deeper into the river, men became ill. We now know they were suffering from "the bends." Roebling himself got the bends and became an invalid. His wife had to take over major supervision of the project.

There are several great pictures here, but show the one of the men working below ground on page 11 and the one on page 17 of E. F. Farrington, the bridge's master mechanic, the first person to actually cross the bridge—in an extremely dramatic way!

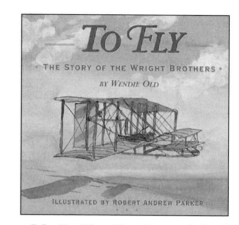

Figure 5.8. *To Fly: The Story of the Wright Brothers* by Wendie Old.

Wendie Old's *To Fly: The Story of the Wright Brothers* tells that when Orville Wright was only seven years old, his father brought home a toy helicopter. Orville and his older brother Wilbur played with it and wondered that it could fly almost 50 feet. Why couldn't humans also fly? People had dreamed that one day they might be able to, but it just looked plain impossible.

Orville went into the kite making business when he was still a kid, and he made good spending money. He learned something that helped him out later: curved wings fly better than flat ones. Together, he and Wilbur went into business, first opening a print shop, and later, when bicycles became very popular, their own bicycle shop. They talked and argued with each other constantly. "They found that by looking at all sides of a problem, everything impossible was eliminated and all that was left was the right answer" (page 13). Just like Sherlock Holmes!

As they got older, the brothers became interested in the problem of controlled flight. People had made gliders successfully, but no one had been able to figure out how to control any kind of flight by human beings. The Wright brothers put their problem-solving abilities to work and created one of the greatest inventions of all time.

Show the picture of the brothers with the toy helicopters on page 6.

More great books on the Wright Brothers, and why not? These two men are icons of ingenuity, stick-to-it-iveness, and turning dreams on paper into hardwired reality. Richard Maurer adds a twist to the saga of Kitty Hawk by showing the story through the eyes of another family member in *The Wright Sister: Katharine Wright and Her Famous Brothers*. On December 17, 1904, Orville Wright sent a telegram to his father and his sister back at home in Dayton, Ohio. Orville and his brother Wilbur were in Kitty Hawk, North Carolina, and they had just accomplished an amazing feat. They had made four flights in an airplane. The longest flight lasted 57 seconds. They were excited and wanted to keep working, but they knew they would be home for Christmas.

Katharine Wright was 30 years old. Her brother Wilbur was 33, and Orville was 37. They also had two older brothers, but it was the three youngest Wrights who formed the strongest bond. Their father was a bishop in the church of the United Brethren and a stern, serious man. Their mother Susan loved and encouraged her children constantly. Unfortunately, she died fairly young. But her nurturing of Orville and Wilbur and encouragement of their curiosity led to one of the most incredible inventions in history.

Katharine spent most of this time at home in Dayton. She had graduated from Oberlin College and become a high school teacher, a job she enjoyed and was good at. She had not married, and soon she became her brothers' business manager. Her brothers said, "In the days of the invention it was all fun and no worry . . . but when we succeeded it was all worry and no fun" (page 86). She also became their housekeeper, companion, and friend, until she fell in love. Read this book to find out about this interesting woman.

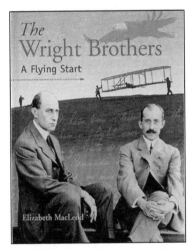

Figure 5.9. *The Wright Brothers: A Flying Start* **by Elizabeth MacLeod.**

Did you know that when the first astronauts landed on the moon in 1969, they carried some material that was in that first plane at Kitty Hawk? As Elizabeth MacLeod reminds us in *The Wright Brothers: A Flying Start,* the two brothers from Ohio changed the world.

Friends of the Wright family said the boys got their engineering smarts from their mother. She could fix and build almost anything. The boys got their names from their father. He figured that Wright was such an ordinary last name that their first names should be more special. Orville once remarked that they were lucky that they grew up in a home where children were encouraged to be curious.

Many people around the world were trying to figure out how to make a plane that could be steered, but no one had quite nailed it yet. Wilbur and Orville started reading and thinking and decided to build a test vehicle. They wrote to the National Weather Bureau to locate the windiest places in the United States. They also talked to another inventor, who recommended that they find soft hills for easy landings. Armed with that information, they went to Kitty Hawk, North Carolina. Lots of wind, and lots of soft sand.

It took the brothers three years from the time they made their first experiment until the time they actually got a plane in the air and steered it. At first, it flew only a few feet. The brothers kept tinkering and tweaking, the machine went farther and farther, and the first real airplane was invented.

Figure 5.10. *Airborne: A Photobiography of Wilbur and Orville Wright* **by Mary Collins.**

In *Airborne: A Photobiography of Wilbur and Orville Wright*, Mary Collins states that part of the reason the Wright brothers succeeded where so many others had failed was that they were both persistent and focused. They were working on only *one project*, the airplane, unlike people like Alexander Graham Bell, who was working on a lot of scientific projects at the same time. They had no wives or children, and their small bicycle shop gave them lots of spare time. They were able to stick with their project and spend a great deal of time on it.

Eventually they needed to test their airplane, and for that they traveled to North Carolina. They made the trip in 1900, 1901, 1902, and in 1903, when they made the first real flight. It wasn't long but it was real, controlled flight.

Show one of the most famous photos in the world, on pages 36–37, of the first controlled powered flight. For that picture, the Wright brothers wore their suits. It was the first day they wore them. Some instinct must have told them that success would smile on them that particular day.

First to Fly: How Wilbur and Orville Wright Invented the Airplane by Peter Busby has excellent paintings by David Craig and clear diagrams by Jack McMaster. And finally, for very young readers, open up Pamela Duncan Edwards's *The Wright Brothers*. What got the brothers so interested in flying? On the endpapers of this book, you can see a time line of what happened to Orville and Wilbur. In 1878, their father bought them a toy helicopter. They loved to play with it, and it made them wonder: If they built a bigger toy helicopter, did it need more power?

This book shows how the brothers made the creative leap from playing with a toy helicopter to making an airplane that could fly. A few little mice comment on their action in this fun, colorful book.

Airplane pilots, as well as ship's pilots, could not travel without the invention featured in Kathryn Lasky's *The Man Who Made Time Travel*. And like many inventions, this one was triggered by a disaster.

On October 22, 1807, three ships crashed off the Scilly Islands, near the southwest English coast. There was a terrible storm, but the storm was only part of the problem. The ships were lost and did not know they were lost. Nearly 2,000 men died that night because no one knew how to figure out exactly where they were.

At that time, sailors could not determine a ship's east–west position. The north–south position was pretty easy to find, and sailors had known how to do it for centuries. But a tragedy like the Scilly Island disaster would not have occurred if both sets of measurements were easily found.

The British government created a prize, under the Longitude Act. Whoever could figure out how to calculate east–west positioning would win £20,000 sterling, which in today's money is worth $12 dollars. The prize set off a lot of brainstorming by scientists and thinkers, and a lot of crackpot ideas were proposed. But one man had a sure grasp on the problem. His name was John Harrison, and no one thought he had the qualifications necessary to perform this seemingly impossible task. They were wrong.

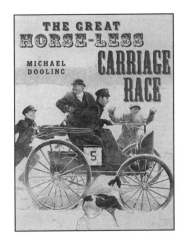

Figure 5.11. *The Great Horse-Less Carriage Race* **by Michael Dooling.**

Do you know what a horseless carriage really is? Michael Dooling explains the term in *The Great Horse-Less Carriage Race*. In 1895, automobiles were new and most people thought if you really wanted to go anywhere you needed a horse.

A Chicago newspaper wanted to prove that the horseless carriage was a good idea, and it sponsored a contest. Six of the new-fangled automobiles entered the contest, but it was not a good day. Snow had fallen the night before, and it was deep. The vehicles were going to have a hard time getting through it, if they didn't break down, which horseless carriages seemed to do a lot. Frank Duryea was a young driver who had the only car completely built in the United States. He wanted to win, but first he had to solve a lot of problems.

This is a fun, and true, story!

Show the picture of Frank's first breakdown.

Thomas Edison, perhaps the most famous inventor of all time, said, "Genius is 1 percent inspiration and 99 percent perspiration"—and he meant it. He worked incredibly hard all of his life. Even when he was a kid, he was trying to invent things, and sometimes he got into trouble for it, especially when what he did was dangerous.

In *Inventing the Future: A Photobiography of Thomas Alva Edison,* Marfe Ferguson Delano tells us that Edison won his first patent when he was 22 years old, for an electric vote recorder. As it turned out, no one wanted to buy it. After that Edison made a rule for himself: only invent things that people were willing to pay for.

Figure 5.12. *Inventing the Future: A Photobiography of Thomas Alva Edison* **by Marfe Ferguson Delano.**

By the time he was 23 years old, Edison had hired 50 employees and opened his own manufacturing company and laboratory in Newark, New Jersey. There he invented the "electric" pen, which could make thousands of copies of handwritten documents. It was an invention that people were definitely willing to pay for. Edison made tons of money, moved his offices to Menlo Park, New Jersey, and started working on improving the telephone. Edison thought it would be a great idea if people could use the phone without having to shout into it. Edison also wanted to record sound, and he invented a device he called the phonograph. It worked the first time he tried it.

Edison went on to invent, perhaps most famously, the light bulb, and then went on to set up power stations extending electrical power throughout America. He also helped invent the motion picture, Portland cement, and the alkaline battery. In all of these things, he had a team of well-paid and much appreciated helpers, but most of the original ideas were his.

Edison was truly one of the most amazing human beings who ever lived. You won't believe all of the incredible things he accomplished!

Speaking of genius-level creators, Leonardo da Vinci may be the greatest creator who ever lived, and Robert Byrd's magnificent book *Leonardo: Beautiful Dreamer* details with hugely appealing color illustrations his triumphs and his failures, as well as a great many of his ideas. It's a great introduction to a complex subject.

In the first paragraph of his introduction, Byrd states,

Think back on the last time you were trying to follow an explanation of how something complicated, like a bird's wing or a poem or the human eye, actually worked. Or perhaps you once tried to draw a leaf or a horse's head or a hand, making every detail exact. Many people—perhaps most—are more than willing to skip the hard parts and rely on someone else's understanding. After all, solving an intricate puzzle or problem can be tough going. And yet, it can also be exhilarating.

Five hundred years ago, a man lived and worked who thrived on the "hard parts."

That man, of course, was, Leonardo, one of the greatest painters in the history of the world, as well as engineer, military advisor, architect, musician, mathematician, animal scientist, writer, and astronomer, a man who studied anatomy, and an inventor.

After Byrd's book, your audience will be familiar with Leonardo's famous paintings, *Mona Lisa* and *The Last Supper*. But Jean Fritz showcases one of the artist's more improbable and magnificent creations in *Leonardo's Horse*. Most people probably never heard of the gigantic bronze horse that Leonardo designed for the city of Milan, Italy. That is because he never got to make it.

Just as Leonardo was about to cast this enormous statue, Milan was threatened by the French army. The Duke of Milan took all of the bronze meant for the horse and hammered and forged it into weapons. Leonardo never got his bronze back. His dream of the huge horse never came true.

Almost 500 years passed, then an American, Charlie Dent, read about the dream horse and decided that *he* needed to complete Leonardo's dream, make the horse, and give it to the city of Milan. How that happened and what happened along the way make for a very interesting read.

This book is just lovely to look at, shaped with a Leonardo-esque dome. Show any of the pictures, although the two-page spread of the horse near the end is great. Did you know that a second horse was made from the same casting molds, and that second horse stands in Grand Rapids, Michigan?

Judith St. George and David Small ask *So You Want to Be an Inventor?* What does it take to be an inventor, to come up with new ideas for new products that hopefully will help people? In this fun book, the same author/illustrator team behind *So You Want to Be President?* show and tell what ingredients help create a creator.

For instance, kids can invent. Ben Franklin invented paddles for his hands and feet to help him swim when he was a kid. Brothers can make a good inventing team, too, as a number of the above titles prove.

If you really want to invent, find something that is needed but does not yet exist—and then make it. You should dream, keep your eyes open, and hang in there. And most important, you shouldn't be upset if people laugh at you.

Women are inventors. Presidents have invented things. Inventors sometimes work alone and sometimes work as part of a team.

Take a look at this fun book filled with colorful illustrations that show people inventing and succeeding—or sometimes failing. Show the picture of Ben Franklin on pages 10–11.

And then show your booktalk audience *How Ben Franklin Stole the Lightning* by Rosalyn Schanzer. Franklin loved kites (when he was a kid, he held on to a kite and lay on his back and let the kite pull him across a pond), and he was fascinated by electricity. He did a very famous and very dangerous experiment with a kite and lightning—and the result of that experiment was probably his most famous and most useful invention. But Franklin did a number of amazing things:

He started the first lending library in the United States.

His post office delivered mail to people's homes—the first to do so.

He helped start a hospital, a school, and a fire department.

This delightful book tells only a part of the story of the imaginative Mr. Franklin. Show the picture of Benjamin and his son William and the kite in the thunderstorm.

SEEKERS, SAILORS, AND AMAZING ACHIEVERS

Catherine Thimmesh starts her book *The Sky's the Limit: Stories of Discovery by Women and Girls* with a great quote from Eleanor Roosevelt: "I think, at a child's birth, if a mother could ask a fairy godmother to endow it with the most useful gift, that gift should be curiosity" (page 6).

Figure 5.13. *The Sky's the Limit: Stories of Discovery by Women and Girls* **by Catherine Thimmesh.**

The women and girls the author describes clearly have or had a lot of curiosity. Vera Rubin worked as an astronomer at the Palomar observatory at a time when so few women were there that the only restroom on the ground floor was labeled "Men." Rubin made a lasting contribution to her field. She was the first to discover that we can actually see only 10 percent of the universe; 90 percent is made of dark matter that cannot be seen.

Denise Schmandt-Besserat realized, after years of observation, that she had found the very beginnings of writing and counting in Mesopotamia over 7,000 years ago.

Jane Goodall found that human beings are not the only animals that use tools. Her beloved chimpanzees use them, too. Once humans were defined as the only creatures that use tools. Famous anthropologist Louis Leakey, the famous paleontologist, remarked, "Now we must redefine man, redefine tool, or accept chimpanzees as human" (page 27). Show the picture of the chimp using tools to fish on page 26.

Sue Hendrickson was fossil hunting in South Dakota in 1990 when she hiked three hours to reach a cliff that she felt had been calling to her for two weeks. It must have been shouting, for within that cliff was buried the most complete skeleton of a *Tyrannosaurus rex* ever found. That dinosaur was named Sue, and it can be seen in the Field Museum in Chicago.

Kids discover things too, and Thimmesh includes some of their stories.

Kathryn Lasky brings to life the story of a boy who was *Born in the Breezes: The Seafaring Life of Joshua Slocum.* Joshua Slocum couldn't help himself. He wanted to go to sea. He wanted to sail ships! But his father made him work in a boot shop, to make fishermen's boots. Living in Nova Scotia, however, he could look out the window and see the ocean.

By the time he was 14, Joshua had run away from home and gotten a job as a cook on a fishing vessel. This was not the exciting, romantic life of the high seas he was expecting. He returned home, and then, when he was 16, his father died. Joshua got a real job on a real ship and decided to learn everything he could about sailing and navigation. By the time he was 25, he had become a captain of his own ship.

Joshua led an incredible life. He married a woman as amazing as he was, who traveled with him wherever he went until she died. Joshua was successful and went all over the world, until the end of the 19th century, when it seemed that sailing ships were a thing of the past. At that point, Joshua decided he wanted to sail around the world completely alone, and he did! The two-page spreads are beautiful. Any will do for showing your audience.

Did you know that Christopher Columbus almost spent his life as a weaver? The inimitable Pete Sis brings his talents to bear on the story of a man we all think we know in *Follow the Dream: The Story of Christopher Columbus.* This is a great introductory bio for very young readers. Ever since he was a young boy, Columbus had loved the story of Marco Polo, who traveled to the fabled Far East. Christopher started thinking that maybe there might be a shorter way to get there. If the world was round like an orange, why couldn't he try just sailing around and getting to it over the ocean, not over the land the way Marco Polo had gone?

Columbus thought it was worth the risk—if he could just get someone to pay for the experiment. Take a look at Sis's unique illustrations. Spend time with them, and find out what really happened to Christopher.

Far Beyond the Garden Gate: Alexandra David-Neel's Journey to Lhasa by Don Brown reveals the story of a woman who had some of the same wanderlust as Columbus and Marco Polo. Alexandra David was born in France in 1868 and made a career for herself singing opera. She had a strong, growing curiosity about Buddhism and Asia. She married Philip Neel in 1904 and kept nurturing her dreams of visiting Asia. Wives were supposed to be submissive and obedient to their husbands in those days, so she asked for Philip's permission to travel. He agreed, and Alexandra took off in 1911. She did not see him again for 14 years!

What Alexandra dared was something that no Western, non-Asian woman had ever done. She set her sights on Lhasa, the holy city where the Dalai Lama lived. She dyed her skin and her hair, took a companion, and embarked on a long and dangerous journey. Read all about it in this interesting book!

Show the very last double-page spread of Alexandra's impossible goal—Lhasa.

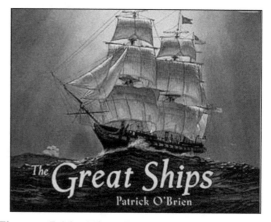

Figure 5.14. *The Great Ships* **by Patrick O'Brien.**

Other famous "she's" that have traveled the world and run into adventures are made of wood and canvas. Ships have names and personalities, and a ship is traditionally referred to as "she." *The Great Ships* by Patrick O'Brien shows us some of the most famous ships in the world and is full of fascinating facts:

- A Viking ship that had been buried in the earth for over a thousand years was found in the grave of a Viking chieftain. It is now on exhibit in a museum.

- In the early 1400s, a Chinese junk commanded by Admiral Cheng Ho sailed over much of the world. "The hull of a junk is built like a large, flat-bottomed box. It is divided inside by watertight wooden walls so that if the junk were to spring a leak, only one area of the hull would fill with water and the junk would not sink" (page 7).

- The *Niña,* the *Pinta,* and the *Santa Maria* were Spanish ships called "caravels." "They were very small and offered the captain and crew almost no shelter from the weather. There were no sleeping quarters for the crew, so at night the sailors just tried to find a comfortable spot on the deck or amid the baggage" (page 9).

- The *Golden Hind,* captained by Sir Francis Drake of England, stole treasure from the Spanish and was the second ship to sail completely around the world.

- The mutiny on the *Bounty* is probably the most famous mutiny of all time. The rebellious sailors set the captain and some other crewmembers adrift. Then the mutineers took off for Tahiti and Pitcairn Island—where their descendants still live.

The most famous warship in the United States is the *Constitution*. During a battle with the British in the War of 1812, an American sailor on the vessel saw the cannonballs bouncing off the thick wooden sides of the ships and yelled "Hurrah! Her sides are made of iron!" (page 21). So the nickname "Old Ironsides" was given to the ship.

Like to solve a mystery? Claudia Logan takes us back to 1924 and reveals *The 5,000-Year-Old Puzzle: Solving a Mystery of Ancient Egypt.* Just two years before the start of the story, the whole world was excited by the discovery of King Tutankhamen's tomb, and everyone is still crazy about pyramids and tombs and mummies. (My mother told me that, as a small child, she had a necklace in which every bead was a mummy!)

In Logan's book, the reader is addressed as a young boy, Will Hunt, whose parents are going on an archaeological expedition, looking for tombs. You get to go along! What will it be like? You promise your best friend that you will write regularly, using a secret code.

Logan's book is fun. She includes pictures of all sorts of things, and the letters Will writes to his friend back in Boston. Will learns that archaeological work is not always thrilling and exciting. A lot of it is really boring. But the rewards can be wonderful.

Logan also tells us that there really *was* such an expedition in 1924. And the archeologists really did find a tomb. Part of the book's mystery is finding out *whose* tomb it was. Almost any of the pictures are fun to show the audience, as they are colorful two-page spreads.

James Rumford reveals another real-life mystery-solver in *Seeker of Knowledge: The Man Who Deciphered Egyptian Hieroglyphs.* When Jean-François Champollion was 11 years old, his brother took him to meet a famous scientist who had been in Egypt with the Emperor Napoleon Bonaparte. The scientist lived in the French city of Grenoble, in a house stuffed with Egyptian treasures. Jean-François was delighted, but he wondered if anyone could read the strange writing on the treasures. The scientist told him no one had been able to figure it out.

Jean-Francois decided that *he* was going to decipher the hieroglyphs. He began to read absolutely everything he could get his hands on about Egypt. This text is loaded with pictures of hieroglyphs and their meanings. Show the picture of Jean-François reading in bed. It will remind some of your booktalk listeners of themselves.

Figure 5.15. *The Mystery of the Maya: Uncovering the Lost City of Palenque* **by Peter Lourie.**

A mystery of the Western Hemisphere comes to life in Peter Lourie's *The Mystery of the Maya: Uncovering the Lost City of Palenque.* He recounts his visit to Palenque, an ancient city of the Maya in Central America. Palenque is enormous, but it is also overgrown by the encroaching jungle. Only 32 buildings out of hundreds have been completely uncovered. The ruins are filled with deadly plants and animals, especially dangerous snakes, such as the poisonous fer-de-lance. Many mysteries surrounding the Maya remain. For example, we don't know why they disappeared from many of their cities.

Palenque was built in about AD 431 and abandoned in AD 799. Many people over the last couple of centuries have explored it, and current descendants of the Maya work for archaeological digs today. This is a good read, with great pictures, about an amazing civilization. Show the photo of the modern Mayan kids on page 41.

Waterhouse Hawkins is one of the most fascinating scientists of the 19th century. In *The Dinosaurs of Waterhouse Hawkins: An Illuminating History of Mr. Waterhouse Hawkins, Artist and Lecturer,* Barbara Kerley remarks, "Waterhouse's models are what first got people excited about dinosaurs. We're still excited, 150 years later" (n.p.). And isn't that the truth? A lot of kids can rattle off the long, hard names of dozens of dinosaurs, and daydreaming and studying about them is a delightful pastime.

In the 1850s not very many people had even heard of dinosaurs. Benjamin Waterhouse Hawkins set out to change that. At the Great Exhibition of 1851 at the Crystal Palace in London, Waterhouse, as he called himself, created huge models of different dinosaurs. With the help of Richard Owen, a scientist who actually invented the word "dinosaur," Waterhouse figured out what they must have looked like. Both men were really guessing, and they guessed wrong pretty often, as we now know,

To introduce the giant models, Waterhouse threw a dinner for some famous scientists. He needed their support. He decided that he would seat his guests in his model of *Iguanodon* (show your audience the picture of that meal). He and *Iguanodon* were a big hit. The marvelous illustrator, Brian Selznick, based his pictures on his own visit to Waterhouse's original models. Lots of Waterhouse's dinos are still around!

BIBLIOGRAPHY

Anderson, M.T. *Handel: Who Knew What He Liked.* Illustrated by Kevin Hawkes. Candlewick Press, 2001. ISBN 0763610461. Unpaged. Grades 1–5.

————. *Strange Mr. Satie.* Illustrated by Petra Mathers. Viking, 2003. ISBN 0670036374. Unpaged. Grades 1–5.

Andrews-Goebel, Nancy. *The Pot That Juan Built.* Pictures by David Diaz. Lee & Low Books, 2002. ISBN 1584300388. Unpaged. Grades K–4.

Armstrong, Jennifer. *Audubon: Painter of Birds in the Wild Frontier.* Illustrations by Jos. A. Smith. Harry N Abrams, 2003. ISBN 0810942380. Unpaged. Grades 1–4.

Batten, Jack. *The Man Who Ran Faster Than Everyone: The Story of Tom Longboat.* Tundra Books, 2002. ISBN 0887765076. 104 p. Grades 5–8.

Brown, Don. *Far Beyond the Garden Gate: Alexandra David-Neel's Journey to Lhasa.* Houghton Mifflin, 2002. ISBN 0618083642. Unpaged. Grades 1–4.

———. *Mack Made Movies.* Roaring Brook Press, 2003. ISBN 0761315381. Unpaged. Grades 1–4.

Burleigh, Robert. *Into the Woods: John James Audubon Lives His Dreams.* Paintings by Wendell Minor. Atheneum Books for Young Readers, 2003. ISBN 0689830408. Unpaged. Grades 1–3.

Busby, Peter. *First to Fly: How Wilbur and Orville Wright Invented the Airplane.* Paintings by David Craig. Diagrams by Jack McMaster. Historical Consultation by Fred. E. C. Culick. A Madison Press Book produced for Crown Publishers New York, 2002. ISBN 0375812873. 32 p. Grades 3–6.

Byrd, Robert. *Leonardo: Beautiful Dreamer.* Dutton Children's Books, 2003. ISBN 0525470336. Unpaged. Grades 4–8.

Christensen, Bonnie. *The Daring Nellie Bly: America's Star Reporter.* Alfred A. Knopf, 2003. ISBN 0375815686. Unpaged. Grades 3–5.

Cline-Ransome, Lesa. *Major Taylor: Champion Cyclist.* Illustrated by James E. Ransome. An Anne Schwartz Book/Atheneum Books for Young Readers, 2004. ISBN 0689831595. Unpaged. Grades K–3.

Collins, Mary. *Airborne: A Photobiography of Wilbur and Orville Wright.* National Geographic, 2003. ISBN 0792269578. 64 p. Grades 3–6.

Curlee, Lynn. *Brooklyn Bridge.* Atheneum Books for Young Readers, 2001. ISBN 0689831838. 36 p. Grades 4–8.

Delano, Marfe Ferguson. *Inventing the Future: A Photobiography of Thomas Alva Edison.* National Geographic Society, 2002. ISBN 792267214. 64 p. Grades 3–6.

Denenberg, Barry. *All Shook up: The Life and Death of Elvis Presley.* Scholastic Press, 2001. ISBN 0439095042. 172 p. Grades 5–up.

Dooling, Michael. *The Great Horse-Less Carriage Race.* Holiday House, 2002. ISBN 0823416402. Unpaged. Grades K–3.

Edwards, Pamela Duncan. *The Wright Brothers.* Illustrated by Henry Cole. Hyperion Books for Children, 2003. ISBN 0786819510. Unpaged. Grades K–3.

Feldman, Jane. *I Am a Skater.* Random House, 2002. ISBN 0375802568. Unpaged. Grades K–4.

Fritz, Jean. *Leonardo's Horse.* Illustrated by Hudson Talbott. G. P. Putnam's Sons 2001. Unpaged. ISBN 0399235760. Grades 3–8.

Gerstein, Mordicai. *What Charlie Heard.* Frances Foster Books, Farrar, Straus & Giroux, 2002. ISBN 0374382921. Unpaged. Grades K–4.

Greenberg, Jan, and Sandra Jordan. *Vincent Van Gogh: Portrait of an Artist.* Delacorte Press, 2001. ISBN 0385900058. 133 p. Grades 5–up.

Grimes, Nikki. *Talkin' About Bessie: The Story of Aviator Elizabeth Coleman.* Illustrated by E. B. Lewis. Orchard Books, an imprint of Scholastic, 2002. ISBN 0439352436. Unpaged. Grades 2–5.

Kerley, Barbara. *The Dinosaurs of Waterhouse Hawkins: An Illuminating History of Mr. Waterhouse Hawkins, Artists and Lecturer.* With drawings by Brian Selznick, many of which are based on the original sketches of Mr. Hawkins. Scholastic Press, 2001. ISBN 0439114942. Unpaged. All ages.

Krensky, Stephen. *Shooting for the Moon: The Amazing Life and Times of Annie Oakley.* Illustrated by Bernie Fuchs. Melanie Kroupa. Books, Farrar, Straus & Giroux, 2001. ISBN 0374368430. Unpaged. Grades 1–4.

Krull, Kathleen. *The Book of Rock Stars: 24 Musical Icons That Shine Through History.* Art by Stephen Alcorn. Hyperion Books for Children, 2003. ISBN 0786819502. 48 p. Grades 4–8.

Lasky, Kathryn. *Born in the Breezes: The Seafaring Life of Joshua Slocum.* Illustrated by Walter Lyon Krudop. Scholastic, 2001. ISBN 0439293057. 48 p. Grades 3–5.

———. *The Man Who Made Time Travel.* Pictures by Kevin Hawkes. Melanie Kroupa Books, Farrar, Straus & Giroux, 2003. ISBN 0374347883. Unpaged. Grades 3–5.

Logan, Claudia. *The 5,000–Year-Old Puzzle: Solving a Mystery of Ancient Egypt.* Illustrated by Melissa Sweet. Melanie Kroupa Books, Farrar, Straus & Giroux, 2002. ISBN 0374323356. 41 p. Grades 3–6.

Lourie, Peter. *The Mystery of the Maya: Uncovering the Lost City of Palenque.* Boyds Mills Press, 2001. ISBN 1563978393. 48 p. Grades 4–up.

MacLeod, Elizabeth. *The Wright Brothers: A Flying Start.* Kids Can Press, 2002. ISBN 1550749331. 32 p. Grades 4–6.

Maurer, Richard. *The Wright Sister: Katharine Wright and Her Famous Brothers.* Roaring Brook Press, 2003. ISBN 0761315462. 128 p. Grades 4–up.

O'Brien, Patrick. *The Great Ships.* Walker & Company, 2001. ISBN 0802787746. 40 p. Grades 4–7.

O'Connor, Jane. *Henri Matisse: Drawing with Scissors* (Smart about Art). Illustrated by Jessie Hartland. Grosset & Dunlap, 2002. ISBN 0448426676. 32 p. Grades 1–3.

Old, Wendie. *To Fly: The Story of the Wright Brothers.* Illustrated by Robert Andrew Parker. Clarion Books, 2002. ISBN 061813347x. 48 p. Grades 1–4.

Orgill, Roxanne. *Mahalia: A Life in Gospel Music.* Candlewick Press, 2002. ISBN 0763610119. 132 p. Grades 5–up

Partridge, Elizabeth. *This Land Was Made for You and Me: The Life & Songs of Woody Guthrie.* Viking, 2002. ISBN 0670035351. 218 p. Grades 5–up.

Ransom, Candice F. *Maria Von Trapp: Beyond the Sound of Music.* Carolrhoda Books, 2002. ISBN 1575054442. 112 p. Grades 4–8.

Ray, Deborah Kogan. *Hokusai: The Man Who Painted a Mountain.* Frances Foster Books, Farrar, Straus & Giroux, 2001. ISBN 0374332630. Unpaged. Grades 3–6.

Rembert, Winfred. *Don't Hold Me Back: My Life and Art.* With Charles and Rosalie Baker. Cricket Books: A Marcato Book, 2003. ISBN 0812627032. 40 p. Grades 4–8.

Rubin, Susan Goldman. *Degas and the Dance: The Painter and the Petits Rats, Perfecting Their Art.* Harry N. Abrams, 2002. ISBN 0810905671. 32 p. Grades 3–6.

———. *There Goes the Neighborhood: Ten Buildings People Loved to Hate.* Holiday House, 2001. ISBN 0823414353. 96 p. Grades 4–up.

Rumford, James. *Seeker of Knowledge: The Man Who Deciphered Egyptian Hieroglyphs.* Houghton Mifflin, 2000. ISBN 039597934x. Unpaged. Grades 3–5.

Ryan, Pam Muñoz. *When Marian Sang: The True Recital of Marian Anderson, the Voice of a Century.* Pictures by Brian Selznick. Scholastic Press, 2002. ISBN 0439269679. Unpaged. Grades 2–4.

Schanzer, Rosalyn. *How Ben Franklin Stole the Lightning.* HarperCollins, 2003. ISBN 0688169937. Unpaged. Grades 1–4.

Sis, Peter. *Follow the Dream: The Story of Christopher Columbus.* Alfred A. Knopf, 1991 (2003 reissue). ISBN 0679806288. Unpaged. Grades K–3.

Slaymaker, Melissa Eskridge. *Bottle Houses: The Creative World of Grandma Prisbey.* Illustrated by Julie Paschkis. Henry Holt, 2004. ISBN 0805071318. Unpaged. Grades 1–3.

Smith, Charles R., Jr. *Hoop Kings.* Candlewick Press, 2004. ISBN 0763614238. 37 p. Grades 3–up.

St. George, Judith. *So You Want to Be an Inventor?* Illustrated by David Small. Philomel Books, 2002. ISBN 0399235930. 50 p. Grades K–3.

Thimmesh, Catherine. *The Sky's the Limit: Stories of Discovery by Women and Girls.* Illustrated by Melissa Sweet. Houghton Mifflin, 2002. ISBN 0618076980. 80 p. Grades 4–8.

Wallner, Alexandra. *Grandma Moses.* Written and illustrated by Alexandra Wallner. Holiday House, 2004. ISBN 0823415384. Unpaged. Grades 1–3.

CHAPTER ———— 6

Inviting a Dragon to Dinner: Poetry, Wordplay, and Telling Stories

Poems, rhymes, and silly songs are the chocolate chips in the cookie dough of a great booktalk. They provide flavor, variety, and surprise if you sprinkle them between the longer, or more serious, subjects in a batch of tasty titles. Sometimes a dazzle of wordplay can wake up a quiet audience. A funny verse can provoke laughter. And if listeners laugh, it means they're listening. Kids respond eagerly and easily to an unexpected rhythm or rhyme. Here's a helping of some of the best ones we've read.

POEMS AND WORDS AT PLAY

If you're looking for humor, try these. Start with X. J. Kennedy's *Exploding Gravy: Poems to Make You Laugh*. This is a colorful book for grades 3 through 5 with fun illustrations and a whole bunch of very silly poems. Read a couple of them out loud to delight and intrigue your listeners—try "Stevie the Internet Addict" on page 83, or "The Vacuum Cleaner Swallowed Will" on page 11.

Then follow that up with *Dogs Rule!* by Daniel Kirk. Only a real dog lover could have written this delightful, funny, dead-on book. When you are booktalking dog books, include a poem or two from this one. Every poem can be sung! A 22-song original CD is included, so, if you dare, sing one yourself or play the appropriate tune. I loved "Red Rubber Ball" on page 8, "Master, I Love You" on page 18, "Stay out of My Yard" on page 20, and "Fire Hydrant" on page 37. Your audience will melt when they stare into the warm, puppy eyes of the cute canines that Kirk illustrates for each poem.

Figure 6.1. *CDC?* by William Steig.

William Steig's minor masterpiece *CDC?* will engage fourth-graders on up with its clever one-sentence puzzles. In a newly released edition, color pictures enliven the classic language book that for 20 years has had kids and adults poring over it, figuring it out, and then sharing it with their friends. The new pictures do, indeed, help with the deciphering, and sometimes you need a lot of help. What, for instance, does U F D-K N U-R K-9 mean in English? Need a clue? Ask Doctor DeSoto. This is great fun!

James Stevenson has two corny collections of verse that he has also illustrated: *Corn-Fed: Poems* and *Corn Chowder*. For a fun break in your booktalk, read "An Old, Familiar Pain" on page 18, or "Responsibility" on pages 6 and 7 in *Chowder*.

For a dash of inspiration along with laughs, open up *I Invited a Dragon to Dinner and Other Poems to Make You Laugh Out Loud,* illustrated by Chris L. Demarest. This selection of funny poems by several poets will provide a good laugh. Show and read "A New View" by Jill Esbaum, and "Closet" by Fonda Bell Miller. And the cool thing about the poets is that all 23 are new. Their poems are the winners in a national contest. Maybe your booktalk listeners have some ideas for poems of their own.

The *Giant Children* in Brod Bagert's book go to a giant school, but otherwise are quite ordinary kids. The speaker in the poem named after them is the classroom hamster! These are very funny rhymes with very funny illustrations and you will delight your audience in a major way when you read and show the accompanying picture of "Booger Love."

Douglas Florian is rapidly becoming one of our favorite rhymesters and funnymen. He writes with wit and bull's-eye humor, and he has several great titles out. *bow wow meow meow: it's rhyming cats and dogs* is a terrific book to use as booktalk filler. We like the poems about the chihuahua (*wha-wha-wha-wha!*) and the pointer, but there are several poems about cats as well. Florian paints with brushes as well as words. Kids will laugh at his whimsical paintings. Notice how the nose on the bloodhound (page 11) looks like another dog. And the hand and cat tail (page 40) are shaped like a question mark to accompany the query: "Who always yanks/The tail off the Manx?"

Almost any poem and its accompanying illustration in *Lizards, Frogs, and Polliwogs* is a big hit with an audience. Try reading aloud a couple of examples of concrete poetry, "The Gecko," "The Skink," or "The Python," or delight kids with the shivery "The Crocodile and the Alligator." *Mammalabilia* is hilarious and insightful. Recommended read-alouds are "The Gorilla" on page 14 and "The Lemurs" on page 34. Be sure to show the pictures too. These are great books for building vocabulary in a fun setting. *Summersaults* is a collection of seasonal poems. Favorites include "What I Hate about Summer" on page 12, "Bees" on page 24, and "Three Words" on page 43.

Figure 6.2. *There's a Frog in My Throat! 440 Animal Sayings a Little Bird Told Me* by Loreen Leedy and Pat Street.

After listening to vivid language and clever wordplay, kids may wonder about the weird, colorful everyday expressions they use themselves, or hear spoken by grown-ups. Is that poetry, too? Here are two titles that find a lot of humor in the way we talk. In *There's a Frog in My Throat! 440 Animal Sayings a Little Bird Told Me*, writer and illustrator Loreen Leedy and Pat Street ask, What the heck is monkey business? Who is a lucky duck? What does "hold your horses" mean? I bet most of you can answer these questions. This book is full of Leedy's typically charming pictures and literally hundreds of animal sayings. See how many you know and how many new ones you can learn. You'll have a grand time. Show any of the double-page spreads.

Does your mother ever say things like:

- "You're the apple of my eye."
- "Money doesn't grow on trees."
- "It's raining cats and dogs."
- "Cat got your tongue?"

Denise Brennan-Nelson's colorful *My Momma Likes to Say* tells us where some of the most common things we say, which are called idioms, maxims, proverbs, and clichés, come from. How did they start? Why do we keep saying them? You'll have a lot of fun trying to figure this all out. Show the "Cat got your tongue" spread.

Poems about school life or classroom subjects are always popular. Betsy Franco's *Mathematickles!* with illustrations by Steven Salerno is a wonderfully creative book combining math, poetry, and art—and can spark a gazillion ideas for kids and parents and teachers.

Nest
–Bird
stringfeatherstwigsleaves

or

ice puddle + snow boot + creakgroanCRACK!

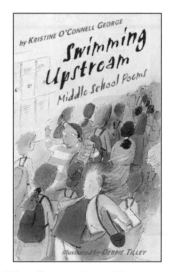

Figure 6.3. *Swimming Upstream: Middle School Poems* **by Kristine O'Connell George.**

Who can't sympathize with Kristine O'Connell George's title, *Swimming Upstream: Middle School Poems*? Middle school audiences will surely identify with the protagonist of these poems, who starts the school year feeling uncertain and out of it, but reaches the end of it, despite bumps along the way, feeling hopeful and confident. Read "Identity" on page 14, or "School I.D. Card" on page 19 (we can all relate to that one!), "The Other Me" on page 27, or "Does He or Doesn't He?" on page 54 for a fine booktalk poetry break.

Carol Diggory Shields bring us *Almost Late to School and More School Poems*. (illustrated by Paul Meisel). This is another fun book of school poems by the author and illustrator of *Lunch Money*. Try reading one of these aloud to liven up your booktalk: "Gotta Go" on page 21 is a good choice, and so is "Jump Rope Rhyme" on pages 30–31. Or ask two kids to read the "Poem for Two Voices" on pages 38–39.

Some of the poems that stick with us the longest are those that reveal sudden glimpses of wonder or beauty in the world around us. For an excellent example of nature poetry return to Barbara Juster Esbensen's *Swing Around the Sun*. These lovely poems were first published in 1965 but have been reissued in a beautiful new edition with gorgeous illustrations by four major children's book artists: Cheng-Khee Chee,

Janice Lee Porter, Mary Grandpre, and Stephen Gammell . Try reading and showing "First Snow" and "Snow Clown," illustrated by Caldecott Medalist Stephen Gammell.

Figure 6.4. *A Chill in the Air: Nature Poems for Fall and Winter* **by John Frank.**

John Frank points out there's *A Chill in the Air: Nature Poems for Fall and Winter*. If it is fall or winter, these poems are great for quick breaks in your booktalk with younger listeners. Read "A Cold October Night" for Halloween, "Footprints" when it snows, and "Scarcity" during a unit on animal hibernation. This is lovely stuff, with wonderful art by Mike Reed.

Kristine O'Connell George teaches us a lot about a special *Hummingbird Nest: A Journal of Poems*. One day, when George was eating breakfast on the patio of her house, a hummingbird almost attacked her. Hummingbirds are tiny, but this one looked like it meant business. She realized that it was building a nest in a plant on her patio—and her whole family got interested. She made the cat stay indoors. The dog became upset because the hummingbird was drinking water out of *his* bowl. And everyone in George's family took a special interest in the nest, and then the eggs, and then the new babies. George's journal is a series of poems about her avian adventure. The pictures are great and the poems are fine. Read it and learn a lot about those beautiful hummingbirds. Read the poem "The Cat Remarks."

Has it ever happened that someone you cared about—a friend, a relative, a classmate—died? What did that feel like? How much did it hurt? Did it ever stop hurting? Nikki Grimes shows us what it is like in *What Is Goodbye?*, a beautiful book of poems about two kids whose older brother has died. Read aloud the poem "Rush," which Jerilyn writes about her mother.

If you are booktalking nonfiction about pets to young children, be sure to include three or four poems from Lee Bennett Hopkins's delightful, easy-to-read book *A Pet for Me: Poems* (An I Can Read Book). Hopkins has put together a wonderful selection. We know you'll love "I Would Like to Have a Pet" by Karla Kuskin, "Old Slow Friend" by Alice Schertle, "Tarantula" by Fran Haraway, and *Ant Farm* by Madeline Comora.

Tony Mitton's *Plum* is a large book with beautiful, colorful illustrations by the magical Mary GrandPre. Read the title poem, "Plum," or "Flightpath" to your audience.

Figure 6.5. *Fireflies at Midnight* **by Marilyn Singer.**

Marilyn Singer's poems in *Fireflies at Midnight* are about animals in nature and are illustrated with glorious precision by Ken Robbins's photographs. Try reading any of them aloud in a booktalk about animals. I recommend "RED FOX."

There are 13 stunning poems and even more illustrations in Patrick J. Lewis's *Freedom Like Sunlight: Praisesongs for Black Americans*. Read a poem about one of these great African Americans, show the picture, and then consider booktalking an entire book about the person you discussed. Show the double-page spread of Martin Luther King being arrested on pages 16–17 and read the poem:

For having told the truth I am alone and cold in Birmingham.
I speak to them. They spit at me because it's Memphis, Tennessee.
The evening news from Selma's jail cannot excuse this brute betrayal.
Though I am tired, I've just begun, but someone's fired the fateful gun.
I hear the shot I feel the pain . . . who bravely fought must fight again.

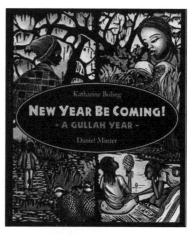

Figure 6.6. *New Year Be Coming! A Gullah Year* **by Katharine Boling.**

Poetry can tell us how other people live. Look into Katharine Boling's *New Year Be Coming! A Gullah Year.* Fine short poems take their listeners month-by-month through a year with the Gullah, who live on the sea islands of Georgia and South Carolina. Read "June" aloud, particularly if you are doing a booktalk on African Americans or the seasons. The illustrations are glorious.

What is it like to live in a different part of a city, in a place called "Chinatown," where wonderful things happen and amazing things can be seen in the shops and on the streets? Kam Mak, who wrote and illustrated *My Chinatown: One Year in Poems,* grew up in Chinatown himself, and, in these lovely poems, he tells how it feels. Read the poem across from the picture of the man holding the bird in the cage.

Have a song in your head that you just can't get rid of? And then you realize it was a song from summer camp years ago? Francine Lessac does us all a service by compiling in *Camp Granada: Sing-Along Camp Songs* all those songs that kids (and we) learned over the years, and still remember. The only problem is that the words are included, but not the music. Some songs are unfamiliar to us, like "Barges," "In a Cabin in the Woods," and "Everywhere We Go," but then of course, we never went to camp. But many of the songs *are* familiar, and the pictures are colorful and appealing. Some of these are hilarious!

For more gut-wrenching laughs (literally) turn next to Alan Wolf's *The Blood-Hungry Spleen and Other Poems About Our Parts.* Wolf was a sixth-grade life sciences teacher when he had his students create a life-sized body chart with a poem for each part. And that got Wolf penning poems. Here are a series of fun and educational rhymes about body parts, humorously illustrated. Read "Your Nose Makes Sense," "Lungs," "Your Muscles Keep you Moving," "Kidney Trouble," and our favorite, "The Story of Ow!"

These next titles are great for integrating into other booktalk topics. The poems teach us something or give us ideas for creating our own poetry and word fun.

You've heard that it's bad luck to have a black cat walk in front of you—or to break a mirror—or to brag about your luck. But if any of these things happen, what should you do? Start out by reading the poems in Janet S. Wong's *Knock on Wood: Poems About Superstitions.* Each describes a different superstition, and some of them suggest what you can do to break the bad luck. At the end of the book is some great background information about some of the most common superstitions. What superstitions do *you* believe in?

You'll have a lot of fun reading Patrick J. Lewis's colorful *A World of Wonders: Geographic Travels in Verse and Rhyme*—and you will learn a little geography painlessly at the same time! Read "Two Animals Talking," "How a Cave Will Behave," and "Did You Know"; show the audience the illustrations; and start a lively discussion!

Figure 6.7 *Wonderful Words: Poems About Reading, Writing, Speaking and Listening* **edited by Lee Bennett Hopkins.**

Wonderful Words: Poems About Reading, Writing, Speaking and Listening edited by Lee Bennett Hopkins is about words and the act of writing itself, and will inspire you to pick up a pen. And maybe to think about language in a new way. Read aloud the classic "METAPHOR," by Eve Merriam, on page 10, and "The End" by Richard Armour on (where else?) the last page.

Wake up House!: Rooms Full of Poems by Dee Lillegard covers a subject not usually the focus of poets. Poems about the furniture, the rooms, and the objects in a house are illustrated with charming illustrations. This is delightful. Have your kids write a poem or a paragraph about something in their houses.

Introduce early readers to concrete poetry with Heidi Roemer's *Come to My Party and Other Shape Poems*. These shape poems with charming, playful pictures by Hideko Takahashi may inspire an entire class to try writing them themselves. These poems might be more fun to show your class before you read them. Have them guess the subject before they even hear the first line. Then read aloud "It's Raining" on page 9, "Camper's Prayer" on page 25, and "Garden Hose" on page 20.

Figure 6.8. *Here's What You Do When You Can't Find Your Shoe (Ingenious Inventions for Pesky Problems)* **by Andrea Perry.**

Another untypical topic for poems is science. Andrea Perry had her own ingenious idea when she wrote *Here's What You Do When You Can't Find Your Shoe (Ingenious Inventions for Pesky Problems)*. Isn't that a great title? These are inventions with enormous appeal to a lot of kids—and maybe some adults too! There are poems about bug homes, foot floss, a spray for grocery carts to eliminate vegetables, and more. Read the "Crumbunny" on page 30, about an animal whose sole purpose is to eat crumbs off your bed. That's even better than a robot vacuum cleaner! This book would work well with a unit on inventions and inventors.

A great companion title is Cherise Mericle Harper's *Imaginative Inventions: The Who, What, Where, When, and Why of Roller Skates, Potato Chips, Marbles, and Pie and More!* These are fun rhymes about some of the world's most famous inventions, and about how people got their ideas for them. Piggy banks, for instance, have been around for a long time, but how the idea happened makes for an unusual tale. You may find it hard to believe that Santa Anna, who led the attack on the Alamo, had something to do with the history of chewing gum. Did you know that potato chips were invented by accident? Show your audience the two-page spread of the invention of eyeglasses on pages 12–13. A fun extra: Most of these poems about inventions will work with "The Yellow Rose of Texas" or "The Battle Hymn of the Republic" if you are willing to be silly and sing them. (The kids will love you for it!)

TELLING THEIR OWN STORY

If you have read the stories about Joey Pigza or Rotten Ralph, you know who Jack Gantos is, a very funny guy and a darn good writer.

But Jack Gantos is something else as well. He's an ex-convict.

Figure 6.9. *Hole in My Life* by Jack Gantos.

In *Hole in My Life*, Gantos tells us that when he was 19 years old, he was using drugs heavily and always looking for ways to make money, preferably easy ways. In the Virgin Islands, someone offered him a great way to make a lot of money in a hurry. All he had to do was smuggle drugs into the United States. Supposedly, he would never get caught.

Gantos relates exactly how he *did* get caught, and what happened to him in federal prison. Whoever reads this book will do their best to stay out of jail! Gantos got out, changed his ways, and is now a famous writer of great books for children and young adults. The first two paragraphs in the book suck you right into the story, and make for a compelling booktalk. Recommended for fifth grade and up.

Dick King-Smith didn't start out to be a writer of books for kids. In fact, he did a lot of other things before he ever put pen to paper, and *Chewing the Cud* is his own story. King-Smith has loved animals all of his life, and he tells us about many of the animals that he loved, and some that inspired the characters in his books. When he got a dachshund puppy named Anna, he was afraid she might be deaf, because she didn't pay any attention to what he said to her. Anna also hated rain, and would not go "to the bathroom" whenever it was raining. Instead, she just hid inside and held it! King-Smith has also loved his wife of many, many years, and he tells us how he met her, how he fought in World War II, and how they were financially unsuccessful at farming for most of their lives. And, then, he decided to try to write a children's book—and he has been writing them like crazy ever since. This is a very funny book that will have you laughing out loud!

William Anderson recounts the life of another American author in *Prairie Girl: The Life of Laura Ingalls Wilder*. Laura Ingalls was a girl at one of the most amazing times in American history. Laura was born in 1867, not long after the Civil War ended. Her sister Mary was two years older, and the two girls lived with their parents in a log cabin near the town of Pepin, Wisconsin. But Laura's pa had his heart set on traveling farther west, moving to wide-open spaces where there was wide-open opportunity for people who were willing to work hard. Laura was only a year old when the family moved to a homestead in Indian Territory, near what is now Independence, Kansas. They didn't stay long. But after returning to Wisconsin, Laura's pa caught the traveling bug again, and Laura spent most of her childhood moving around the Great Plains.

Laura's life experiences are hard for us to imagine today. But her keen observations and memory help us see life through the eyes of a 19th-century American pioneer girl. She wrote her own story in the *Little House on the Prairie*, but she left a lot out—such as the birth and death of her little brother, and the family's time living in Iowa, working at a hotel. William Anderson, who is probably the world's greatest expert on Laura Ingalls, fills in the missing pieces. This is a great book for people who have fallen in love with Walnut Grove and Plum Creek.

One of America's most beloved poets is the subject of Penelope Niven's *Carl Sandburg: Adventures of a Poet*. Carl Sandburg was one of seven kids born to Swedish immigrants in Galesburg, Illinois. Born in 1878, he grew up wanting to travel on the railroad where his father worked. When he was 19 years old, Sandburg started hopping illegally on freight trains and traveling around the country. Thus began his love of travel. He joined up to fight in the Spanish–American war, and he wrote home reports about it to the Galesburg newspaper. He decided to become a journalist, and then a poet—and always he remained true to himself.

This is Sandburg's fascinating story, and includes many of his own writings and poems. Do you know the most famous one, about "The Fog"?

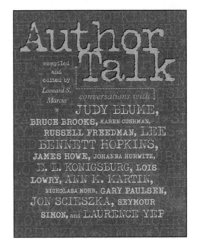

Figure 6.10. *Author Talk: Conversations with Judy Blume, Bruce Brooks, Karen Cushman, Russell Freedman, Lee Bennett Hopkins, James Howe, Johanna Hurwitz, E. L. Konigsburg, Lois Lowry, Ann M. Martin, Nicholasa Mohr, Gary Paulsen, Jon Scieszka, Seymour Simon, and Laurence Yep* compiled and edited by Leonard Marcus.

If you like to read, or be read to, at least one of your favorites is probably listed in Leonard Marcus's neat survey *Author Talk: Conversations with Judy Blume, Bruce Brooks, Karen Cushman, Russell Freedman, Lee Bennet Hopkins, James Howe, Joanna Hurwitz, E.L. Konigsburg, Lois Lowry, Ann M. Martin, Nicholasa Mohr, Gary Paulsen, Jon Scieszka, Seymour Simon and Laurence Yep*. Listen to this cool writing advice from Bruce Brooks: "Try . . . to write a paragraph describing a room that, without the use of a single negative adjective, makes the reader absolutely not want to go into that room" (page 15). Brooks also says is that "building self-respect . . . is basically what being a kid is all about" (page 14). What a great idea!

Russell Freedman, one of our greatest living authors, says that a nonfiction writer is "A storyteller . . . who has taken an oath to tell the truth" (page 22).

Both Lois Lowry and Johanna Hurwitz say that their favorite books when they were kids were the Betsy-Tacy books by Maud Hart Lovelace.

Gary Paulsen had a terribly hard childhood and youth. He was pretty much on his own by the time he was seven or eight. His parents were both alcoholics and they hated each other. He says:

> At one time, when we were living in an apartment in a small Minnesota town, I moved down into the basement of our building by myself. My parents were so drunk, they didn't know the difference. I had found a place in back of the furnace, a sort of alcove, with a half-sized couch and a light hanging from the ceiling. That became my home. I'd usually take down a quart of milk and would eat grape jelly and peanut butter sandwiches there. I made a lot of airplane models. And I slept there at night. Or I would take off for a week and go stay with an uncle to work on his farm or go hunting. Half the time my parents wouldn't know I was gone. (page 77)

Jon Scieszka must have been as funny when he was a kid as he is today. He had four little brothers, and he would tell them if they were naughty that he was going to call the Bad Boy's Home to come and take them away. They always promised to do anything he said after that! These authors are not only fine writers, but they have great stories to tell about their own lives.

Kids become the storytellers in *It's Back to School We Go! First Day Stories from Around the World* by Ellen Jackson. In 11 different countries around the globe, children tell what the first day of school is like where they live. In Kenya, they attend school six days a week between January and November, but they have almost no books or paper. Japanese school begins in April, and children attend classes as American children do, Monday through Friday. But they also add two Saturday mornings each month. In Peru, near the Amazon River, a schoolteacher may be only 14 years old, and many students arrive by canoe. In Nunavut, Canada, Inuit children study their own Inuit language along with English. In colder weather, they wear traditional Inuit clothing. School is different everywhere—but some of it is also the same. Lovely illustrations.

When Chris Crutcher was a kid, growing up in the fifties and sixties, he was pretty much of a dork. He didn't read much, he couldn't get girls to even look at him, and he was a weakling when it came to sports. In spite of the fact that his family nickname was "Lever" for the *simplest* machine, somehow he pulled through. Crutcher tells in *King of the Mild Frontier: An Ill-Advised Autobiography* how he hated working in his dad's service station wearing *really* nerdy clothes, how he had huge pimples, how his mother was an alcoholic, and how he grew up in a tiny town in the middle of Idaho.

This is one of the funniest books around. Imagine this nightmare of a letterman initiation: All the kids who are eligible for lettering are stark naked, each is given a number of pitted olives, and then they are forced to race carrying the olives from one point to another *without* using their hands or mouths. You'll laugh so hard you'll be shaking. Today Chris Crutcher is a famous writer and a man who has made a difference for the better in our world. You'll have a blast getting to know him!

BIBLIOGRAPHY

Anderson, William. *Prairie Girl: The Life of Laura Ingalls Wilder*. Illustrations by Renee Graef. HarperCollins, 2004. ISBN 0060289732. 74 p. Grades 2–5.

Bagert, Brod (poems by). *Giant Children*. Pictures by Tedd Arnold. Dial Books for Young Readers, 2002. ISBN 0803725566. Unpaged. Grades 1–5.

Boling, Katharine. *New Year Be Coming! A Gullah Year*. Illustrated by Daniel Minter. Albert Whitman, 2003. ISBN 0807555908. Unpaged. Grades 1–3.

Brennan-Nelson, Denise. *My Momma Likes to Say*. Illustrated by Jane Monroe Donovan. Sleeping Bear Press, 2003. ISBN 1585361062. 32 p. Grades K–3.

Crutcher, Chris. *King of the Mild Frontier: An Ill-Advised Autobiography*. Greenwillow Books, an imprint of HarperCollins, 2003. ISBN 0060502509. 260 p. Grades 6–up.

Esbensen, Barbara Juster. *Swing Around the Sun.* Art by Cheng-Khee Chee, Janice Lee Porter, Mary Grandpre, Stephen Gammell. Carolrhoda Books, 2003. ISBN 0876141432. Unpaged. Grades K–3.

Florian, Douglas. *Bow Wow Meow Meow: It's Rhyming Cats and Dogs.* Harcourt, 2003. ISBN 0152163956. 48 p. Grades K–4.

———. *Lizards, Frogs, and Polliwogs.* Harcourt, 2001. ISBN 015202591x. 48 p. Grades 2–5.

———. *Mammalabilia.* Poems and paintings by Douglas Florian. Voyager Books/Harcourt, 2003. ISBN 0152050248. 48 p. Grades 2–5.

———. *Summersaults.* Poems and paintings by Douglas Florian. Greenwillow Books, an imprint of HarperCollins, 2002. ISBN 0060292687. 48 p. Grades 2–5.

Franco, Betsy. *Mathematickles!* Illustrations by Steven Salerno. Margaret K. McElderry Books, 2003. ISBN 0689843577. Unpaged. Grades 1–5.

Frank, John. *A Chill in the Air: Nature Poems for Fall and Winter.* Illustrated by Mike Reed. Simon & Schuster Books for Young Readers, 2003. ISBN 0689839235. Unpaged. Grades K–3.

Gantos, Jack. *Hole in My Life.* Farrar, Straus & Giroux, 2002. ISBN 0374399883. 200 p. Grades 5–up.

George, Kristine O'Connell. *Hummingbird Nest: A Journal of Poems.* Illustrated by Barry Moser. Harcourt, 2004. ISBN 0152023259. Unpaged. Grades 1–4.

———. *Swimming Upstream: Middle School Poems.* Illustrated by Debbie Tilley. Clarion Books, 2003. ISBN 0618152504. 80 p. Grades 5–9.

Grimes, Nikki. *What Is Goodbye?* Illustrated by Raul Colon. Hyperion Books for Children, 2004. ISBN 0786807784. Unpaged. Grades 3–8.

Harper, Cherise Mericle. *Imaginative Inventions: the Who, What, Where, When, and Why of Roller Skates, Potato Chips, Marbles, and Pie and More!* Megan Tingley Books/Little, Brown, 2001. ISBN 0316347256. 32 p. Grades 1–4.

Hopkins, Lee Bennett (selected by). *A Pet for Me: Poems* (An I Can Read Book). Pictures by Jane Manning. HarperCollins, 2003. ISBN 0060291117. Unpaged. Grades K–3.

———. *Wonderful Words: Poems About Reading, Writing, Speaking and Listening.* Illustrated by Karen Barbour. Simon & Schuster Books for Young Readers, 2001. ISBN 0689835884. 32 p. Grades 1–5.

I Invited a Dragon to Dinner and Other Poems to Make You Laugh Out Loud. Illustrated by Chris L. Demarest. Philomel Books, 2002. ISBN 0399235671. Unpaged. Grades 2–5.

Jackson, Ellen. *It's Back to School We Go! First Day Stories from Around the World.* Illustrated by Jan Davey Ellis. Millbrook Press, 2003. ISBN 076132362x. 32 p. Grades 2–5.

Kennedy, X. J. *Exploding Gravy: Poems to Make You Laugh*. Illustrated by Joy Allen. Little, Brown, 2002. ISBN 0316384232. 128 p. Grades 3–5.

King-Smith, Dick. *Chewing the Cud*. Illustrated by Harry Horse. Alfred A. Knopf, 2001, 2003. ISBN 0375814590. 197 p. Grades 5–up.

Kirk, Daniel. *Dogs Rule!* Hyperion Books for Children, 2004. ISBN 0786819499. 48 p. Grades 1–4.

Leedy, Loreen, and Pat Street. *There's a Frog in My Throat! 440 Animal Sayings a Little Bird Told Me*. Illustrated by Loreen Leedy. Holiday House, 2003. ISBN 0823417743. 48 p. Grades 1–4.

Lessac, Francine. *Camp Granada: Sing-Along Camp Songs*. Henry Holt, 2003. ISBN 0805066837. 45 p. Grades K–6.

Lewis, J. Patrick. *Freedom Like Sunlight: Praisesongs for Black Americans*. Illustrations by John Thompson. Creative Editions, 2000. 40 p. ISBN 1568461631. Grades 5–up.

———. *A World of Wonders: Geographic Travels in Verse and Rhyme*. Pictures by Alison Jay. Dial Books for Young Readers, 2002. ISBN 0803725795. Unpaged. Grades 2–5.

Lillegard, Dee. *Wake up House!: Rooms Full of Poems*. Illustrated by Don Carter. Alfred A. Knopf, 2000. ISBN 0679883517. Unpaged. Grades K–3.

Mak, Kam. *My Chinatown: One Year in Poems*. HarperCollins, 2002. ISBN 0060291915. Unpaged. Grades 1–4.

Marcus, Leonard, comp. and ed. *Author Talk: Conversations with Judy Blume, Bruce Brooks, Karen Cushman, Russell Freedman, Lee Bennett Hopkins, James Howe, Johanna Hurwitz, E. L. Konigsburg, Lois Lowry, Ann M. Martin, Nicholasa Mohr, Gary Paulsen, Jon Scieszka, Seymour Simon, and Laurence Yep*. Simon & Schuster Books for Young Readers, 2000. ISBN 068981383x. 103 p. Grades 4–8.

Mitton, Tony. *Plum*. Illustrated by Mary GrandPre. Arthur A. Levine Books/An Imprint of Scholastic Press, 1998, 2003. ISBN 0439364094. Unpaged. Grades 2–5.

Niven, Penelope. *Carl Sandburg: Adventures of a Poet*. With Poems and Prose by Carl Sandburg. Illustrated by Marc Nadel. Harcourt, 2003. ISBN 0152046860. Unpaged. Grades 4–6.

Perry, Andrea. *Here's What You Do When You Can't Find Your Shoe (Ingenious Inventions for Pesky Problems)*. Illustrated by Alan Snow. Atheneum Books for Young Readers, 2003. ISBN 068983067x. 32 p. Grades 2–4.

Roemer, Heidi. *Come to My Party and Other Shape Poems*. Illustrated by Hideko Takahashi. Henry Holt, 2004. ISBN 0805066209. 48 p. Grades K–3.

Shields, Carol Diggory. *Almost Late to School and More School Poems*. Illustrated by Paul Meisel. Dutton Children's Books, 2003. ISBN 0525457437. 40 p. Grades 2–5.

Singer, Marilyn. *Fireflies at Midnight.* Pictures by Ken Robbins. Atheneum Books for Young Readers, 2003. ISBN 0689824920. Unpaged. Grades K–3.

Steig, William. *CDC?* Farrar, Straus & Giroux, 1984, 2003. ISBN 0374312338. 58 p. Grades 4–up.

Stevenson, James. *Corn Chowder.* With illustrations by the author. Greenwillow Books, an imprint of HarperCollins, 2003. ISBN 006053059. 48 p. Grades 3–6.

———. *Corn-Fed: Poems.* With illustrations by the author. Greenwillow Books, an imprint of HarperCollins, 2002. ISBN 006000598x. 43 p. Grades 3–6.

Wolf, Alan. *The Blood-Hungry Spleen and Other Poems About Our Parts.* Illustrated by Greg Clark. Candlewick Press, 2003. ISBN 076361565x. 53 p. Grades 4–7.

Wong, Janet S. *Knock on Wood: Poems About Superstitions.* Illustrated by Julie Paschkis. Margaret K. McElderry Books, 2003. ISBN 0689855125. Unpaged. Grades 1–4.

CHAPTER 7

Freaky, Funny, Gross, and Cool

GROSS AND GRUESOME

Have you heard the horrifying tale of Phineas Gage, a man who lived with a metal bar through his brain? Read on in John Fleischman's *Phineas Gage: A Gruesome But True Story About Brain Science.* It's 1848, in a small town in Vermont. Phineas Gage is the construction foreman working on laying railroad tracks. Gage is working with a sharp iron bar when, in a ghastly instant, it shoots straight up through his head, leaving a hole in his cheek and another one in the top of his skull. Show the illustration on page 16, and the computer reconstruction on page 71. But, and this is even more amazing, Gage is still able to walk, to talk, and get himself to a doctor, to whom he said, "Well, here's work enough for you, Doctor" (page 8).

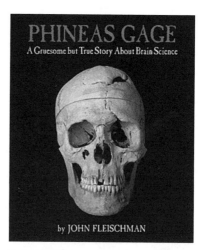

Figure 7.1. *Phineas Gage: A Gruesome But True Story About Brain Science* **by John Fleischman.**

In Gage's day no one knew about sterilization. No one realized the importance of keeping themselves especially clean when working with the sick. The workings of the brain were unknown territory. One doctor who examined Gage wrote up the tale of the railroadman's survival, but readers did not believe it. In one sense they were right. The old Phineas did not really survive. He was alive, but due to the considerable brain damage, his personality suffered a massive transformation. What scientists know now is that Gage lost his ability to socialize.

You will not believe the gruesome things you will read in this true story. Phineas's grave in San Francisco was dug up six years after his death, his body exhumed and beheaded, and his perforated skull taken back for study.

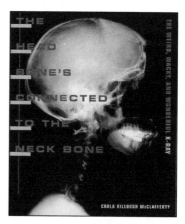

Figure 7.2. *The Head Bone's Connected to the Neck Bone: The Weird, Wacky and Wonderful X-Ray* **by Carla Killough McLafferty.**

Gage's physicians could certainly have benefited from an X-ray machine. Unfortunately, it wasn't invented for another 50 years. Have you ever had an X-ray? If the answer is yes, were you scared? Excited? Or was it just plain ordinary? In Carla Killough McLafferty's *The Head Bone's Connected to the Neck Bone: The Weird,*

Wacky and Wonderful X-Ray we learn that Dr. Wilhelm Conrad Roentgen was experimenting with cathode rays in 1895 when he noticed something unusual. He realized he could see inside his own hand. He could actually see his bones!

Using the amazing new ray—which Roentgen insisted on calling the "x-ray" because x is the mathematical symbol for the unknown—people could see things they had never imagined. In their overexcitement, scientists and amateurs experimented with the strange new rays. They never dreamed their experiments were dangerous, even fatal. Overexposure to the rays caused a terrible new disease, radiation sickness, and many people died horrible, painful deaths. People who used their hands to show others that X-rays were safe sometimes had to have those same hands amputated.

Today we take X-rays for granted. And today, we can use them to

- look inside a mummy without destroying it,

- look inside a fossil,

- find out if bones are broken,

- find out if teeth have cavities,

- find out if paintings are faked, and

- find out where a bullet is located in a gunshot victim.

And that is just the beginning. An imaginative use of X-rays has told us that ancient Egyptians could have used dental braces. Most pharaohs had buck teeth!

This is a good read and will astonish you. Show the picture of the hands deteriorating from exposure to radiation on page 71.

Can't get enough of bones and skeletons? Then you'll dig one of our favorite picks, Natalie Jane Prior's *The Encyclopedia of Preserved People: Pickled, Frozen and Mummified Corpses from Around the World.* The stories are copious and satisfactorily gruesome. Prior goes around the world, pinpointing locales where preserved people have been discovered. Not all of them are preserved on purpose, like mummies. Some specimens have just accidentally survived. Prior describes an 1828 English murderer, whose skin was removed when he died and used to bind a book about his crime. You can see the book today in the Bury St. Edmund's Museum—or on the Web at www.stedmundsbury.gov.uk/rbexhib.htm. Prior's book could use more and bigger pictures, but it is great fun.

Scientists believe that the first time human beings caught the disease we call smallpox was 8,000 years ago. Somehow, those ancient, unfortunate humans caught it from an animal. According to Albert Marrin's *Dr. Jenner and the Speckled Monster: The Search for the Smallpox Vaccine,* the first person we know for certain who contacted smallpox was a pharaoh, Ramses V. He died in 1157 BC, and his mummy shows a great number of pockmarks.

On of the more horrible results of smallpox is that if it did not kill you or make you blind, it scarred you for life. Before modern medicine, a third of smallpox's victims died; one out of six went blind in one or both eyes. After Britain's Elizabeth I had it, she lost her hair and her eyebrows. The Virgin Queen wore thick makeup for the rest of her life to cover the scars.

Careful observers of the deadly disease, however, noted that if you had smallpox once, you did not get it again. In China, over 1,000 years ago, one such brainy observer had the idea that if people got a mild case of smallpox, they would remain immune the rest of their lives. Marrin remarks that, while no one knows the exact details, perhaps this nameless person made powder out of smallpox scabs and then blew the powder up the noses of healthy people. This primitive control group got smallpox, but only a light case. By the 1600s, this unusual practice had spread all across Asia. Soon, instead of inhaling the medicine, a drop or two of pus was removed from a person with a mild case of smallpox, a scratch was made in a healthy patient's arm, and the pus was rubbed into the scratch. Voila! The world's first inoculation.

In the 1700s, Lady Mary Montagu, a scarred smallpox survivor and the wife of the English ambassador to Turkey, heard about the inoculations and tried them on her own children. The practice spread through Western Europe. In Newgate prison, for instance, three men and three women, all condemned to death by hanging, were offered the chance to be inoculated. If they survived, they would be set free.

Later, Dr. Edward Jenner realized that milkmaids never caught smallpox. The reason: They had already caught a form of pox from the cows they worked with, and thereby became immune. Jenner thought to inoculate people with cowpox rather than smallpox, and how he did it makes for an astounding story. Twenty years ago, everyone believed that smallpox was a disease of the past. No one would ever get it again. Now they are not so sure. Is it still around? You can read all about it and its history here.

Show the frontispiece photo of the man whose arms and legs are covered with pustules.

Another disease that always grabs the headlines is influenza. David Getz tells the remarkable story of the *Purple Death: The Mysterious Flu of 1918.*

In a personal note, Kathleen remembers her mother often telling her about her neighbors near the farm where she grew up. In 1918, when her mother was a toddler, the neighbor's only child, a beloved son, enlisted and was sent to France. He never made it. Like most of the rest of the men in his platoon, he died of influenza on the way over, and he was buried at sea. His parents did not find out about it until weeks later.

The poor boy was not alone. According to Getz, in World War I 85 out of every 100 soldiers died not in battle but of the flu. There were not enough doctors, nurses, coffins, or even space for the dead bodies. It was a pandemic.

"A 'pandemic' is a disease that quickly spreads through populations and crosses over borders to infect thousands, even millions of people" (page 11). In Nashville, Tennessee, over 40,000 people caught the disease; over 15,000 of them died. Scientists believe that 20 to 40 million people around the world died in one six-month period.

And they did not know what caused it. Scientists are still searching for the virus. Some medical workers have dug up the frozen bodies of victims who died in 1918 and were buried in cold places. The virus remains one of the world's most terrifying and disturbing mysteries.

Thank goodness for modern medicine! Kathryn Senior warns in her book, *You Wouldn't Want to Be Sick in the 16th Century: Diseases You'd Rather Not Catch.* If you like gross information, this is the book for you. Senior looks through the eyes of an imaginary kid of 12 arriving in London to become a barber surgeon's apprentice. Along the way the young kid learns (and so do you):

- A popular way to diagnose illnesses is to look at people's urine. It is examined three times, once when fresh, once after cooling for about an hour, and then once completely cold. Sometimes the urine is even tasted to find out whether it is sweet or sour!

- Barber surgeons believe that bloodletting helps cure the sick, because blood has bad stuff in it. If the surgeons are not careful, however, patients can bleed to death.

- Amputation saws are never cleaned between operations, and they are frequently dropped in the mud. No wonder that almost anyone who has a limb amputated dies!

- Women may have to sit in a birthing chair to give birth. That way they can preserve their modesty.

Show the picture of the amputation on page 15. Once you finish Senior, you'll be happy you live in the 21st century.

Figure 7.3. *Bury the Dead: Tombs, Corpses, Mummies, Skeletons, & Rituals* **by Christopher Sloan.**

Great photographs enliven a morbidly fascinating look at funeral rituals in Christopher Sloan's *Bury the Dead: Tombs, Corpses, Mummies, Skeletons and Rituals.* Throughout recorded history, and for a considerable time before, people have used many rituals in burying their dead. Today in North America, some of the customs used in these rituals may seem strange, but all of them helped in dealing with grief. Even in modern times, "babies are buried in trees on the island of Sulawesi in Indonesia; bodies are fed to vultures and other birds in Tibet, and in the Amazon rain forest, the Yanomami are burned, crushed, and then eaten" (page 7).

Scientists studying ancient skeletons have determined that people took care of the elderly and sick as long as 60,000 years ago. Some of the bones they have examined belonged to people who had broken or missing limbs, or severe arthritis, or other diseases that would prevent them from taking care of themselves. Clearly, others took care of them, and that included burying them.

Some skeletons have utensil marks on them, which probably means the bodies were eaten. This was not necessarily because survivors were hungry. It may have been part of the funerary ritual.

Studying graves can lead to important information about what people wore and about their health. A 12,000-year-old grave found in Southeast Asia, for example, included a child buried with a puppy. This is the first real evidence that people kept pets that long ago. Perhaps the most famous funerary rituals in the world were in ancient Egypt, where people and animals were mummified, and entire towns became industrial centers for the funeral business. Amazing Scythian tombs, filled with gold, have been found in Russia. Getz also discusses the wondrous tomb in China that contains thousands of life-sized terracotta soldiers.

Show your audience the picture on page 61 of "the Dani people of Uruan Jaya who preserve their great warriors by smoking them. They believe this will preserve their fighting spirit" (page 60).

Any booktalk on the gross and gruesome has to include a few titles on that perennially favorite topic among kids: human waste. A good place to start is Nicola Davies's *Poop: A Natural History of the Unmentionable*. Davies isn't afraid to mention it. And she gives us a great biology lesson along the way. Did you know that hippos leave a tiny trail of poop when they waddle out of their safe riverbanks and go foraging for food at night? In the pitch dark, the hippo merely has to sniff its way back home. A truly gross variation on the old Hansel-and-Gretel breadcrumb trick.

Which animal poops the least? The slow-moving sloth, of course. It climbs down from its tree every four or five days and deposits a little hill of waste at the bottom of the trunk. Then it climbs back up, slowly, slowly, to start eating again. And ants literally eat poop! They "harvest" greenflies, whose diet is mostly sugar derived from plants. That means their poop is also mostly sugar, and nutritious to ants. Yum!

Davies tells us that serious poop scientists are hard at work. For example, they look closely at the droppings of bats and then count the legs and eyes and wings of eaten critters embedded in the waste. Droppings tell us a lot about the creatures who emit them. Fun stuff! And always a crowd pleaser.

For another look at the subject, open up Susan E. Goodman's *The Truth About Poop*. As much as adults don't like to talk about it, we all poop fairly often. It's a good thing, too. We would die if we didn't.

This book gives us the lowdown on poop, human and animal. Did you know:

- Sharks can smell poop over a mile away. So don't ever poop in the water.

- In Ephesus, a city in the ancient Roman Empire, rich people sent their slaves to public bathrooms to warm up their toilet seats for them!

- People use the toilet, on the average, four to five times a day. But only one of those four times is to poop.

- Camels' poop comes out so dry that you can burn it immediately.

- Most people produce about an ounce of poop for each 12 pounds of body weight.

- A Japanese toilet manufacturer makes a toilet with a blow-dry feature. It saves money on toilet paper.

- Astronauts wear diapers.

- "During World War II, 'poop' could kill. The British knew that the German tank drivers fighting in the desert thought it was good luck to drive over camel dung. So the Brits made explosives that looked exactly like the stuff. One pass over the poop—and the tanks were out of action. 'Drivers thought they were safe and . . . BOOM!' " (page 39).

Figure 7.4. *Oh Yuck! The Encyclopedia of Everything Nasty* **by Joy Masoff.**

You will be telling your friends all the amazing things you learn about poop!

And then to sum up the world of grossness, there's nothing better than Joy Masoff's magnificently disgusting *Oh Yuck! The Encyclopedia of Everything Nasty.* Look it up, A to Z, acne to zits, in this hilarious tome on all things gross and gruesome. Among other things:

- Snakes can swallow objects *three times* the size of their heads.

- If a fire ant bites you, it feels like you've just been hit by a blowtorch.

- The reason bats hang upside down is because their legs are not strong enough to support their weight. Bats can't stand up; they topple over.

- The reason that the spiciest foods are served in the hottest places (e.g., India or Mexico) is that those foods cool down your body by activating your sweat glands.

- There have been cannibals in the United States! Read all about them on page 28.

- Slime eels are completely covered with mucus, like the stuff that comes out of your nose. Other sea creatures will not eat them. Slime eels themselves eat by boring into the mouths or eyes or butts of dead or dying creatures on the sea floor. Then they suck up everything but bones and skin. Scientists call them "hagfish" or "slimehags."

- About a hundred years ago in France, a performer called "Let Petomane" would fart onstage. He would even play tunes with his farts! People paid to see him do it. "Le Petomane" means "the Fartiste." Show the picture on page 56.

- Jellyfish move very slowly. "Make a fist with your hand. Now extend all your fingers. Now, make a fist again. And extend your fingers again. Keep doing this until you have propelled yourself across the Atlantic Ocean! Just kidding, but that's kind of how jellyfish move from here to there, by contracting and opening their bell-shaped bodies" (page 86).

Ask your booktalk audience to name the most dangerous animal in the world. How many of them will guess the mosquito? This nasty bug wins the top rank because it spreads so many other bugs—dangerous diseases. So all of us have probably killed at least one of the most dangerous animals in the world!

FOOD, GLORIOUS FOOD

Have you ever wondered where ice cream comes from? I mean where it really comes from, and how it is made? Maybe all you ever think about ice cream is how good it tastes! Elisha Cooper's *Ice Cream* tells us that it takes a lot of people and a lot of time and a lot of cows to make ice cream. This book will show you how it happens. And did you know that ice cream companies insure the tongues of their ice cream tasters? Wouldn't *that* be a fun job?

Show the pictures of the ice cream cartons and the ice cream taster.

You can't think of ice cream without thinking of ice cream cones, and Elaine Greenstein takes on the tastier invention in *Ice Cream Cones for Sale!* In 1904, Saint Louis had a World's Fair, and five people there claimed to have invented something new and exciting—ice cream cones. Until that time ice cream was served only in dishes. Apparently a waffle-maker offered (or was asked for) a waffle in which to place the ice cream, and this fun book tells the story of how the cone took shape. That's the legend, anyway. Greenstein next pulls a cool trick by filling us in on the *real* information: The cone was actually invented by an Italian immigrant, a street vendor, several years before the fair. I'm sure your booktalk audience will have fun discussing their favorite flavors.

Your audience will gasp and their mouths will water at the astonishing pictures in this next delightfully delicious book. Take a look at *The Secret Life of Food* by Clare Crespo and see if you can figure out how the author, who is obviously a brilliantly creative cook, made some of these culinary creations. What on earth are they made of? They look absolutely real.

Show your audience the photos of the Tarantula Cookies on page 12, the Monsterhead Potatoes on page 34, the Handpunch on page 44, and the Jell-o Aquarium on page 52. Ask your audience if they think they could do this at home—and watch the book fly out of the library.

Ask your booktalk audience to list their favorite foods. They will usually name something sweet or salty. Do kids in other parts of the world like eating the same kinds of things? We all have the same taste buds, right? Find out in Beatrice Hollyer's *Let's Eat! What Children Eat Around the World.* This appealing book takes five kids, from

France, India, Thailand, South Africa, and Mexico, and asks them what they eat and what there favorite foods are. You may be surprised at their answers!

In South Africa, eight-year-old Thembe eats mostly foods that the family grows in their garden. Store-bought treats are uncommon. As she says on page 7, "When I grow up, I would like a well-paying job so we can spend less time thinking about food." Her favorite food is a cereal called Weetabix, but she also likes to chew on a piece of sugarcane.

Aa in Thailand just loves eggs, knows how to cook them, and eats them at almost every meal. In India, Yamini loves fruit, and especially a coconut dessert called naryal ladoo. Peter in France loves pretty much the same foods as American kids do, but he also just loves oysters. Each kid's story includes a section on what foods are served on special days. This is a fun book!

Figure 7.5. *How Sweet It Is (and Was): The History of Candy* **by Ruth Freeman Swain.**

No surprise here. Ruth Freeman Swain's *How Sweet It Is (and Was): The History of Candy* tells us that all over the world, people love candy. The word derives from an Arabic word, "gandi," which comes from an old Sanskrit Indian word "Khanda," meaning a piece of sugar. India is where people first took sweet juice from sugar cane.

In ancient Rome and Egypt, sugar did not exist. People sweetened their foods with honey. Sugar didn't make its way into Europe until after the Crusades. But then folks didn't know what to do with it. In 1659 some bright soul combined sugar with chocolate and then everyone went candy crazy!

This has great information about candy throughout history:

- More candy is bought for Halloween than for any other holiday—almost $2 billion worth in the United States alone in 2000.

- The average American eats 25 pounds of candy a year. Are *you* average?

- Mottos were first put on pastel candy hearts for Valentine's Day in 1866 by the Oliver R. Chase Company of Massachusetts.

- Thomas Adams invented flat sticks of gum in 1875.

- Good & Plenty candy was introduced in 1893 and is the oldest brand name candy still being sold.

- Snickers bars were introduced in 1929. They were named after a horse belonging to the Mars family!

Here's something they don't always tell you about two of the world's greatest explorers: Tenzig Norgay and Sir Edmund Hillary ate peppermints at the top of Mount Everest!

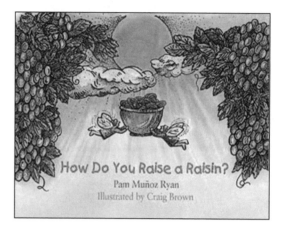

Figure 7.6. *How Do You Raise a Raisin?* **by Pam Muñoz Ryan.**

Another treat is the subject of *How Do You Raise a Raisin?* by Pam Muñoz Ryan. Almost everyone knows that raisins are dried grapes, but where do they come from, and how exactly are they dried? Pam Ryan tells us the answers with bouncy, tasty illustrations by Craig Brown.

- About 90 percent of the raisins sold in the United States come from a single place: an area near Fresno, California.

- Most raisins are left to dry naturally in the sun.

- Raisins bake in the sun for two to three weeks, then are wrapped into bundles and left a few more days to make sure they are really dry.

- It takes four and a half pounds of grapes to make one pound of raisins!

And, of course, raisins are very nutritious and are naturally sweet.

More than just cool recipes fill the charming *Inside the Secret Garden: A Treasury of Crafts, Recipes, and Activities* by Carolyn Strom Collins and Christina Wyss Erickson, with illustrations by Tasha Tudor and Mary Collier. Do you like *The Secret Garden*, by Frances Hodgson Burnett? Burnett's book was published in 1912 and immediately became a best seller. Movies, TV shows, and even a Broadway musical have been based on the original story.

It's about a little girl, Mary Lennox, who grew up in India, but now her parents are both dead and she must go to live with her uncle in the north of England. Mary meets strange new people, mainly servants in her uncle's home, who help her change and grow. And when she discovers a seemingly abandoned secret garden and decides she wants to rescue it, Mary not only rescues the garden, but also herself and her sickly cousin. It's a wonderful story!

Collins and Erickson's book relates a wealth of information about the real homes and gardens that inspired the story. It tells us where Mrs. Burnett lived, who she visited, and how those places became Mary's garden and her uncle's house. There are great-looking recipes, crafts to do, and information on how to create your own secret garden! This is a wonderful companion to Burnett's original book.

MARTIANS, WRESTLERS, PETS, AND POTPOURRI

Imagine that you are in the car, in the dark, the night before Halloween, driving around and listening to the radio. Then imagine hearing a horrifying news bulletin. Invaders from Mars have landed in a small town in New Jersey, and they are killing innocent people. It can't be true! But the reporter is clearly terrified! Suddenly, the reporter's voice vanishes. Static. Then a new voice: a professor from Princeton, New Jersey. He says the Martians just moments ago fired a deadly heat ray weapon. One of the 40 people killed in the attack was the reporter you were just listening to.

The New Jersey National Guard is sent out. There are 7,000 of them, and the Martians kill them all almost immediately. The Martians are heading for New York City! And where are you going to head? Where can you go? Now the U.S. Army is wiped out. Spaceships are landing in Buffalo, in Chicago, in Saint Louis—all over the country!

What are you going to do?

Something almost exactly like this happened in 1938. Kathleen Krull tells the tale in *The Night the Martians Landed: Just the Facts (Plus the Rumors) About Invaders from Mars*. The story on the radio was just that, an imaginary story broadcast for Halloween. It was a play based on H. G. Wells's science fiction story *The War of the Worlds*, but the actors playing the parts were so good that everyone believed they were hearing about something that was truly happening. People were going crazy! Back in 1938, of course, people had no television to rely on for verifiable news. Radio was the major source of all information and entertainment. And in this bizarre instance, the two became frighteningly confused. Krull tells us about one of the most unforgettable Halloweens in American history.

Figure 7.7. *The Essential Worldwide Monster Guide* **by Linda Ashman.**

Linda Ashman surveys more than Martians in *The Essential Worldwide Monster Guide*. This fun guidebook for younger readers describes some of the unusual creatures and characters that populate the world's various cultures. At the beginning of the book there is a world map. A short poem and a whimsical picture (by David Small) describe one kind of monster you might see in each of the countries you could visit. Some of the names are familiar. Have you heard of trolls? Where exactly do they prowl? Everyone's heard of the Loch Ness Monster, but where is Loch Ness?

Lesser-known monsters also lurk here, such as the Tengu of Japan, the swamp-loving Hotots, and the fierce, doglike Adlet of Inuit tradition. Read the poem about the last monster described, Bigfoot, and show the audience the illustration.

Some people fear snakes more than monsters. Others are charmed by them, or charm them. *Snake Charmer* by Ann Whitehead Nagda tells the true story of Vishnu, the oldest son of Sher Singh, who is a snake charmer. Sher works with cobra snakes and "charms" them with his flute to make them dance. Vishnu wants to be a snake charmer like his father, but his father says Vishnu must be educated and get a better job. Does your booktalk audience think it would be fun watch a snake charmer? Nagda shows us exactly how Vishnu lives and how he and his father find the snakes they use in the act. Show the picture of the hooded cobra. Yikes!

Gibbs Davis takes us on a tour of more cuddly creatures in *Wackiest White House Pets*. About 400 pets have lived in the White House. You might expect cats, dogs, fish, birds, and horses, but there are some pretty surprising others. The first unusual pets to live there arrived as gifts to our third president, Thomas Jefferson. The explorers Lewis and Clark sent him two grizzly bear cubs. Jefferson liked them so much he had a cage built for them on the south lawn so the public could share his enjoyment. He also liked to go for walks around the garden with them. A few years later, James Madison's wife Dolley often entertained with her parrot perched on her shoulder. She loved that parrot dearly. When the British attacked Washington, D.C., Dolley fled with only three possessions: a famous portrait of George Washington, the Declaration of Independence, and her bird. President Andrew Jackson had a parrot, too. His parrot, Poll, screamed curse words during his funeral

John Quincy Adams was visited by the Revolutionary War hero the Marquis de Lafayette in the 1820s. Lafayette brought along his pet alligator, and President Adams let the alligator stay in the East Room for two months.

President James Buchanan was sent a gift of elephants by the King of Siam (he turned most of them over to a zoo), President Lincoln issued a presidential pardon to the turkey his son Tad loved (so the turkey wouldn't be eaten for Thanksgiving dinner), and President Theodore Roosevelt had a lot of kids and more than 40 pets. His oldest daughter, Alice, liked to scare people. She hid a green garter snake in her purse. At parties, she liked to open up her purse and let the snake slither out, scaring everyone around.

Want to *really* scare someone? Tell them their computer crashed! Or has a virus. Or is being hacked. Compared to most crimes that have been around for thousands of years, computer crime is something new. And in *Computer Evidence*, Michael Dahl shows young readers how expert detectives solve these kinds of cases.

The book opens with a case of computer terrorism: Someone has been sending threatening letters and e-mails to a group of stores. Who would do such a thing? How can the police find someone who works hard to remain anonymous?

Have your booktalk listeners heard of hacking? Or shoulder-surfing? That's when someone sneaks a peek over your shoulder and watches you punch in your secret code number at an ATM machine. A number of notorious cyber crimes are explained here. A specialized crime is called "phreaking," when hackers find numbers of phone-calling cards and use them to make long-distance telephone calls (forcing other people to pay for them).

Another crime, probably the most well-known today, is to create and/or spread viruses. "A virus is a damaging computer program attached to another program or document. The virus starts after the program or document is opened. Viruses can make copies of themselves and affect other computers" (page 13). Worms are similar to viruses. And sometimes kids create viruses and worms just for fun. Show the photo of the teenager (on page 15) who created the destructive Blaster Worm! And then ask how many kids know the meanings of words like s*pam*, *glitch*, and *ping*. This book shows how the world of cyber-crime has its own specialized lingo, criminals, and detectives.

Want to check your puppy's I.Q.? D. Caroline Coile explains the wonderful woofy world of cynology, the scientific study of dogs, in *How Smart Is Your Dog?* She gives us great explanations of doggy skin, ears, tails, teeth, even taste buds. Dogs don't appreciate salty treats as much as people. And when they eat something sweet, dogs don't get the sugary blast until it hits the back of their tongues. (This is different from humans, who have their sweet sensors on the tips of their tongues.) Coile tells how dogs register pain, heat, and happiness. And there is a great section on body language: how dog owners can interpret their dog's feelings according to posture and movement. For example, when a dog seems to be bowing down, but its head is up, it's saying, "Please don't be mad at me!" Aww. Coile packs her book with lots of fun experiments you can do with canines, like the Yawn Test on page 43.

And which dog do you think is the smartest? In the opinion of most trainers and judges, the most intelligent is the border collie, Followed by the poodle! Learn how to keep your dog safe and comfortable in extreme temperatures. Take a nose print of your pup. And even test if your puppy has ESP! Woof!

Lots of girls want to be cowgirls when they grow up, and, incredible as it may seem in today's modern world, some of them really do get to be cowgirls. Even before they grow up, they work with horses and cattle, usually on family ranches.

Marc Talbert talked to and spent time with four cowgirls, and he divides *Holding the Reins: A Ride Through Cowgirl Life* by the seasons of the year as he describes all the interesting work the girls do.

Katy Whitlock lives with her family on their Wyoming ranch, where she is homeschooled, partly because the nearest public school is an hour's drive away. She does all sorts of work on the ranch, which has old-fashioned horses rather than new-fangled machinery. All four girls help out. The branding and cutting of the animals is not a job for folks with weak stomachs. The descriptions of the actual work can get pretty gruesome. Kids who want to be cowgirls or cowboys probably don't realize that this kind of thing would be a part of their normal, day-to-day work.

A lot of people would think that Sarah Mills is very lucky, because she lives on a horse farm called Willow Tree Farm. According to Judy Wolfman in *Life on a Horse Farm*, Sarah's grandfather raised racehorses and he taught her father how to do it. Now the whole family helps raise horses.

About 25 horses live on the farm. Most of them belong not to the family but to people who pay to breed their mares at the farm and then have Sarah's family raise the mare's foal. The family does own a stallion called Like a Brother, although they call him Mikey, and he is the father of the foals. Mikey's own father won the Kentucky Derby, one of the most famous horse races in the world.

Sarah tells us what it's like to live on a horse farm and how the family trains and takes care of the foals. If you like horses, you will love reading this book and looking at the photographs.

Show the picture on page 17 of the just-born foal.

Figure 7.8. *Stealth Bombers: The B-2 Spirits* **by Bill Sweetman.**

Boys who prefer mega horsepower will goggle over Bill Sweetman's books on warplanes. First, in *Stealth Bombers: The B-2 Spirits,* the author states that the stealths are basically flying wings. Most of the parts we are used to seeing on airplanes simply do not exist on a B-2, which is one reason they are so extraordinary.

All stealth bombers are based at Whiteman Air Force Base in Missouri. A single plane costs $1.3 *billion* to build. The shape of the plane makes it highly difficult to detect by radar. On most radar screens the plane appears no bigger than a bird. There are radar stations that can detect the planes if they are directly overhead so, of course, stealth pilots must always avoid those particular stations. The first B-2 went into service in 1993. Today, no more are built because they are so costly. The Air Force expects to make do with the ones we have until 2020. When the U.S. attacks, it is a good thing to have a stealth bomber to do the job.

Figure 7.9. *Supersonic Fighters: The F-16 Fighting Falcons* by **Bill Sweetman.**

Sweetman takes us for a ride on the best fighter planes ever made, *Supersonic Fighters: The F-16 Fighting Falcons.* In fact, the F-16s have been so successful that over 4,000 of them have been made. Their pilots nickname them "Vipers," saying they are as fast and deadly as viper snakes.

These planes can do the work of two different aircraft, bombers and fighters. They carry an arsenal of bombs, missiles, and machine guns, and they can fly incredibly fast. F-16s can go twice the speed of sound. When they climb rapidly, the planes generate a lot of g force, which is a measure of the force of gravity on an object. The crews of the F-16s are required to wear special G-suits designed specifically to protect them against this force. Show the picture of the plane on page 10.

Figure 7.10. *Stone Cold: Pro Wrestler Steve Austin* **by Michael Burgan.**

Another book that will appeal to lovers of speed and power is Michael Burgan's *Stone Cold: Pro Wrestler Steve Austin.* Steve Austin is one of the all-time great wrestlers. Steve's real name is not Steve Austin, but when he first became a wrestler, he found that another wrestler already had his name, Steve Williams. Since Steve was from Austin, Texas (and still lives there), that seemed like a good choice. Later, he needed a catchy, showy nickname. His wife had once told him to drink his tea before it got stone cold. Steve liked that term, and decided it would work perfectly as his nickname. And now the world knows him as "Stone Cold."

When Steve became world champion in 1998, he accidentally knocked out the referee during the fight. The match had to finish without a referee!

Readers who think that only stupid people would ever choose wrestling as a serious profession should meet Steve. He was a member of the National Honor Society in high school, he was a good student, and he loved sports. Steve has had a lot of injuries. He has had to take a lot of time out to recover from various injuries over the years, but he is still one of the very best.

In *Go Fly a Bike! The Ultimate Book About Bicycle Fun, Freedom & Science,* Bill Haduch tells us right away that "riding your bike is a lot like being a bird, because cycling is very similar to flying. The way you overcome gravity with your muscles, the way you balance, the way you turn, the way you cut through the wind, even the way cycling makes you feel—free as a bird" (page 3).

Think about it. As he says, when you ride a bike, you feel the freedom and fun of flying! The Wright brothers figured that out. They owned a bicycle shop and they got interested in flying because of that. They even attached wing parts to bicycles to see how those parts would move when they rode them in the wind. The Wrights understood that balance is a key to understanding how to fly, and bicyclists know almost automatically a lot about balance. In fact, you will be surprised to learn how many tricky maneuvers you do all of the time when you are bike riding, most of them without even thinking. Haduch describes the different styles of bikes, such as mountain bikes, road bikes, hybrid bikes, and more, and how to safely ride each one.

Mountain bikes are the most popular today; 80 percent of the bikes sold are mountain bikes. Road bikes are best for long rides on good roads. Serious racers and long-distance riders use them. About 10,000 people every year ride all the way across the United States, and most of them use road bikes. You'll learn all sorts of great stuff about bikes and biking:

- Bikes may have been invented over 200 years ago, but they really caught on around 1861. By the 1880s, safety bikes that resemble the ones we have to-day were very popular, and also very expensive. In today's money they would cost $2000.

- You can test your riding positions to see which is the most efficient—and make a great science fair project out of the results!

- It's easier to follow another biker than it is to be the first one to disturb the air. That's why riders take turns being in front.

- The fastest sprint speed record is now over 80 miles an hour.

Bike riding is incredibly healthy for you—as long as you follow basic safety rules.

Figure 7.11. *Follow the Money!* **by Loreen Leedy.**

Have you got any money in your pocket? Do you know whose picture is on the money you have? Have you ever wondered where it came from and where it might go next? Loreen Leedy's book *Follow the Money!* will have your booktalk audience all thinking about it.

All money is created at a U.S. mint. Then the coins are wrapped in tight rolls, sent to a Federal Reserve Bank, and then on to local banks. That's when money takes on a life of its own. Someone comes to the bank needing coins. Coins can end up in a pocket, in a store, or given back to you as change. What do you do with that change? What kind of places would a coin go during a typical day? Show the picture of the boy getting his allowance and adding his quarter to his state quarter collection.

A book on money naturally leads into discussions of numbers and math. A good title that makes math fun is Greg Tang's *Math Appeal: Mind-Stretching Math Riddles.* Tang's popular, colorful book features two-page spreads that each include a poem and a problem to be solved creatively. In *Math Appeal,* kids are encouraged to look for patterns and symmetries. A clue is included in each poem. Excellent for problem-solving and math exercises.

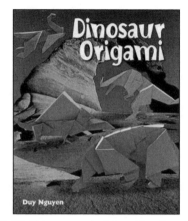

Figure 7.12. *Dinosaur Origami* **by Duy Nguyen.**

Two more titles that include problem solving in a more hands-on approach are both by Duy Nguyen. In *Dinosaur Origami,* delightful color photographs show the origami dinosaurs in natural settings. There are directions for making 14 different dinosaurs, and the directions are clearly written. Basic directions for origami are included in the front of the book. Great fun. And if you are talking books on dinosaurs, be sure to include this one as a special treat.

Figure 7.13. *Fantasy Origami* **by Duy Nguyen.**

For more paperfolding pleasure, Nguyen's *Fantasy Origami* gives you some great ideas and directions. Did you ever want to make a paper swordfish, rattlesnake, dragon, killer whale, or Pegasus? Directions for these and more are in this colorful book with great photographs. Show the picture of Pegasus on page 36. Nguyen's books are for grades 4 and up.

Kids love to keep secrets. And they like to share them. Satisfy both itchy impulses by tapping into Paul B. Janeczko's *Top Secret: A Handbook of Codes, Ciphers, and Secret Writing.* Learn how to crack the toughest codes. Memorize the Zigzag Cipher, the Cardano Grille, and the St. Cyr Slide. Learn how spies conceal their messages.

One German spy hand-knit his message into his sweater! The knots in the yarn stood for different letters of the alphabet. Did you know that Mary Queen of Scots lost her head because one of her secret codes was captured and deciphered by her enemies?

Tell your older readers the story of the Beale Cipher. This famous coded message claims to reveal the hidden location of a wagonload of gold and silver buried somewhere in Virginia. And if your readers can solve this 100-year-old puzzle, they will discover a treasure worth $20 million. It's still out there! This fun book has loads of info, and even a recipe for making your own invisible ink.

We all know what birthday celebrations are like in the United States. One thing that *always* happens is that everyone sings "Happy Birthday to You." And that seems the case for birthday celebrations in many parts of the world. But *Birthdays Around the World* by Mary D. Lankford tells us what birthday parties are like in other places. Find out in which country children wear blindfolds while trying to eat a soft cookie hanging on a string. Find out where children play a game called "Share the Chocolate."

You can also discover your own birthday gemstone and your birthday flower, and how to host an "Around the World Birthday Party." Birthdays everywhere have one thing in common—they are fun! Read this to find out more.

Show the picture of the cookie game on page 17.

The Legend of Saint Nicholas by Demi answers the question, Who was the real, the original Santa Claus, that fellow named Saint Nicholas? The real-life Nick was probably born around 1,700 years ago in a country now called Turkey. He loved to pray and help people. He made a vow to help people everywhere in every way possible. And, as he grew older, that is just what he did. Nicholas even performed miracles, including bringing back people from the dead! And just as Demi did in her book *Muhammad*, here she beautifully fits the artwork to the time and tone of the tale. A glorious gold leaf cover hides treasures within. Open this book and learn how the real St. Nicholas was transformed into the lovable Santa Claus. And learn why he is admired, loved, and prayed to around the world.

In Aliki's wonderful *Ah, Music* she writes, "If you hum a tune, play an instrument, or clap out a rhythm, you are making music. You are listening to it, too" (page 7). The author introduces us to every possible aspect of music—its history, the instruments, the conductor, dance, voice, harmony, jazz, popular music, and more. Music is melody. Music is rhythm. Music is voice. Music is even used for therapy. Show and read the frontispiece that tells how music can make us feel.

Figure 7.14. *Chickens May Not Cross the Road and Other Crazy (But True) Laws* **by Kathi Linz.**

You won't believe some of the laws described in *Chickens May Not Cross the Road and Other Crazy (But True) Laws.* Some of them are really stupid, but author Kathi Linz swears that all of them are real. When the laws were made, someone, somewhere must have thought they were important.

Find out that:

- In Santa Ana, California, swimming on dry land is illegal.

- In Marshalltown, Iowa, it is illegal for horses to eat fire hydrants. (Show the picture of the horse nibbling a hydrant.)

- In Memphis, Tennessee, you will get in big trouble if you drive while you are asleep

- In International Falls, Minnesota, it is illegal for cats to chase dogs up telephone poles!

These are just a few of the great laws described in the book. You will laugh your head off!

Good thing there's no law against reading great nonfiction books!

BIBLIOGRAPHY

Aliki. *Ah, Music.* HarperCollins, 2003. ISBN 006028719548. 48 p. Grades 1–3.

Ashman, Linda. *The Essential Worldwide Monster Guide.* Illustrations by David Small. Simon & Schuster Books for Young Readers, 2003. ISBN 0689826400. Unpaged. Grades K–3.

Burgan, Michael. *Stone Cold: Pro Wrestler Steve Austin* (Pro Wrestlers). Capstone High-Interest Books, 2002. ISBN 0736809201. 48 p. Grades 4–up.

Coile, D. Caroline, *How Smart Is Your Dog? 30 Fun Science Activities with Your Pet.* Sterling Publishing, 2003. ISBN 0806976772. 96 p. Grades 4–7.

Collins, Carolyn Strom, and Christina Wyss Erickson. *Inside the Secret Garden: A Treasury of Crafts, Recipes, and Activities.* Illustrations by Tasha Tudor and Mary Collier. HarperCollins, 2002. ISBN 0060279222. 130 p. Grades 4–up.

Cooper, Elisha. *Ice Cream.* Greenwillow Books, an imprint of HarperCollins, 2002. ISBN 0060014237. Unpaged. Grades K–3.

Crespo, Clare. *Secret Life of Food.* Photographs by Eric Staudenmaier. A Melcher Media Book Hyperion Books for Children, 2002. ISBN 0786808462. 108 p. All ages.

Dahl, Michael. *Computer Evidence.* (Edge Books: Forensic Crime Solvers). Capstone Press, 2004. ISBN 073682698x. 32 p. Grades 3–9.

Davies, Nicola. *Poop: A Natural History of the Unmentionable.* Illustrated by Neal Layton. Candlewick Press, 2004. ISBN 0763624373. 61 p. Grades 4–7.

Davis, Gibbs. *Wackiest White House Pets.* Illustrated by David A. Johnson. Scholastic Press, 2004. ISBN 0439443733. Unpaged. Grades 3–5.

Demi. *The Legend of Saint Nicholas.* Margaret K. McElderry Books, 2003. ISBN 0689846819. Unpaged. Grades K–3.

Fleischman, John. *Phineas Gage: A Gruesome But True Story About Brain Science.* Houghton Mifflin, 2002. ISBN 0618052526. 96 p. Grades 4–up.

Getz, David. *Purple Death: The Mysterious Flu of 1918.* Illustrations by Peter McCarty. Henry Holt, 2000. ISBN 080505751x. 86 p. Grades 4–8.

Goodman, Susan E. *The Truth About Poop.* Illustrated by Elwood H. Smith. Viking, 2004. ISBN 0670036749. 40 p. Grades 2–5.

Greenstein, Elaine. *Ice Cream Cones for Sale!* Arthur A. Levine Books/An Imprint of Scholastic Press, 2003. ISBN 0439327288. Unpaged. Grades K–3.

Haduch, Bill. *Go Fly a Bike! The Ultimate Book About Bicycle Fun, Freedom & Science.* Illustrated by Chris Murphy. Dutton Children's Books, 2004. ISBN 0525470247. 83 p. Grades 4–6.

Hollyer, Beatrice. *Let's Eat! What Children Eat Around the World.* Introduction by Jamie Oliver. Henry Holt, in association with Oxfam, 2003. ISBN 0805073221. 41 p. Grades 3–5.

Janeczko, Paul B. *Top Secret: A Handbook of Codes, Ciphers, and Secret Writing.* Illustrated by Jenna LaReau. Candlewick Press, 2004. 136 pp. Grades 4–7.

Krull, Kathleen. *The Night the Martians Landed: Just the Facts (Plus the Rumors) About Invaders from Mars.* Illustrations by Christopher Santoro. HarperCollins, 2003. ISBN 0688172474. 74 p. Grades 2–4.

Lankford, Mary D. *Birthdays Around the World.* Illustrated by Karen Dugan. HarperCollins, 2002. ISBN 068815431x. 32 p. Grades K–3.

Leedy, Loreen. *Follow The Money!* Holiday House, 2002. ISBN 0823415872. Unpaged. Grades K–3.

Linz, Kathi. *Chickens May Not Cross the Road and Other Crazy (But True) Laws.* Illustrated by Tony Griego. Houghton Mifflin, 2002. ISBN 061811257x. Unpaged. Grades 1–4.

Marrin, Albert. *Dr. Jenner and the Speckled Monster: The Search for Smallpox Vaccine.* Dutton Children's Books, 2002. ISBN 0525469222. 120 p. Grades 4–8.

Masoff, Joy. *Oh Yuck! The Encyclopedia of Everything Nasty.* Illustrated by Terry Sirrell. Workman, 2000. ISBN 0761100711. 212 p. Grades 4–9.

McLafferty, Carla Killough. *The Head Bone's Connected to the Neck Bone: The Weird, Wacky and Wonderful X-Ray.* Farrar, Straus & Giroux, 2001. ISBN 0374329087. 136 p. Grades 4–8.

Nagda, Ann Whitehead. *Snake Charmer.* Henry Holt, 2002. ISBN 0805064990. Unpaged. Grades K–3.

Nguyen, Duy. *Dinosaur Origami.* Sterling Publishing, 2002. ISBN 0806976993. 96 p. Grades 4–up.

———. *Fantasy Origami.* Sterling Publishing, 2003. ISBN 0806980079. 96 p. Grades 4–up.

Prior, Natalie Jane. *The Encyclopedia of Preserved People: Pickled, Frozen and Mummified Corpses from Around the World.* Crown, 2003. ISBN 0375822879. 64 p. Grades 4–8.

Ryan, Pam Muñoz. *How Do You Raise a Raisin?* Illustrated by Craig Brown. Charlesbridge, 2003. ISBN 1570913978. Unpaged. Grades 1–3.

Senior, Kathryn. *You Wouldn't Want to Be Sick in the 16th Century: Diseases You'd Rather Not Catch.* Illustrated by David Antram. Created and designed by David Salariya. Franklin Watts, a division of Scholastic, 2002. ISBN 0531163660. 32 p. Grades 4–8.

Sloan, Christopher. *Bury the Dead: Tombs, Corpses, Mummies, Skeletons, & Rituals.* National Geographic, 2002. ISBN 0792271920. 64 p. Grades 2–5.

Swain, Ruth Freeman. *How Sweet It Is (and Was): The History of Candy.* Illustrated by John O'Brien. Holiday House, 2003. ISBN 0823417123. Unpaged. Grades3–6.

Sweetman, Bill. *Stealth Bomber: The B-2 Spirits* (War Planes). Capstone, 2001. ISBN 0736807918. 32 p. Gr. 4–up.

———. *Supersonic Fighters: The F-16 Fighting Falcons* (War Planes). Capstone, 2001. ISBN 0736807928. 32 p. Gr. 4–up.

Talbert, Marc. *Holding the Reins: A Ride Through Cowgirl Life.* Photographs by Barbara Van Cleve. HarperCollins, 2003. ISBN 0060292555. 105 p. Grades 4–up.

Tang, Greg. *Math Appeal: Mind-Stretching Math Riddles.* Illustrated by Henry Briggs. Scholastic Press, 2003. ISBN 0439210461. Unpaged. Grades K–4.

Wolfman, Judy. *Life On a Horse Farm.* Photographs by David Lorenz Winston. Carolrhoda Books, 2002. ISBN 0575055171. 48 p. Grades 3–5.

Acknowledgments

Chapter 1

Cover from Jane Yolen and Heidi Elisabet Yolen Stemple, *Roanoke: The Lost Colony: An Unsolved Mystery from History*. Illustrated by Roger Roth. New York: Simon & Schuster Books for Young Readers, 2003. Reprinted with permission.

Cover from *Under the Ice: A Canadian Museum of Nature Book* written by Kathy Conlan and the Canadian Museum of Nature. Used by permission of Kids Can Press Ltd., Toronto. Cover photograph © Kathy Conlan 2002 Canadian Museum of Nature.

Cover from James Rumford, *Traveling Man: The Journey of Ibn Battuta, 1325–1354*. Boston: Houghton Mifflin Company, 2001.

Cover from Debbie S. Miller, *The Great Serum Race: Blazing the Iditarod Trail*. Illustrated by Jon Van Zyle. New York: Walker & Company, 2002. Reprinted with permission.

Cover from Carmen Bredeson, *After the Last Dog Died: The True-life, Hair-raising Adventure of Douglas Mawson and His 1911–1914 Antarctic Expedition*. Washington, DC: National Geographic Society, 2003. Reprinted with permission of the National Geographic Society.

Chapter 2

Cover from Joanne Mattern, *The Ragdoll Cat* (Learning about Cats). Bloomington, MN: Capstone Press, 2002. Reprinted with permission.

Cover from Francine Jacobs, *Lonesome George the Giant Tortoise*. Illustrated by Jean Cassels. New York: Walker & Company, 2003. Reprinted with permission.

Cover from Gail Gibbons, *Polar Bears*. New York: Holiday House, 2001. Reprinted with permission.

Cover from Caroline Arnold, *When Mammoths Walked the Earth*. Illustrated by Laurie Caple. New York: Clarion Books, 2002. Reprinted with permission.

Cover from Kelly Milner Halls, *Dinosaur Mummies: Beyond Bare-Bone Fossils*. Illustrated by Rick Spears. Plain City, OH: Darby Creek Publishing, 2004. Copyright © Darby Creek Publishing. All rights reserved.

Cover from Hannah Bonner, *When Bugs Were Big, Plants Were Strange, and Tetrapods Stalked the Earth: A Cartoon Prehistory of Life Before Dinosaurs*. Washington, DC: National Geographic Society, 2003. Reprinted with permission of the National Geographic Society. All rights reserved.

Cover from Shelley Tanaka, *New Dinos: The Latest Finds! The Coolest Dinosaur Discoveries!* Illustrated by Alan Barnard. Toronto: An Atheneum Book for Young Readers/Madison Press Books, 2003. Reprinted with permission.

Cover from Donna M. Jackson, *The Bug Scientists.* Boston: Houghton Mifflin Company, 2002. Reprinted with permission.

Cover from Sy Montgomery, *The Tarantula Scientist.* Photographs by Nic Bishop. Boston: Houghton Mifflin Company, 2004.

Cover from Cathy Camper, *Bugs Before Time: Prehistoric Insects and Their Relatives.* Illustrated by Steve Kirk. New York: Simon & Schuster Books for Young Readers, 2002. Reprinted with permission.

Cover from Charles Micucci, *The Life and Times of the Ant.* Boston: Houghton Mifflin Company, 2003. Reprinted with permission.

Cover from Linda George, *Vipers.* Bloomington, MN: Capstone High Interest Books, 2002. Reprinted with permission.

Cover from Sy Montgomery, *Encantado: Pink Dolphin of the Amazon.* Photographs by Dianne Taylor-Snow. Boston: Houghton Mifflin Company, 2002.

Cover from Sneed B. Collard III, *The Deep-Sea Floor.* Illustrated by Gergory Wenzel. Watertown, MA: Charlesbridge Publishing, 2003. Used with permission by Charlesbridge Publishing, Inc.

Cover from Christopher Sloan, *Supercroc and the Origin of Crocodiles.* Washington, DC: National Geographic Society, 2002. Reprinted with permission of the National Geographic Society. All rights reserved.

Cover from Sandra Markle, *Growing Up Wild: Penguins.* New York: Atheneum Books for Young Readers, 2002. Reprinted with permission.

Cover from Irene Kelly, *It's a Hummingbird's Life.* New York: Holiday House, 2003. Reprinted with permission.

Cover from Gail Gibbons, *Chicks & Chickens.* New York: Holiday House, 2003. Reprinted with permission.

Cover from Sneed B. Collard III, *Beaks!* Illustrated by Robin Brickman. Watertown, MA: Charlesbridge Publishing, 2002. Used with permission by Charlesbridge Publishing, Inc.

Cover from Steve Jenkins and Robin Page, *What Do You Do With a Tail Like This?* Boston: Houghton Mifflin Company, 2003. Reprinted with permission.

Cover from Lynda Graham-Barber, *Spy Hops & Belly Flops: Curious Behavior of Woodland Animals.* Illustrated by Brian Lies. Boston: Houghton Mifflin Company, 2004.

Cover from Kelly Milner Halls, *Albino Animals.* Plain City, OH: Darby Creek Publishing, 2004. Copyright © Darby Creek Publishing. All rights reserved.

Cover from Deborah Heiligman, *Babies: All You Need to Know*. Illustrated by Laura Freeman-Hines. Washington, DC: National Geographic Society, 2002. Reprinted with permission of the National Geographic Society. All rights reserved.

Cover from Elaine Landau, *Popcorn!* Illustrated by Brian Lies. Watertown, MA: Charlesbridge Publishing, 2003. Used with permission by Charlesbridge Publishing, Inc.

Cover from Barbara Seuling, *Flick a Switch: How Electricity Gets to Your Home*. Illustrated by Nancy Tobin. New York: Holiday House, 2003. Reprinted with permission.

Cover from Barbara Seuling, *From Head to Toe: The Amazing Human Body and How It Works*. Illustrated by Edward Miller. New York: Holiday House, 2002. Reprinted with permission.

Cover from Seymour Simon and Nicole Fauteux, *Let's Try It Out with Towers and Bridges: Hands-On Early-Learning Science Activities*. Illustrated by Doug Cushman. New York: Simon & Schuster Books for Young Readers, 2003. Reprinted with permission.

Cover from Steve Jenkins, *Life on Earth: The Story of Evolution*. Boston: Houghton Mifflin Company, 2002.

Cover from Steve "The Dirtmeister®" Tomecek, *Dirt*. Illustrated by Nancy Woodman. Washington, DC: National Geographic Society, 2002. Reprinted with permission of the National Geographic Society. All rights reserved.

Chapter 3

Cover from Ronald J. Drez, *Remember D-Day: The Plan, the Invasion, Survivor Stories*. Washington, DC: National Geographic Society, 2004. Reprinted with permission of the National Geographic Society. All rights reserved.

Cover from David A. Adler, *A Hero and the Holocaust: The Story of Janusz Korczak and His Children*. Illustrated by Bill Farnsworth. New York: Holiday House, 2002.

Cover from James Cross Giblin, *The Life and Death of Adolf Hitler*. New York: Clarion Books, 2002. Reprinted with permission.

Cover from Diana Preston, *Remember the* Lusitania! New York: Walker & Company, 2003. Reprinted with permission.

Cover from Catherine M. Andronik, *Hatshepsut: His Majesty, Herself*. Illustrated by Joseph Daniel Fiedler. New York: Atheneum Books for Young Readers, 2001. Reprinted with permission.

Cover from Yona Zeldis McDonough, *Peaceful Protest: The Life of Nelson Mandela*. Illustrations by Malcah Zeldis. New York: Walker & Company, 2002. Reprinted with permission.

Cover from Diane Hoyt-Goldsmith, *Celebrating Ramadan*. Photographs by Lawrence Migdale. New York: Holiday House, 2001. Reprinted with permission.

Cover from Susan Campbell Bartoletti, *Black Potatoes: The Story of the Great Irish Famine, 1845–1850.* Boston: Houghton Mifflin Company, 2001. Reprinted with permission.

Cover from Peter Lourie, *Tierra del Fuego: A Journey to the End of the Earth.* Copyright © 2002 by Peter Lourie. Published by Boyds Mills Press, Inc. Reprinted by permission.

Cover from Caroline Arnold, *Uluru, Australia's Aboriginal Heart.* Photographs by Arthur Arnold. New York: Clarion Books, 2003. Reprinted with permission.

Cover from Lynn Curlee, *Seven Wonders of the Ancient World.* New York: Atheneum Books for Young Readers, 2004. Reprinted with permission.

Cover from Dyan Blacklock, *The Roman Army: The Legendary Soldiers Who Created an Empire.* Illustrated by David Kennett. New York: Walker & Company, 2004. Reprinted with permission.

Cover from Melvin Berger and Gilda Berger, *The Real Vikings: Craftsmen, Traders, and Fearsome Raiders.* Washington, DC: National Geographic Society, 2003. Reprinted with permission of the National Geographic Society. All rights reserved.

Cover from Margaret Cooper, *Exploring the Ice Age.* New York: Atheneum Books for Young Readers, 2001. Reprinted with permission.

Chapter 4

Cover from Cheryl Harness, *The Revolutionary John Adams.* Washington, DC: National Geographic Society, 2003. Reprinted with permission of the National Geographic Society. All rights reserved.

Cover from Candace Fleming, *Ben Franklin's Almanac: Being a True Account of the Good Gentleman's Life.* New York: An Anne Schwartz/Atheneum Books for Young Readers, 2003. Reprinted with permission.

Cover from Lynn Curlee, *Capital.* New York: Atheneum Books for Young Readers, 2003. Reprinted with permission.

Cover from Dennis Brindell Fradin, *The Signers: The 56 Stories Behind the Declaration of Independence.* Illustrated by Michael McCurdy. New York: Walker and Company, 2002. Reprinted with permission.

Cover from Russell Freedman, *In Defense of Liberty: The Story of America's Bill of Rights.* New York: Holiday House, 2002.

Cover from Deborah Chandra and Madeleine Comora, *George Washington's Teeth.* Illustrated by Brock Cole. New York: Farrar Straus Giroux, 2003. Used with permission of Farrar Straus Giroux.

Cover from Patricia Lauber, *Who Came First? New Clues to Prehistoric Americans.* Washington, DC: National Geogrpahic Society, 2003. Reprinted with permission of the National Geographic Society. All rights reserved.

Cover from Susan Campbell Bartoletti, *Kids on Strike!* Boston: Houghton Mifflin Company, 1999. Reprinted with permission.

Cover from Rosalyn Schanzer, *How We Crossed the West: The Adventures of Lewis & Clark.* Washington, DC: National Geographic Society, 1997. Reprinted with permission of the National Geographic Society. All rights reserved.

Cover from Peter Lourie, *On the Trail of Lewis and Clark: A Journey up the Missouri River.* Copyright © 2002 by Peter Lourie. Published by Boyds Mills Press, Inc. Reprinted by permission.

Cover from Ginger Wadsworth, *Words West: Voices of Young Pioneers.* New York: Clarion Books, 2003. Reprinted with permission.

Cover from Connie Nordhielm Wooldridge, *When Esther Morris Headed West: Women, Wyoming, and the Right to Vote.* Illustrated by Jacqueline Rogers. New York: Holiday House, 2001. Reprinted with permission.

Cover from Russell Freedman, *In the Days of the Vaqueros: America's First True Cowboys.* New York: Clarion Books, 2001.

Cover from Andrea Warren, *We Rode the Orphan Trains.* Boston: Houghton Mifflin Company, 2001. Reprinted with permission.

Cover from Raymond Bial, *Tenement: Immigrant Life on the Lower East Side.* Boston: Houghton Mifflin Company, 2002. Reprinted with permission.

Cover from David A. Adler, *A Picture Book of Harriet Beecher Stowe.* Illustrated by Colin Bootman. New York: Holiday House, 2003. Reprinted with permission.

Cover from Dennis Brindell Fradin and Judith Bloom Fradin, *Fight On! Mary Church Terrell's Battle for Integration,* New York: Clarion Books, 2003. Reprinted with permission.

Cover from Peter Burchard, *Frederick Douglass: For the Great Family of Man.* New York: Atheneum Books for Young Readers, 2003. Reprinted with permission.

Cover from Christine King Farris, *My Brother Martin: A Sister Remembers: Growing Up with the Rev. Dr. Martin Luther King Jr.* Illustrated by Chris Soentpiet. New York: Simon & Schuster Books for Young Readers, 2003. Reprinted with permission.

Cover from Cheryl Harness, *Ghosts of the Civil War.* New York: Simon & Schuster Books for Young Readers, 2002. Reprinted with permission.

Cover from Harold Holzer, *The President Is Shot! The Assassination of Abraham Lincoln.* Copyright © 2004 by Harold Holzer. Published by Boyds Mill Press, Inc. Reprinted by permission.

Cover from Thomas B. Allen, *Remember Pearl Harbor: American and Japanese Survivors Tell Their Stories.* Washington, DC: National Geographic Society, 2001. Reprinted with permission of the National Geographic Society. All rights reserved.

Cover from Michael L. Cooper, *Remembering Manzanar: Life in a Japanese Relocation Camp.* New York: Clarion Books, 2002. Reprinted with permission.

Cover from Melissa Abramovitz, *The U.S. Marine Corps at War*. Bloomington, MN: Capstone High Interest Books, 2002. Reprinted with permission.

Cover from Karen Levine, *Hana's Suitcase: A True Story*. Morton Grove, IL: Albert Whitman & Company, 2002. Reprinted with permission.

Cover from David A. Adler, *A Picture Book of Dwight David Eisenhower*. New York: Holiday House, 2002. Reprinted with permission.

Cover from Deborah Heiligman, *High Hopes: A Photobiography of John F. Kennedy*. Washington, DC: National Geographic Society, 2003. Reprinted with permission of the National Geographic Society. All rights reserved.

Cover from Betsy Harvey Kraft, *Theodore Roosevelt: Champion of the American Spirit*. New York: Clarion Books, 2003. Reprinted with permission.

Cover from Kay Winters, *Abe Lincoln: The Boy Who Loved Books*. Illustrated by Nancy Carpenter. New York: Simon & Schuster Books for Young Readers, 2002. Reprinted with permission.

Cover from Jim Murphy, *An American Plague: The True and Terrifying Story of the Yellow Fever Epidemic of 1793*. New York: Clarion Books, 2003. Reprinted with permission.

Cover from Laurie Halse Anderson, *Thank You, Sarah: The Woman Who Saved Thanksgiving*. Illustrated by Matt Faulkner. New York: Simon & Schuster Books for Young Readers, 2002. Reprinted with permission.

Cover from Eileen Christelow, *Vote!* New York: Clarion Books, 2003. Reprinted with permission.

Cover from Iris Van Rynbach, *Safely to Shore: America's Lighthouses*. Watertown, MA: Charlesbridge Publishing, 2003. Used with permission by Charlesbridge Publishing, Inc.

Cover from Teresa Bateman, *Red, White, Blue, and Uncle Who? The Stories Behind Some of America's Patriotic Symbols*. Illustrated by John O'Brien. New York: Holiday House, 2001. Reprinted with permission.

Chapter 5

Cover from Alexandra Wallner, *Grandma Moses*. New York: Holiday House, 2004. Reprinted with permission.

Cover from Deborah Kogan Ray, *Hokusai: The Man Who Painted a Mountain*. New York: Frances Foster Books, 2001. Used with permission of Farrar Straus Giroux.

Cover from Mordicai Gerstein, *What Charlie Heard*. New York: Frances Foster Books, 2002. Used with permission of Farrar Straus Giroux.

Cover from Robert Burleigh, *Into the Woods: John James Audubon Lives His Dream*. Paintings by Wendell Minor. New York: Atheneum Books for Young Readers, 2003. Reprinted with permission.

Cover from Lesa Cline-Ransome, *Major Taylor, Champion Cyclist.* Illustrated by James E. Ransome. An Anne Schwartz Book. New York: Atheneum Books for Young Readers, 2004. Reprinted with permission.

Cover from Susan Goldman Rubin, *There Goes the Neighborhood: Ten Buildings People Loved to Hate.* New York: Holiday House, 2001. Reprinted with permission.

Cover from Lynn Curlee, *Brooklyn Bridge.* New York: Atheneum Books for Young Readers, 2001. Reprinted with permission.

Cover from Wendie Old, *To Fly: The Story of the Wright Brothers.* Illustrated by Robert Andrew Parker. New York: Clarion Books, 2002. Reprinted with permission.

Cover of *The Wright Brothers: A Flying Start,* written by Elizabeth MacLeod is used by permission of Kids Can Press Ltd., Toronto. Photos from Eyewire, Library of Congress, and Wright State University.

Cover from Mary Collins, *Airborne: A Photobiography of Wilbur and Orville Wright.* Washington, DC: National Geographic Society, 2003. Reprinted with permission of the National Geographic Society. All rights reserved.

Cover from Michael Dooling, *The Great Horse-Less Carriage Race,* New York: Holiday House. © 2002.

Cover from Marfe Ferguson Delano, *Inventing the Future: A Photobiography of Thomas Alva Edison,* reprinted with permission of the National Geographic Society. All rights reserved.

Cover from Catherine Thimmesh, *The Sky's the Limit: Stories of Discovery by Women and Girls.* Illustrated by Melissa Sweet. Boston: Houghton Mifflin Company, 2002. Reprinted with permission.

Cover from Patrick O'Brien, *The Great Ships.* New York: Walter & Company, 2001. Reprinted with permission.

Cover from Peter Lourie, *The Mystery of the Maya: Uncovering the Lost City of Palenque.* Copyright © 2001 by Peter Lourie. Published by Boyds Mills Press, Inc. Reprinted by permission.

Chapter 6

Cover from William Steig, *CDC?* New York: Farrar Straus Giroux, 1984. Used with the permission of Farrar Straus Giroux.

Cover from Loreen Leedy and Pat Street, *There's a Frog in My Throat! 440 Animal Sayings a Little Bird Told Me.* Illustrated by Loreen Leedy. New York: Holiday House, 2003. Reprinted with permission.

Cover from Kristine O'Connell George, *Swimming Upstream: Middle School Poems.* Illustrated by Debbie Tilley. New York: Clarion Books, 2002.

Cover from John Frank, *A Chill in the Air: Nature Poems for Fall and Winter.* Illustrated by Mike Reed. New York: Simon & Schuster Books for Young Readers, 2003.

Cover from Marilyn Singer, *Fireflies at Midnight*. Pictures by Ken Robbins. New York: Atheneum Books for Young Readers, 2003. Reprinted with permission.

Cover from Katharine Boling, *New Year Be Coming! A Gullah Year*. Illustrated by Daniel Minter. Morton Grove, IL: Albert Whitman & Company, 2002. Reprinted with permission.

Cover from Lee Bennett Hopkins, *Wonderful Words: Poems about Reading, Writing, Speaking, and Listening*. Illustrated by Karen Barbour. New York: Simon & Schuster Books for Young Readers, 2004. Reprinted with permission.

Cover from Andrea Perry, *Here's What You Do When You Can't Find Your Shoe (Ingenious Inventions for Pesky Problems)*. Illustrated by Alan Snow. New York: Atheneum Books, 2003. Reprinted with permission.

Cover from Jack Gantos, *Hole in My Life*. New York: Farrar Straus Giroux, 2002. Used with the permission of Farrar Straus Giroux.

Cover from Leonard Marcus (compiler and editor), *Author Talk: Conversations with Judy Blume, Bruce Books, Karen Cushman, Russell Freedman, Lee Bennett Hopkins, James Howe, Johanna Hurwitz, E. L. Konigsburg, Lois Lowry, Ann M. Martin, Nicholasa Mohr, Gary Paulsen, Jon Sciesczka, Seymour Simon, and Laurence Yep*. New York: Simon & Schuster Books for Young Readers, 2000.

Chapter 7

Cover from John Fleischman, *Phineas Gage: A Gruesome but True Story About Brain Science,* Boston: Houghton Mifflin Company, © 2002. Reprinted with permission.

Cover from Carla Killough McClafferty, *The Head Bone's Connected to the Neck Bone: The Weird, Wacky, and Wonderful X-Ray*. New York: Farrar Straus Giroux, 2001. Used with the permission of Farrar Straus Giroux.

Cover from Christopher Sloan, *Bury the Dead: Tombs, Corpses, Mummies, Skeletons, & Rituals*. Washington, DC: National Geographic Society, 2002. Reprinted with permission of the National Geographic Society. All rights reserved.

Cover from Joy Masoff, *Oh Yuck! The Encyclopedia of Everything Nasty*. Illustrated by Terry Sirrell. New York: Workman Publishing, 2000. Reprinted with permission.

Cover from Ruth Freeman Swain, *How Sweet It Is (and Was): The History of Candy*. Illustrated by John O'Brien. New York: Holiday House, 2003. Reprinted with permission.

Cover from Pam Muñoz Ryan, *How Do You Raise a Raisin?* Illustrated by Craig Brown. Watertown, MA: Charlesbridge Publishing, 2003. Used with permission of Charlesbridge Publishing, Inc.

Cover from Linda Ashman, *The Essential Worldwide Monster Guide*. Illustrated by David Small. New York: Simon & Schuster Books for Young Readers, 2003. Reprinted with permission.

Cover from Bill Sweetman, *Stealth Bombers: The B-2 Spirits.* Bloomington, IN: Capstone Press, 2001. Reprinted with permission.

Cover from Bill Sweetman, *Supersonic Fighters: The F-16 Fighting Falcons.* Bloomington, IN: Capstone Press, 2001. Reprinted with permission.

Cover from Michael Burgan, *Stone Cold: Pro Wrestler Steve Austin.* Bloomington, IN: Capstone High Interest Books, 2002. Reprinted with permission.

Cover from Loreen Leedy, *Follow the Money!* New York: Holiday House, 2002. Reprinted with permission.

Cover from Duy Nguyen, *Dinosaur Origami.* New York: Sterling Publishing Co., Inc., 2002. Courtesy of Sterling Publishing Co., Inc.

Cover from Duy Nguyen, *Fantasy Origami.* New York: Sterling Publishing Co., Inc., 2003. Courtesy of Sterling Publishing Co., Inc.

Cover from Kathi Linz, *Chickens May Not Cross the Road and Other Crazy (But True) Laws.* Illustrated by Tony Griego. Boston: Houghton Mifflin Company, 2002. Reprinted with permission.

Author and Illustrator Index

Title Index

About the Authors

KATHLEEN A. BAXTER served as the Coordinator of Children's Services in the Anoka County Library, for over twenty-five years. She has written "The Non Fiction Booktalker" column for *School Library Journal* since 1997. She has presented at hundreds of national and state library and reading conferences all over the country. Kathleen has also taught classes in children's literature, served on the 2001 Newbery Committee, consults for publishers, and now presents all-day seminars on children's books for the Bureau of Education and Research.

MICHAEL DAHL is the author of over 50 fiction and nonfiction books for children and young adults. He has twice won the Distinguished Achievement Award from the Association of Educational Publishers for his nonfiction. Among his fiction, his Finnegan Zwake series was named among the five best mystery books of 2002 for children by the Agatha Awards. Dahl is a conference speaker on mysteries and children's nonfiction, and also conducts writing workshops for students. He is based in Minneapolis, Minnesota and can be reached at dahl@mysteryworks.com.